STATE-LOCAL RELATIONS

STATE-LOCAL RELATIONS

A PARTNERSHIP APPROACH

Joseph F. Zimmerman

PRAEGER SPECIAL STUDIES • PRAEGER SCIENTIFIC

Library of Congress Cataloging in Publication Data

Zimmerman, Joseph Francis, 1928–
    State-local relations.

    Bibliography: p.
    Includes index.
    1. State-local relations—United States.
2. Intergovernmental fiscal relations—United
States. I. Title.
KF5300.Z53 1983   342. 73'042   82–19004
ISBN 0-03-063184-X   347. 30242

Published in 1983 by Praeger Publishers
CBS Educational and Professional Publishing
a Division of CBS Inc.
521 Fifth Avenue, New York, New York 10175 U.S.A.

456789 052 98765432

Printed in the United States of America

PREFACE

One of the most neglected areas of the literature on the U.S. governance systems is state-local relations. The neglect is most surprising in view of the fact that the bulk of the public services are provided to the citizenry by general purpose local governments that are subject to varying degrees of control by their respective state governments. In part, the neglect is explainable by the great diversity in state-local relations within the typical state as well as between states. The legal and fiscal relationships vary from one type of political subdivision to another within most states and obviously differ greatly from one state to another. Explaining state-local relations in a relatively short book is a formidable undertaking, yet the need for such an explanation is great.

This book builds upon earlier studies conducted by the author for the U.S. Advisory Commission on Intergovernmental Relations. The studies deal with intergovernmental service agreements, transfers of functional responsibility, state mandates, and local discretionary authority. The last study mentioned produced the first index of local discretionary authority for each type of general purpose local government in each of the 50 states.

All local governments were subject to stringent control by the state legislature until the last quarter of the nineteenth century. The so-called home rule movement, one of several governmental reform movements originating in the late 1800s, has been successful in broadening the discretionary authority of general purpose political subdivisions. However, major controversies revolved around the best approach to granting local discretionary authority and the role of the judiciary as a referee of state-local conflicts. The controversies remain today and one purpose of this book is to present a model of state-local relations that will produce broad discretionary authority for local governments and a partnership approach between the state governments and its political subdivisions for the solution of public problems.

A book dealing with a subject as complex as state-local relations reflects the contributions of experts in the 50 states too numerous to acknowledge. Nevertheless, a special debt of gratitude must be expressed to my colleague Ronald M. Stout as well as Dr. David B. Walker and Dr. Carl W. Stenberg, assistant directors of the U.S. Advisory Commission on Intergovernmental Relations, for their constructive criticisms of the manuscript, which was typed by Edith K. Connelly.

CONTENTS

PREFACE   v

Chapter

**1   PATERNALISM OR PARTNERSHIP: STATE-LOCAL
      RELATIONS IN THE UNITED STATES**   1

    Formal Power Distribution   2
    State-Local Tensions and Problems   10
    Notes   14

2   THE LEGAL RELATIONSHIP   17

    The Ultra Vires Rule   17
    Freedom from State Control   21
    Local Discretionary Authority   36
    Summary and Conclusions   44
    Notes   45

3   STATE-LOCAL FISCAL RELATIONS   49

    Constitutional and Statutory Fiscal Provisions   51
    General Property Tax   57
    Local Nonproperty Taxing Authority   62
    The Mandate Problem   64
    State Financial Assistance   70
    Summary and Conclusions   79
    Notes   80

4   STATE RESPONSE TO LOCAL PROBLEMS   85

    The State as Inhibitor   87

The State as Facilitator 90

The State as Initiator 96

Summary and Conclusions 124

Notes 126

5 THE FEDERAL INFLUENCE 133

Expansion of National Powers 134

The Impact of Federal Preemption 138

Federal Financial Assistance 145

Summary and Conclusions 153

Notes 154

6 STATE-LOCAL RELATIONS: A PARTNERSHIP APPROACH 159

Expansion of Local Discretionary Authority 160

A State-Local Relations Model 161

A Defender of Local Discretionary Authority 168

A Partnership Approach 169

Notes 170

APPENDIX 171

BIBLIOGRAPHY 183

INDEX 227

ABOUT THE AUTHOR 241

STATE-LOCAL RELATIONS

CHAPTER 1

Paternalism or Partnership: State-Local Relations in the United States

The most important type of government in the United States, measured in terms of delivery of service to citizens and number of employees, is local government. Many of the nearly 80,000 local governments, governed by approximately 474,971 elected officials and supported by nearly 12.6 million employees, are Lilliputian in size and also are part-time governments with one individual holding several offices (see Table 1.1). Substate units historically have possessed relatively little discretionary authority and have been tightly controlled by their respective state governments.

While local governments are the important providers of services, a 1980 national public opinion poll by the Opinion Research Corporation revealed that only 26 percent of the interviewees felt that local governments provide "the most for your money" while 33 percent cited the federal government and 22 percent cited state government.[1] By way of contrast, a 1980 poll of the members of the Citizens Public Expenditure Survey, Inc., a New York State taxpayers' organization, discovered that 84 percent of its members believe that local governments provide "the best level of services considering the cost of taxpayers" and only 3 percent of the respondents cited the federal government or the state government.[2]

State dominance of substate governments or local autonomy has been one of the most controversial issues of state politics since the end of the Revolutionary War. While each state initially determined the nature of the local governance system, the typical state has partially relinquished its position as a controller of local government and has allowed the electorate a

TABLE 1.1 Local Governments Classified by Type and Number of Elected Officials, 1977

Type	Number of Units	Number of Elected Officials	Average per Unit
Counties	3,042	62,922	20.7
Municipalities	18,862	134,017	7.1
Townships	16,822	118,966	7.1
Schools districts	15,174	87,062	5.7
Other special districts	25,962	72,377	2.8
Total	79,862	474,971*	6.0

*Adjusted to avoid duplicate counting of elected officials serving both a county and another local government.
Source: 1977 Census of Governments, vol. 1, no. 2: *Popularly Elected Officials* (Washington, D.C.: U.S. Government Printing Office, 1979), p. 1.

considerable degree of authority relative to the structuring of a local governmental system.

Two competing theories relating to the most desirable degree of concentration of political power influenced the legal nature of state-local relations in the United States. One paradigm stresses the integration of political authority, while the other supports the fragmentation of such authority. The clash may be viewed as one between elitist theory and democratic theory. The key question is on what level of government policy should be made.

The open town meeting form of local government, which originated in the Massachusetts Bay Colony, often is cited as an example of "pure" or "direct" democracy, and the conclusion has been drawn that the early town meeting possessed unrestricted discretionary authority over town affairs. Did such a "golden age" of unfettered local self-government ever exist? A brief examination of Massachusetts historical records in Chapter 2 is most revealing with respect to the suggested grass roots tradition of local self-governance.

FORMAL POWER DISTRIBUTION

Although the U.S. Constitution, drafted in 1787, might have been designed to allocate specific powers to the three levels of government (national, state, and local), a decision was made to have the Constitution delegate enumerated powers only to the national government and to reserve all other powers (not prohibited) to the states and the people. No mention was made of local governments since they were assumed to be creatures of the states.

Included among the delegated or expressed powers were exclusive powers—such as foreign affairs, coinage of money, post offices, and declaration of war—which states were forbidden to exercise.[3] The Congress and the states were denied other powers—bill of attainder, ex post facto law, and granting titles of nobility—by the Constitution.[4]

Two types of concurrent powers are provided for by the Constitution. The first type includes the power to tax, which is not subject to formal preemption.[5] The second type of concurrent power includes powers granted to the Congress and not prohibited to the states. In the event of a direct conflict between a federal statute and a state statute, the supremacy clause of the Constitution provides for the prevalence of the federal law by nullifying the state law.[6] In other words, the exercise of this type of concurrent power by a state is subject to complete or partial preemption by Congress.

The Constitution also contains a list of powers that states may exercise only with the consent of Congress; examples include the levying of import and tonnage duties, keeping of troops in time of peace, and entrance into compacts with other states.[7] The U.S. Supreme Court, however, has not interpreted these powers to mean that in all cases they may be exercised only with the consent of the Congress. The Court ruled in 1893 that congressional consent is required only if states desire to enter into political compacts affecting the balance of power between the states and the Union.[8] In 1975 the Court held that the prohibition of levying duties on imports without the consent of Congress does not prohibit levying a property tax on imported products.[9]

In spite of *Publius'* assurances in *The Federalist Papers* that federal powers would be limited under the proposed Constitution, fear of a strong centralized government induced the proponents of the document to agree to the adoption of a Bill of Rights in order to gain sufficient support for ratification of the proposed Constitution.[10] To clarify that the national government possessed only enumerated powers, the Tenth Amendment to the U.S. Constitution stipulates that "the powers not delegated to the United States by the Constitution, nor prohibited by it to the States, are reserved to the States respectively, or to the people." This division-of-powers approach to government—an *Imperium in Imperio*—often is labelled "dual" or "layer cake" federalism. As Chapters 4 and 5 make clear, there is a sharing of many powers by the three principal levels of government—federal, state, and local—rather than the complete division of powers suggested by the term "dual federalism."[11]

The federal sphere of power since 1788 has been broadened appreciably, as explained in more detail in Chapter 5, by accretion of power from constitutional amendments, statutory elaboration of delegated powers, and judicial interpretation. The involvement of the national government in areas considered to be the responsibilities of the states and their political subdivisions has produced a continuing ideological debate over the proper role of the national government. Suggestions have been advanced that informal and formal federal preemption is responsible for the erosion of local discretionary authority during the past quarter century.

State-Local Power Division

In view of the fact that the U.S. Constitution does not delegate or reserve political power to local governments, it is apparent that local governments must obtain their powers from the states. The early state constitutions contained few references to local governments or local officials, and the references typically were to counties that historically in every state were quasi-municipal corporations serving as administrative arms of the state and possessing no legislative powers. In the absence of constitutional status, local governments were at the mercy of the state legislature, which imposed the Ultra Vires Rule on local governments; for example, a political subdivision could exercise only the powers specifically granted to it, and these powers were to be interpreted narrowly by the courts.

Acting upon the basis of the Ultra Vires Rule, state legislatures in the nineteenth century enacted numerous special laws affecting individual local governments. Some of these special laws properly recognized that political subdivisions were different in many respects, including climate, industry, population, topography, and transportation systems. Other special laws, frequently referred to as "ripper laws," represented an abuse of legislative power and were used as a means of arbitrarily controlling local governments.

In the nineteenth century, abuses of the legislature's plenary power to enact special laws led voters in several states to approve constitutional amendments prohibiting the legislature from enacting special laws relating to specific topics.[12] This prohibition was followed in some states by the adoption of a constitutional provision stipulating that all "special city" acts were subject to a suspensory veto by the concerned cities.[13]

The authority to draft, adopt, and amend a charter and to supersede special laws and certain general laws was the next power granted to cities, and later to other units in some states, by constitutional amendments or statute. Chapter 2 describes and analyzes the two constitutional approaches utilized by states in granting discretionary authority to their political subdivisions.

In terms of the distribution of political power within a state, three broad spheres can be identified—a local controlling sphere, a state controlling sphere, and a shared state-local sphere. In practice, many

State					
Mississippi	—	—	—	Yes	MCA § 21-17-1
Missouri	art. VI, §§ 18-19	Yes	No	Yes	MSA, chap. 46-55 & 70-99
Montana	art. XI	No	No	Yes	RCM, tit. 11 & 16
Nebraska	art. XI, § 22-5	No	No	Yes	RSN, chap. 14-19 & 22
Nevada	art. VIII, § 8	No	No	Yes	NRS, chap. 265-73
New Hampshire	—	—	—	Yes	NHRS, § 49A
New Jersey	—	—	—	Yes	NJSA, §§ 40:20-1, 40:23-1, 40:48-1
New Mexico	art. X, § 6	No	Yes	Yes	NMS, §§ 15-37-1 to 15-37-41
New York	art. IX	No	Yes	Yes	Mun. Home Rule Law, Gen. Mun. Law.
North Carolina	—	—	—	No	NCGS, chap. 153A & 160A
North Dakota	art. VI, § 130	No	No	Yes	NDCC, tit. 11 & 40
Ohio	art. XV, §§ 3 & 7 & art. X	Yes	No	Yes	ORCA, §§ 705.01 et seq.
Oklahoma	art. XVIII	Yes	No	Yes	OSA, tit. 11 & 19
Oregon	art. IV, VI, XI	Yes	No	Yes	ORS, §§ 203 & 215
Pennsylvania	art. IX	Yes	No	Yes	PA.SA, tit. 16 & 53
Rhode Island	art. XXVIII, §§ 1-12	Yes	No	Yes	RIGL, § 45-2-1
South Carolina	art. VII-VIII	No	No	Yes	SCCL, tit. 14 & 47
South Dakota	art. IX, § 2	Yes	Yes	No	SDCL, chap. 6-9
Tennessee	art. XI, § 9	Yes	No	Yes	TCA, tit. 5-6
Texas	art. XI, § 5	Yes	No	Yes	TACS, tit. 28 & 33-37
Utah	art. XI, § 5	Yes	Yes	Yes	UCA, tit. 10 & 17
Vermont	—	—	—	No	VtSA, tit. 24, § 703
Virginia	—	—	—	Yes	VC, tit. 15.1, § 839
Washington	art. XI, § 10	Yes	No	Yes	RCW, §§ 35.22.570, 32.21.620, 35.22.900
West Virginia	art. VI, § 39a	Yes	Yes	Yes	WVC, chap. 8
Wisconsin	art. XI, § 3; art. IV, § 23	No	No	No	WSA, tit. 8, §§ 66.01-66.99
Wyoming	art. XIII, § 1	Yes	No	Yes	WSA, tit. 15 & 18

9

statutory grant of local discretionary authority and in effect limited cities to selecting one of four statutory forms of government and determining the dates of local elections.[17] In Vermont the statutory home rule provision is not employed by cities and towns because bond counsels contend the provision violates the state constitution.

Public understanding of the amount and type of discretionary authority possessed by substate units has been inhibited by the failure of the state constitution to define terms, for example, "local concerns" and "municipal affairs." This has resulted in courts resolving state-local conflicts on a case-by-case basis. Poorly drafted provisions—the use of "not inconsistent" or "denied" in the Massachusetts Constitution—cause problems since a proposed city or town action that is not denied by the commonwealth's constitution or statutes is inconsistent if the action does not follow the existing statutes.

STATE-LOCAL TENSIONS AND PROBLEMS

That tensions should exist in the relations between a state and its political subdivisions is not surprising in view of the fact that the state possesses plenary legal authority to control local governments, which naturally prefer to operate independently of higher levels of government. While local government officials typically desire additional discretionary authority and the failure of the legislature to grant such authority may heighten state-local tensions, the major source of poor relations between the two levels of government is direct legislative action to solve local problems. In its formal policy statement, the League of Kansas Municipalities in 1980 maintained that "the state legislature should avoid unwarranted intervention in matters of local affairs and government, and should act to encourage and promote the exercise of authority and assumption of responsibility by locally elected, locally responsible governing bodies."

While municipal leagues and county associations decry what is labelled "state interference" in local affairs, these organizations seek additional state financial assistance and prefer it in the form of "string-free" revenue sharing, a subject examined in Chapter 3. They also seek state reimbursement of costs associated with state mandates (a directive that a local unit provide a service or undertake an activity) and a requirement that all bills affecting local governments carry a fiscal rate indicating the costs being imposed upon political subdivisions.

As one would anticipate, local officials representing a single jurisdiction of a given type lobby continually during sessions of the state legislature in favor of certain bills and in opposition to other bills. Where possible, local officials form coalitions with other interest groups to amass sufficient political power to gain their legislative goals but often encounter strong opposition from public employee unions. The latter not only oppose certain goals of the local officials but also seek legislative approval for state mandates upon political subdivisions. Unions and associations representing firefighters and police officers tend to have the most political strength among public employee unions lobbying the legislature.

State-Local Issues

Of the various issues contributing to poor relations between states and their local governments, Table 1.3 reveals that the issue of state mandates in general has the greatest impact in all regions of the United States in the view of state and local officials and experts on state-local relations surveyed in 1981. Interest groups unable to achieve their goals on the local level often turn their attention to the state legislature in the knowledge that the legislators possess the constitutional authority by general law to order local governments to initiate or stop specific actions and in the hope that the legislators will be more sympathetic to the groups' goals than local officials. A typology of and rationale for state mandates are presented in Chapter 3.

Table 1.3 reveals that perceptions concerning the severity of the state mandate issue vary considerably from region to region with 85 percent of the respondents in the northeast and 55 percent of the respondents in the north central region rating the issue as a major problem, as compared to only 34 percent of the western respondents and 39 percent of the southern respondents.

The next most important issue in state-local relations, according to the perceptions reported in Table 1.3, is state financial assistance to education, which is viewed as a most serious problem by north central and northeastern respondents. State financial assistance to local governments also is perceived to be a major problem.

Survey respondents rated compulsory binding arbitration of police and fire union impasses, a specific state mandate, as a major issue in the northeast only. The reason for the regional differences in perceptions on this issue is the fact that several states in the industrial northeast have adopted compulsory binding arbitration laws for the settlement of collective bargaining impasses involving local governments and their fire and police unions.

The key question in state-local relations is the extent to which states can permit local self-determination without the danger that actions taken by one political subdivision will cause problems for other subdivisions or result in the abuse of the rights of minorities within the subdivision. Concerning the latter, federal intervention to protect minority rights has increased sharply during the past two decades.

TABLE 1.3 Perceptions of State-Local Relations Problems by Region, 1981

Problem Area	Northeast			North Central			South			West		
	Major Problem	Minor Problem	Not a Problem	Major Problem	Minor Problem	Not a Problem	Major Problem	Minor Problem	Not a Problem	Major Problem	Minor Problem	Not a Problem
	No. %	No. %	No. %	No. %	No. %	No. %	No. %	No. %	No. %	No. %	No. %	No. %
Special laws not requested	6 18	10 29	19 56	6 14	16 38	18 43	7 12	30 53	20 35	8 21	12 32	15 39
State mandates	29 85	8 24	1 3	23 55	15 36	4 10	22 39	26 46	9 16	24 63	13 34	0 0
State administrative supervision	4 12	24 71	8 24	6 14	19 45	13 31	14 25	24 42	17 30	5 13	21 55	10 26
Compulsory binding arbitration of police and fire impasses	22 65	10 29	3 9	6 14	9 21	24 57	4 7	8 14	44 77	6 16	8 21	18 47
State creation of special Districts	1 3	6 18	30 88	6 14	15 36	19 45	6 11	19 33	32 56	3 8	18 47	13 34
State tax limits	10 29	6 18	18 53	20 48	12 26	10 24	18 32	15 26	23 40	22 58	10 26	6 16
State debt limits	4 12	8 24	24 71	9 21	15 36	16 38	7 12	23 40	26 46	5 13	18 47	11 29

State financial assistance to local governments	21 62	12 35	4 12	27 64	13 31	6 14	29 51	16 28	11 19	17 45	14 37	5 13
State financial assistance for local education	26 76	7 21	3 9	23 55	13 31	6 14	18 32	22 39	14 25	12 32	11 29	13 34
State-mandated functional transfers	7 21	13 38	15 44	7 17	13 31	21 50	6 11	18 32	33 58	4 11	17 45	17 45
Use of initiative and referendum to put a lid on borrowing	1 3	7 21	29 85	3 7	4 10	32 76	1 2	9 16	45 79	5 13	4 11	26 68
Use of initiative and referendum to put a lid on spending	6 18	8 24	22 65	8 19	5 12	23 55	2 4	9 16	42 74	14 37	7 18	16 42

Geographic regions—**Northeast** includes the New England and Mid-Atlantic divisions, including the states of Connecticut, Maine, Massachusetts, New Hampshire, New Jersey, New York, Pennsylvania, Rhode Island, and Vermont; **North Central** includes the East and West North Central divisions, including the states of Illinois, Indiana, Iowa, Kansas, Michigan, Minnesota, Missouri, Nebraska, North Dakota, Ohio, South Dakota, and Wisconsin; **South** includes the South Atlantic and West South Central divisions, including the states of Alabama, Arkansas, Delaware, Florida, Georgia, Kentucky, Louisiana, Maryland, Mississippi, North Carolina, Oklahoma, South Carolina, Tennessee, Texas, Virginia, and West Virginia; **West** includes the Mountain and Pacific Coast divisions, including the states of Alaska, Arizona, California, Colorado, Hawaii, Idaho, Montana, Nevada, New Mexico, Oregon, Utah, Washington, and Wyoming.

The second key question involves the state's role in local government problem solving. The state as the superior government can play, as described in Chapter 4, one or more of the following three roles: inhibitor, facilitator, and initiator. States traditionally have inhibited the solution of substate problems by failing to delegate to political subdivisions sufficient authority to cope with the problems. As a facilitator, the state can grant additional discretionary authority to local government, including authorization to enter into intergovernmental service agreements and transfer functions or functional components to other governments. The most controversial role tends to be that of an initiator of solutions for local problems because such actions are often perceived by many local officials and many citizens as a violation of home rule, a subject analyzed in Chapter 2.

Chapter 5 examines the influence of the federal government on state-local relations. Addressing the National Association of Counties in 1974, Governor Calvin Rampton of Utah admitted that states have not responded adequately to local problems:

> The past several years have seen a tendency arise for local governments, both city and county, to circumvent state government and take their problems directly to Washington. In all candor, I must say that a large share of the blame for this disenchantment on the part of local officials with state government lies with the States themselves. We as States have failed fully to meet our responsibility to units of local government, and they have turned to the federal government in desperation.[18]

The federal government since the late 1940s increasingly responded in a favorable manner to numerous requests by local governments for assistance in solving problems. Chapter 5 describes and analyzes the impact of national government actions upon local governments and state-local relations in the form of pass-through mandates.

A detailed examination of state-local relations commences in Chapter 2. The changing legal relationships between a state and its political subdivisions will be analyzed, and information will be presented on the amount of discretionary authority possessed by each type of local government.

NOTES

1. *1980: Changing Public Attitudes on Governments and Taxes* (Washington, D.C.: U.S. Advisory Commission on Intergovernmental Relations, 1980), p. 2.

2. *CPES Membership Questionnaire on Issues: Summary of Results* (Albany: Citizens Public Expenditure Survey, 1980), p. 2.

3. *U.S. Constitution*, art I, § § 8, 10.

4. Ibid., art. I, § § 9, 10.

5. Ibid., art. I, § 8; and the Tenth Amendment.

6. Ibid., art. VI, § 2.

7. Ibid., art. I, § 10.

8. *Virginia v. Tennessee*, 148 U.S. 503 (1893).

9. *Michelin Tire Corporation v. Wages*, 423 U.S. 276 at 286 (1975).

10. *The Federalist Papers* (New York: New American Library, 1961), p. 292.

11. For the historical development of cooperative federalism, see Daniel J. Elazar, *American Federalism: A View from the States*, 2nd ed. (New York: Thomas Y. Crowell, 1972); and Morton Grodzins, *The American System* (Chicago: Rand McNally, 1967). The latter work was edited by Daniel J. Elazar after the death of Professor Grodzins.

12. For an example, see the *Constitution of the State of New York*, art. III § 18 (1874).

13. See ibid., art. XII, § 2 (1894).

14. The Appendix contains indexes of the amount of discretionary authority possessed by each type of local government in each of the 50 states.

15. Elazar, *American Federalism*, pp. 86–126.

16. *Constitution of Vermont*, § 72.

17. *Hogan v. City of South Charleston*, 260 S.E.2d 283 (1979). See also David A. Bingham, "No Home Rule in West Virginia," *National Civic Review* 69, April 1980, pp. 213–14.

18. Calvin L. Rampton, "An Address to the National Association of Counties, July 1974," in *States' Responsibilities to Local Governments: An Action Agenda* (Washington, D.C.: National Governors' Conference, 1975), p. iii.

CHAPTER 2

The Legal Relationship

The most desirable degree to which political power should be decentralized by a state government to local governments has been a source of major controversy since the end of the Revolutionary War. Numerous attempts have been made by local governments to secure protection from state interference and a relatively broad grant of discretionary authority to be exercised intramurally. The exercise of governmental power by two or more levels of government over a common geographical area automatically produces occasional conflicts and raises the question of which jurisdiction should prevail in cases of conflict.

A brief historical examination of the legal position of local governments in the period prior to 1875 will assist one in understanding the current legal position of political subdivisions of a state.

THE ULTRA VIRES RULE

Local governments historically have been subject to the Ultra Vires Rule, which holds that political subdivisions possess only the powers expressly conferred by charter or law and no other powers. In other words, the rule provides for a narrow interpretation of the powers of local governments and makes explicit that a substate government may engage only in an activity specifically sanctioned by the superior government. The Ultra Vires Rule is based upon powers reserved to the states by the Tenth Amendment to the U.S. Constitution.

Town-Colony Relations in Massachusetts

Local government in its currently recognizable form is traceable to the Massachusetts Bay Colony in the second quarter of the seventeenth century, when town government first appeared and its inferior legal status was established.

An inspection of the records of the Massachusetts Bay Company reveals the subordinate status of towns and the controls the Massachusetts General Court (legislature) exercised during the 1630s and 1640s over these units, including regulation of the establishment of new towns, local boundary adjustments, and appointment of constables in Charlestown, Dorchester, Roxbury, and Watertown.[1] Specific directives often were issued to towns, such as keeping a watch at night, establishing a pound "for swine found in cornfields," repairing highways, and providing a system of weights and measures.[2] If a town failed to carry out an order, the town was fined.[3]

Town-colony relations apparently were good, as evidenced by town records indicating ready compliance with orders of the general court.[4] The removal of the royal government subsequent to the start of the Revolutionary War and the widespread popularity of the social contract theory enabled towns to exercise broad discretionary authority for a period of three to four years until the Massachusetts Constitution was adopted in 1780. It was only during this brief period that a so-called golden age of unfettered local self-government existed in Massachusetts.

Special Charters

Municipalities in the colonial period were created by the colonial legislature or royal charter issued by the lieutenant governor-in-council. Following the end of the Revolutionary War, all municipal corporations were established by the state legislature, which was free to grant or to withhold specific municipal powers. In effect, there was an unwritten constitutional principle —a common law of municipal corporations—holding that each local government was completely subordinate to the state legislature. Legislative favoritism in granting charters and specific powers led to a movement in the nineteenth century to amend the state constitution to prohibit special legislation.

In addition to creating municipal corporations, the legislature established quasi-municipal corporations. The most important quasi-municipal corporation was the county, which functioned as an arm of the state government for convenience in administration. In contrast to a municipal corporation, the historic county possessed no charter and no sublegislative powers, performed no proprietary or business functions, was established without the consent of the voters, and had the same immunity from suit as the state. A municipality, on the other hand, possessed a charter and sublegislative powers, typically was formed upon petition of its residents, and was liable to suit when performing a proprietary function.

Dillon's Rule

Although it was not known as Dillon's Rule until 1868, the Ultra Vires Rule is really Dillon's Rule, or the rule of strict construction of the powers of local governments. The rule is attributable to Judge John Dillon of Iowa who issued two decisions in 1868 construing narrowly the powers of municipal corporations. In *City of Clinton v. Cedar Rapids and Missouri Railroad Company*, he ruled:

> Municipal corporations owe their origin to, and derive their powers and rights wholly from the Legislature. It breathes into them the breath of life, without which they can not exist. As it creates, so may it destroy. If it may destroy, it may abridge and control. Unless there is some constitutional limitation on the right, the Legislature might, by a single act, if we can suppose it capable of so great a folly and so great a wrong, sweep from existence all municipal corporations of the State, and the corporations could not prevent it. We know of no limitation on this right as the corporations themselves are concerned. They are, so to phrase it, the mere tenants at will of the Legislature.[5]

In a second opinion in the same year, Judge Dillon reinforced his original ruling relative to the powers of municipal corporations:

> In determining the question now made, it must be taken for settled law, that a municipal corporation possesses and can exercise the following powers and no others: First, those granted in express words; second, those necessarily implied or necessarily incident to the powers expressly granted; third, those absolutely essential to the declared objects and purposes of the corporation—not simply convenient, but indispensable; fourth, any fair doubt as to the existence of a power is resolved by the courts against the corporation.[6]

A challenge to Dillon's Rule was issued by Judge Thomas Cooley of the Michigan Supreme Court in 1871 when he ruled that municipalities possess certain inherent rights of local self-government and that all local legislation should be general in nature.[7] Cooley's Rule was followed for a short period of time by courts in Indiana, Iowa, Kentucky, and Texas. It is interesting to note that Judge Cooley in his treatise on the legislative power of states subsequently accepted Dillon's Rule:

> They [municipalities] have no inherent jurisdiction to make laws or adopt regulations of government; they are governments of enumerated powers, acting by a delegated authority; so that while the State Legislature may exercise such powers of government coming within a proper designation of legislative power as are not expressly or impliedly prohibited, the local authorities can exercise those only which are expressly or impliedly conferred, and subject to such regulations or restrictions as are annexed to the grant.[8]

The U.S. Supreme Court was first called upon to determine the validity of Dillon's Rule in 1903 and upheld it:

> Such corporations are the creatures, mere political subdivisions of the State for the purposes of exercising a part of its powers. They may exert only such powers as are expressly granted to them, or such as may be necessarily implied from those granted. What they lawfully do of a public character is done under the sanction of the State. They may be created, or, having been created, their powers may be restricted or enlarged, or altogether withdrawn at the will of the Legislature; the authority of the Legislature, when restricting or withdrawing such powers, being subject only to the fundamental condition that the collective and individual rights of the people of the municipality shall not be destroyed.[9]

In 1923 the Court again refused to recognize an inherent right of local self-government for a municipality.[10]

Dillon's Rule allows the legislature to control local governments completely in terms of their structure of government, methods of financing activities, procedures, and authority to undertake functions. Ruling by special act, the legislature typically served as a "super city council" and made decisions affecting only a single municipality. During much of the nineteenth century, many cities were subject to punitive state action administered on a partisan basis. The legislative delegation from a city usually possessed more power than the city council since the legislature typically would approve or reject a special bill on the basis of "legislative courtesy," that is, the delegation's recommendation. Members of the delegation often held views differing from those of municipal officials and frequently were political competitors of municipal officials. Interest groups were able to influence legislative decisions to the detriment of municipalities. The principal irritants in state-local relations typically are state restraints and mandates on local governments, a product of interest group action and a subject discussed in more detail in Chapter 3.

The ability of local governments to respond quickly to changing conditions in the latter half of the nineteenth century was limited by Dillon's Rule, since no new municipal action could be undertaken without permission of the state legislature, which typically met in a short biennial session. Nevertheless, local governments in a Dillon's Rule state may possess relatively broad discretionary powers because of the political power of the local governments in the legislature or because the latter chooses not to control its political subdivisions closely. In New Jersey today, local governments operate under a relatively broad statutory grant of discretionary authority. Dillon's Rule, however, generally requires that local officials spend a considerable amount of time lobbying the legislature to approve bills granting authority to local governments and disapprove bills restraining or imposing mandates upon them.

FREEDOM FROM STATE CONTROL

Special laws can recognize the unique problems of individual local governments and assist in the solution of their problems. These laws also can be employed to control political subdivisions arbitrarily, but such use represents an improper use of the legislature's superordinate power. Abuses of the plenary power of state legislatures in the nineteenth century encouraged voters to approve constitutional amendments restricting the power of the legislature to enact local laws.

Prohibition of Special Laws

In 1850 Michigan adopted the first constitutional amendment prohibiting a special law: the legislature was forbidden to enact a law "vacating or altering" any road laid out by highway commissioners.[11] In 1874 New York State voters approved a constitutional amendment, which still is in effect, forbidding the legislature to enact a special bill laying out or discontinuing roads, draining swamps, locating or changing county seats, or incorporating villages.[12] Presently, 41 state constitutions have been amended to prohibit all special legislation.

Legislative ingenuity, however, has been employed to evade the constitutional prohibition to some extent. The ineffectiveness of the New York constitutional prohibition of special legislation is illustrated by the enactment of 1,284 laws affecting the 30 cities in the period 1884 to 1889.[13] In 1886 alone, 380 (61.5 percent) of the bills approved by the New York State legislature were special acts.[14]

The most common method of evasion involves the use of classified laws. In general, state courts have not invalidated classified legislation—such as cities of the first class—if the laws reasonably distinguish between the classes in terms of the goals of the legislation.[15] In 1944, however, the New York Court of Appeals invalidated a law applicable to counties with a population of 200,000 to 250,000 and containing a city with a population greater than 125,000 because the law applied only to Albany County and hence violated the constitutional ban on special legislation.[16] Nevertheless, 12 years later, the court upheld as a "general" law a statute that applied to cities with a population over 1 million even though New York City was the only city with a population exceeding that amount.[17] With a few exceptions, courts have not invalidated the use of population classes as the basis for classified legislation but have struck down classified laws based upon geography.[18]

In some states, classified charters based upon population have necessitated a charter change as a city's population grew, even though the city was satisfied with its existing charter.

Procedural Requirements

Recognizing that special legislation may be needed at times by local governments, constitutional amendments have been adopted specifying a procedure that must be followed when a local law is being enacted. A new constitution, approved by the voters in New York in 1894, contained a provision that all "special city" acts were subject to a suspensory veto by the concerned cities.[19] A special act could not be transmitted directly to the governor by the legislature, since the act first had to be sent to the mayor and/or city council of the concerned city for review and a possible suspensive veto.[20] To protect Chicago against the enactment of "Ripper laws," the pre-1970 Illinois Constitution granted Chicago a suspensory veto over special acts applying to that city.[21]

The current Massachusetts Constitution allows the general court to enact a special law under two conditions: (1) receipt of a petition from the mayor and city council, or a town meeting, or the voters of the concerned political subdivision; or (2) receipt of a recommendation from the governor for approval of a local bill and its approval by a two-thirds vote of each house of the general court.[22]

Minimum Number of Classes

The power of the legislature to control local governments has been limited in several states by adoption of a constitutional provision establishing a maximum number of classes and/or a minimum number of political subdivisions in any class. According recognition to the fact that classified local legislation may be an euphemism for special legislation, Jefferson Fordham included in his 1953 recommendations for a constitutional grant of local discretionary authority a provision limiting the number of classes of local governments to four and stipulating that each class must contain a minimum of two local governments.[23]

In granting constitutional local discretionary authority, Massachusetts followed in general the recommendations of Professor Fordham and adopted a provision specifying that each class must contain a minimum of two local governments.[24]

Uniform Law Application

The Wisconsin Constitution contains a provision illustrating a fourth approach designed to make the evasion of the constitutional prohibition of special legislation impossible. The provision restricts the legislature to approving only statewide bills uniformly affecting every city or village.[25] The constitutional prohibition of special legislation often has not prevented the legislature from evading the prohibition through the use of classified legislation. The uniform law application provision of the Wisconsin Constitution, however, has been interpreted strictly, and a city may override a state-classified statute dealing primarily with a matter of local concern.[26]

Acceptance Statutes

To provide local governments with additional discretionary authority to meet what may be relatively unique conditions, state legislatures have enacted general laws in the form of "acceptance" statutes that become effective within a political subdivision only if the governing body or electorate votes to accept the laws.

Acceptance statutes are of two types. The first type, representing the market basket approach, is a general law containing optional charters for local governments. Not all local governments, however, may be eligible to adopt one of the standard charters contained in an optional charter law. In Massachusetts, for example, city voters may adopt one of six optional charters,[27] but town voters are not accorded this privilege even though Massachusetts towns are municipal corporations, possessing the same basic authority as cities, and strong interest has been expressed in optional town charters. (An optional town charter can be adopted quicker and at less expense than a locally drafted and adopted charter following constitutional procedures for drafting and adopting a charter.)

New York voters in 1935 approved a constitutional amendment that, among other things, directed the legislature to provide counties with

alternative forms of government.[28] Although the legislature enacted the
Optional County Government Law in 1937, no county has adopted one of
the alternative forms: county mayor, county manager, county director, or
county board form.[29]

The second type of acceptance statute authorizes a political subdivision accepting the law to exercise the grant of discretionary authority
contained in the statute. Revocation of the acceptance may be a complica-
ted matter. Until 1979 the general laws in Massachusetts stipulated that a
town with a population under 15,000 may vote to rescind its previous
acceptance of a special law with the exceptions of those: (1) providing for a
different method of rescission; (2) relating to the pension statute and tenure
of employees of the town; (3) involving participation of the town in a special
district; or (4) authorizing a capital expenditure.

In 1970 the Supreme Judicial Court restricted the authority of a city or
a town with a population over 15,000 by ruling that a special statute may be
repealed only by the general court or by drafting and adopting a charter
revoking the previous acceptance of the statute.[30] In view of the very large
number of acceptance statutes adopted by Massachusetts cities and towns
over the years, this decision was of major importance until 1979 when the
general court authorized towns with a population over 15,000 and cities to
rescind acceptance statutes.[31]

The complexities involved in the rescission of acceptance statutes are
illustrated by Lynn, Massachusetts, whose city council voted to accept a
rent control act and subsequently petitioned the general court for enactment of a special law permitting a referendum to be held on the question of
the termination of rent control. Although voters in 1972 decided to continue
rent control, the city council two years later voted to abolish rent control.
The action of the council was challenged and the Supreme Judicial Court
rejected the argument that rent control could be terminated only by a
referendum vote because the original act authorizes the city council to
revoke its acceptance of the act.[32]

A Positive Grant of Power

The prohibition of special legislation, precedural requirements imposed on
the state legislature, constitutional establishment of a minimum number of
classes of local government and a minimum number of units in each class,
and a constitutional uniform local law requirement may be viewed as
negative actions designed to prevent the legislature from interfering
arbitrarily in the affairs of an individual local government. While acceptance statutes represent a positive grant of power, many local governments
have been reluctant to accept these statutes because they may not be

tailored to meet specific needs, and/or the difficulty of repealing the statutes in certain states limit their value to local governments. The reader should be aware that the type of power sought by local governments can not be exercised extramurally, that is, beyond the walls or boundary of each local government.

Local government officials and reformers who are proponents of a broad grant of discretionary authority by the state to local governments advance seven major arguments to support their recommendation. The first six arguments are closely interrelated. First, a broad grant of intramural power will promote citizens' interest in their governments and local problems since the local governments possess the authority to initiate discretionary activities. A related argument is that civic education will be advanced because local officials and citizens will have to study major problems before decisions on corrective action can be taken. Formation of study committees and public hearings will assist in educating the citizenry.

Third, since local citizens have the most detailed knowledge of community problems, employment of this knowledge will result in the most expeditious solution of the problems.

A fourth argument holds that local government experimentation in problem solving and providing services more effectively and efficiently will be encouraged. Successful experiments by one local government will induce other local governments to initiate similar actions with necessary modifications to meet special conditions.

Fifth, greater discretionary authority is essential in a period of resource scarcity to ensure the most effective and efficient allocation of funds to high priority needs.

The sixth argument maintains that political alienation may be reduced since responsibility for solving problems is transferred from state legislators and bureaucrats, who are not directly involved with the problems, to local officials and citizens.

From the standpoint of the state government and its problems, the most important argument in favor of a broad grant of local discretionary authority is that such a grant will remove the necessity for the state legislature to spend an inordinate amount of time considering special bills and provide the legislature with additional time to devote to the study of statewide problems.

In 1953 Executive Director Carl Chatters of the American Municipal Association argued that "municipal governments can be neither free nor responsible unless they are guaranteed the right (and the compulsion) to decide purely local matters for themselves."[33] Whether there is agreement on what constitutes purely local matters is a topic that will be examined in a subsequent section.

Included typically within a broad grant of discretionary authority is the power to draft, adopt, and amend a charter. The 1875 Missouri Constitution was the first state constitution to authorize a local government to draft and adopt a charter.[34]

Alabama, Kentucky, and Virginia do not allow the adoption of a locally drafted charter. In other states, the power to adopt a locally drafted charter is limited to specific types of political subdivisions (counties in Georgia and cities and towns in Massachusetts), and in still other states the power is restricted to units with a specified minimum population size (cities with a population of 3,500 or more in Arizona and cities exceeding 5,000 in Texas).

A 1979 survey reveals that authorized local governments often do not adopt a new charter and the principal reason for adopting a charter is to achieve greater structural and administrative discretion.[35] The failure of local governments to utilize their charter-making powers more often is explainable in terms of their satisfaction with charters adopted years ago or their preference for optional or general law charters containing a broad grant of discretionary power. The same survey also revealed that local governments do not amend their charters often, and most amendments tend to be minor ones.

Two avenues have been followed by states in their attempts to grant reasonably broad discretionary authority to local government, that is, *Imperium in Imperio* and devolution of powers. In 24 states, the constitutional grant is self-executing and no implementing legislation is necessary. The Nevada constitutional grant has not been implemented by the legislature.

Imperium in Imperio

In 1921 the National Municipal League, a good government association founded in 1894, proposed a model constitutional provision recognizing that it would be undesirable to confer unlimited power upon local governments and attempted to divide powers precisely between the state and its political subdivisions, thereby establishing a type of dual federalism within the state. Called the separate entity approach, the league favored the establishment of a state within a state, or *Imperium in Imperio*, by insulating local government in part from state interference.

Whenever a conflict occurred between the state and one of its local governments, state courts applied *expressio unius est excusio alterius*, which is the rule of exclusion. In other words, a constitutional listing of specified local government powers automatically reserves all other governmental powers to the state. In addition, the courts followed the principle of *noscitur a sociis*; that is, a specific word is interpreted in concord with other words on the same subject.

From a theoretical standpoint, the *Imperium in Imperio* or enumerated powers method of granting exclusive authority in certain areas to local governments is undesirable since the distribution of authority can be changed only by adoption of a constitutional amendment, which is a difficult and time-consuming process in most states. Where adopted, the separate entity approach generally has not achieved its goals because courts interpreted the scope of municipal or local affairs narrowly.

The tendency of courts to uphold the paramountcy of the state legislature under the *Imperium in Imperio* approach when there is a conflict between a state power, such as the police power, and a local power is illustrated by a 1929 New York Court of Appeals decision. In 1923 New York voters approved a constitutional amendment forbidding the legislature to enact any law relating to the "property, affairs, or government" of a city if the law was "special or local in terms of its effects."[36]

In 1929 the state legislature enacted a multiple dwelling law applicable to cities with a population over 800,000.[37] Since New York City was the only city affected by the law, the conclusion was drawn by many officials that the law was unconstitutional. The court of appeals interpreted the 1923 constitutional amendment in a different light and ruled that the voters had inserted "property, affairs, or government" of a city in the state constitution "with a Court of Appeals' definition and not that of Webster's Dictionary." [38]

Developing a "state concern" doctrine, Judge Benjamin N. Cardozo pointed out that it was impossible to place each governmental function in a state government category or a local government category. He ruled that the state legislature may enact a law in a functional area provided there is a substantial state concern even "though intermingled with it are concerns of the locality."[39] Put simply, Judge Cardozo announced that whether the legislature could pass a special law would be determined by the courts.

Judge Cuthbert Pound agreed with Judge Cardozo and added in a concurring opinion that the multiple dwelling law was designed to protect the health and promote the welfare of citizens, which is a police power responsibility of the state legislature.[40]

The state concern doctrine does not necessarily mean that courts always rule in favor of the state. New York State Court of Appeals decisions in the period 1960 to 1963, when the state operated under the traditional *Imperium in Imperio* grant of local discretionary authority, were examined by Frank Macchiarola, who reported that 32 out of 46 of the decisions were in the favor of the concerned local government.[41]

In adopting a new constitutional local government amendment in 1963, New York retained the *Imperium in Imperio* provision but also provided for devolution of powers by the legislature.[42] The intent of the amendment was to broaden the scope of local discretionary authority. In a

1980 study, Jon A. Baer discovered only one court of appeals decision in the period 1969 to 1980 that he could characterize "as broadly construing local governmental powers, and that was merely a memorandum opinion holding that municipal corporations' constitutional and statutory authority to acquire transit facilities extends to charter and school buses."[43] According to Baer, the court of appeals employed the state concern doctrine in interpreting narrowly municipal powers in the five major decisions rendered during the period of his study.[44]

An *Imperium in Imperio* constitutional grant of local discretionary authority had as one of its major goals the prevention of state interference in what local officials believed to be their own affairs. The governmental system was less complex when this "layer cake" approach initially was promoted, and many functions did not appear to have a clear state concern. Nevertheless, the courts in major state-local disputes typically found a state concern and upheld the state action. The *Imperium in Imperio* approach was criticized severely in 1955 by Dean Jefferson Fordham of the University of Pennsylvania Law School, who maintained that the "general-local distinction ranks with the governmental-proprietary test in tort and other matters as a major contributor to the fuzziness of local government law doctrine and relatively high unpredictability in application."[45]

Devolution of Powers

Somewhat surprisingly, local government officials and their associations did not develop a new approach to granting local discretionary authority immediately after realizing that the *Imperium in Imperio* approach was relatively ineffective because of narrow judicial interpretation of the grant of local powers.

In 1952 the American Municipal Association engaged Dean Fordham to investigate state-local relations. In his 1953 report, Dean Fordham included model constitutional provisions for a new approach to the granting of local discretionary authority that would hopefully avoid the problem of strict judicial interpretation of the powers of political subdivisions.[46] Fordham recommended that the state constitution delegate to a municipal corporation adopting a charter all powers capable of delegation subject to preemption by general law with the exceptions of the powers to enact "civil law governing civil relations" and "define and provide for the punishment of a felony." The judicial state concern doctrine is obliviated since the devolution of powers approach does not distinguish between state and local concerns. Dean Fordham pointed out:

> The familiar distinction between state or general concerns and
> municipal or local affairs, with which courts are confronted in certain

existing home rule states, has not been susceptible to satisfactory application. It has served to shift largely political questions to the judicial forum for decision. The approach here taken avoids this difficulty.[47]

The devolution of powers approach to granting local discretionary authority has been labelled the "residual powers" approach.[48] Devolution of powers, however, is a preferable term since the term "residual powers" is typically employed to refer to the powers reserved to the states by the Tenth Amendment to the U.S. Constitution.

Under the Fordham plan, the self-executing constitutional grant would be triggered by the adoption of a charter, and voters in a municipality would possess the right to repeal the charter by referendum and return the municipality to its precharter status or adopt an optional state charter. Many states, including Massachusetts, New York, and Wisconsin, in adopting a devolution of powers constitutional provision provided that the grant of power may be exercised by a general purpose local government without the adoption of a new charter.

By charter or local law, a municipality may supersede special state laws and certain general state laws. The Washington State Constitution specifically authorized each city with a population over 20,000 to draft and adopt a charter superseding "all special laws inconsistent with such charter."[49] In 27 states, some or all of the general purpose political subdivisions may supersede special state laws and certain general laws by adoption of a charter or a local law, bylaw, or ordinance. According to a 1979 survey, supersession of state laws often or occasionally was reported by 37 percent of the respondents.[50]

A local government does not have to exercise a discretionary power if the unit prefers to operate under a state statute. However, as the Wisconsin Supreme Court pointed out in 1968, "a city or village is to manifest its election not to be governed by a State law by the passage of a charter ordinance."[51]

The devolution of powers approach represents a partial restoration of faith in the state legislature since it, rather than the courts, would be empowered to draw and redraw the dividing line between state and local powers. In effect, the devolution of powers approach is a type of Dillon's Rule approach in that the legislature possesses the supreme power of determining how much discretionary authority should be possessed by political subdivisions but differs from Dillon's Rule, which prevents a local government from exercising a power unless specifically authorized to do so by the legislature. Under the devolution of powers approach, a local government is free to initiate action authorized by the constitutional grant of power unless the legislature adopts a general law preempting specified powers. One can argue that the devolution of powers approach automatically establishes an *Imperium in Imperio*, a division of powers between the two levels of government, unless the legislature exercises its power of preemption.

Because the devolution of powers approach is a legislative supremacy approach to state-local relations, local governments must keep a watchful eye on bills in the legislature and lobby for and against particular bills. Since no devolution of powers constitutional provision grants local governments broad discretionary financial powers, except in Alaska and Pennsylvania, substate units continually pressure the legislature to appropriate additional state financial assistance, a topic addressed in Chapter 3.

In contrast to a local government charter adopted under Dillon's Rule, a devolution of powers charter is a considerably shorter document since it contains restrictions upon the exercise of devolved powers rather than an enumeration of delegated powers.

As pointed out in a preceding section, Dean Fordham recommended that the constitutional amendment authorize the legislature to classify municipalities on the basis of population into a maximum of four classes with a minimum of two units in a class.

A dual or tripartite system of state-local relations exists in most states with a constitutional devolution of powers provision for two reasons. First, the devolution of powers provision applies to only certain types of political subdivisions in several states, and the other types are completely subject to Dillon's Rule. Second, the state constitution, with the exception of Alaska, Montana, and Pennsylvania, does not devolve upon any type of local government all the powers recommended by Dean Fordham. In 1974 the Alaska Supreme Court interpreted the constitutional grant of local discretionary authority as a type of *Imperium in Imperio*.[52]

Since Dean Fordham proposed the devolution of all powers capable of delegation with two exceptions, he did not foresee the need for a provision authorizing the enactment of a special law since each municipality would possess sufficient authority to enact all needed laws in the form of municipal ordinances. In view of the fact that several states adopted a modified devolution of powers constitution provision that does not devolve all the powers that Dean Fordham recommended be devolved, these constitutional provisions recognize the need for special acts. The New York State Constitution, for example, provides that the state legislature may enact a special law affecting the "property, affairs, or government" of a local government "only (a) on request of two-thirds of the total membership of its legislative body or on request of its chief executive officer concurred in by a majority of such membership, or (b) except in the case of the City of New York, on certificate of necessity from the Governor reciting facts which in his judgment constitute an emergency requiring enactment of such law and, in such latter case, with the concurrence of two-thirds of the members elected to each house of the Legislature."[53] As pointed out earlier, the Massachusetts Constitution contains a somewhat similar provision.

Provided the state legislature periodically reexamines the powers devolved upon local governments and takes preemptive action as needed to meet changing conditions, the courts to a great extent are relieved of the responsibility for determining the scope of local discretionary authority. A constitutional directive to the legislature to enact and periodically revise a code of restrictions (powers that may not be exercised) upon the powers of local governments would significantly reduce resorting to the judicial forum for the settlement of state-local disputes since local officials would have a relatively clear understanding of the extent of their powers. Lacking a constitutional requirement for a code of restrictions, the legislature in partially or totally preempting responsibility for functions by general law is apt to scatter the preemptive laws throughout the statute books, thereby making it difficult for local officials to determine all restrictions on their powers.

It is important to recognize that the devolution of powers approach does not eliminate state-local conflicts entirely because the exercise by the legislature of the police power—to protect public health, safety, welfare, morals, and convenience—may conflict with the exercise of a discretionary power by a local government. Currently, only Alaska, Montana, and Pennsylvania have completely adopted the devolution of powers approach. Experience with this approach reveals that the courts still are called upon to interpret the scope of local discretionary authority and issue separation of powers decisions.

That courts continue to play a role in delimiting the extent of powers devolved upon political subdivisions is not surprising since it is impossible for even the most conscientious state legislature, which reexamines on a continuing basis the distribution of political power in the state, to anticipate every type of case that may arise. In 1963 the Washington Supreme Court rejected the argument that a state law requiring a motorist to have a valid operator license preempted a local government from enacting an ordinance containing a similar requirement since the state law did not expressly preempt and there was no conflict between the ordinance and the state law.[54] The Wisconsin Supreme Court in 1977 rejected the preemption doctrine and ruled that local governments may exercise power over subjects of statewide concern provided there is no conflict between the two levels of government.[55]

A constitutional amendment adopted in Oregon grants city and town voters broad discretionary "power to enact and amend their municipal charters, subject to the Constitution and criminal laws of the State of

Oregon. . . ."[56] The Oregon Supreme Court consistently has interpreted the grant broadly and in 1962 wrote that the grant was based upon "the concept that the closer those who make and execute the laws are to the citizens they represent the better are those citizens represented and governed in accordance with democratic ideals."[57] The court, however, pointed out that the state and a city both may have an interest in the matter under contention, and the key question is "whether the State's interest or that of the city is paramount."[58]

In 1937 the Wisconsin Supreme Court ruled that the fact the state legislature enacted a law does not prevent a city from legislating to complement the state law in the same area provided the legislature did not by express language limit the authority of cities.[59]

Court decisions have been both broad and narrow, even within the same state. Decisions by the Rhode Island Supreme Court in 1976 and 1977 illustrate conflicting interpretations of the scope of powers of cities and towns. In 1976 the court ruled that cities and towns may require their employees to be residents of the employing unit, but the next year the court held that a state senator could retain his senate seat even though the Woonsocket city charter forbids the holding of more than one public office.[60] Joseph E. Coduri reported that the narrow judicial interpretation of city and town powers by the courts has resulted in the enactment of special acts, at local request, which in effect establish a separate set of laws for each city and town superseding many sections of the general laws.[61]

Court decisions in Connecticut also have vacillated between broad and narrow. The Connecticut Supreme Court in 1965 held that the act granting local discretionary authority did not restrict a city's power to amend a city charter provision establishing a civil service system.[62] In the same year, the court issued a decision that the statutory grant of power did not allow a town with a locally drafted charter to divest the town zoning commission of its exclusive powers to enact and amend zoning regulations or to change zonal boundaries.[63]

The problem of broad versus narrow interpretations of the discretionary authority of local governments is illustrated by two Wisconsin Supreme Court decisions. In 1968 the court ruled that whether a retired policeman can receive a pension while employed as a school teacher was predominantly a local concern.[64] In the same year, the court held in a case involving waste disposal facilities that "when the Legislature deals with matters that are primarily of state-wide concern, it may deal with them free of any restriction contained in the home-rule amendment."[65]

Special legislation has not been eliminated by the adoption of the devolution of powers approach in Massachusetts. The Legislative Research Council in 1972 released a study revealing that 1,563 special municipal bills were introduced in the general court between 1968 and 1971 with only 322 of the bills dealing with matters reserved by the constitution to the general court.[66] A similar study by the Massachusetts Department of Community Affairs in 1975 identified 546 special municipal bills introduced in the general court between 1972 and 1975; only 115 bills dealt with matters reserved to the general court.[67]

Why do local government officials seek the enactment of special state laws relating to subjects that fall within the discretionary authority of the concerned local governments? Depending upon the state, as many as six reasons may be offered as explanations for the filing of these bills. First, a charter commission may have to be created to research a matter and place a proposed charter amendment on the ballot in order to enable the municipality to take a certain action. Charter amendment is more expensive and slower than the enactment of a special law in some states.

Second, the failure of the state legislature to recodify all local governments laws and clearly identify the powers reserved by the legislature has produced uncertainty in the minds of many local officials who decided to take the conservative approach by seeking the enactment of a special law.

Third, local officials occasionally have found it to be politically expedient to avoid a controversial issue by seeking the enactment of a special law, thereby transferring the controversy to the arena of the state legislature.

Fourth, part-time local government attorneys do not always conduct adequate research to determine the scope of local powers and find it easier to recommend that the local government seek the enactment of a special state law. If the attorney was trained under Dillon's Rule and the state only recently adopted a devolution of discretionary powers constitutional provision, the force of habit and a cautious conservative nature may induce the attorney to recommend that the local government seek legislative permission to take many actions falling within the political subdivision's discretionary authority.

Fifth, courts have issued both broad and narrow interpretations of local government powers in the same state, thereby adding to the uncertainty in the minds of local officials concerning the scope of their powers.

A sixth reason applies in Massachusetts because the drafters of the constitutional amendment granting local discretionary authority employed two phrases interchangeably in a proviso. A power may be exercised by a municipality provided the power is "not inconsistent" with the state constitution or laws enacted by the legislature under its reserved powers, or "denied" to the municipalities by their respective charters.[68] A local ordinance or bylaw not following an existing statute is "inconsistent" with state law even though the action is "not denied" by the state constitution and laws or the local charter.

Role of Advisory Opinions

Local government action is guided not only by constitutional and statutory provisions and court decisions. In every state, the attorney general may issue either formal or informal opinions with the former being binding in nature. In addition, the state auditor (state comptroller) and the superintendent of public instruction (commissioner of education) may issue advisory opinions to local governments, including school districts. Counsels for various departments of the state government are also frequently asked for their opinion as to whether a local government possesses the legal authority to institute a specific action.

In issuing advisory opinions, state officials generally are conservative in interpreting the discretionary authority of political subdivisions. That the opinions tend to be narrow in terms of local powers is not surprising since the officials attempt to base their decisions to a large extent on court decisions and typically cite various decisions as support for the advisory opinions.

Local officials and their attorneys would be foolish not to follow the advice contained in an opinion issued by a state official since they might be subject to court action and harsh public criticism if they choose to act contrary to the advisory opinion. The result of the issuance of advisory opinions by state officials historically has been a reluctance by local officials to initiate an action where the authority to do so has been questioned and to seek the enactment of a special law by the state legislature, thereby adding to the time required to initiate an action and placing an additional burden upon the legislature.

A major change in the type of advisory opinion issued by the attorney general and the state comptroller occurred in 1979 in New York State shortly after newly elected officials assumed these offices. George Braden, a longtime advocate of broad powers for local governments, was appointed an assistant attorney general by Attorney General Robert Abrams. Braden in his first major opinion concerning local discretionary authority in 1979 superseded contrary informal opinions issued since 1958 and advised that a reference in the state constitution to county clerks, district attorneys, registers, and sheriffs did not make them officers of the state. If they were considered officers of the state they would be prohibited from receiving an increase or a decrease in salary during their term of office.[69]

In a second opinion, Braden advised the counsel of a community development agency that while one could argue that the agency lacks the corporate power to assist the town by preparing papers the town would use to enter into a contractual relationship with third parties, Braden could "see no harm in this limited assistance to the Town" provided no state or local funds financed the paperwork.[70]

On June 5, 1980, Braden issued an advisory opinion that has the potential for greatly broadening the discretionary authority of municipal corporations. The state constitution defines a general law as one applying "alike to all counties, all counties other than those wholly included within a city, all cities, all towns or all villages."[71] Braden, referring to the provision in section 81 of the General City Law containing the phrase "except a city having a population of more than one million people," advised that the authorization in the law for a mayor of a city to appoint a board of zoning appeals is a special law and not a general law restricting the authority of a city.[72] In other words, unless the legislature covers all municipal corporations in a law, these units possess the power to amend the law by enacting a local law.

On August 12, 1980, Attorney General Robert Abrams, acting on the advice of Braden, in effect removed what had been perceived as a restriction on the powers of a municipality when he issued an advisory opinion pointing out "the danger of imputing legislative intent retroactively to cover a different Federal-State relationship."[73] Under the General Municipal Law, state aid for an urban renewal project is limited to a maximum of 50 percent of the net cost of a project exclusive of any federal aid or assistance.[74] Braden concluded "that block grant funds used to meet the local grant-in-aid requirement under a Federal urban renewal project are not Federal aid or assistance to be excluded in computing a local government's contribution to the project."[75] He reasoned that the municipality's reliance on the U.S. Department of Housing and Urban Development's

> ... policy of permitting use of block grant funds to meet a municipality's local grant-in-aid contribution ought not to be upset long after the event because the municipality, if it had known in advance that such use would penalize it, could have rearranged its use of block grant funds in a manner that would have permitted it to use its own money to meet its urban renewal commitment.[76]

On April 23, 1981, Braden issued an opinion reversing a 1974 opinion of the attorney general that a county could not charge towns for the sheriff's road patrol or limit the road patrol to towns that enter into a contract with the county providing for the payment by the towns of the cost of the service.[77] Braden advised that a 1979 court of appeals decision made clear that a sheriff was a local and not a state official and, hence, a charter county could amend its charter to stipulate that the road patrol will be made available only on a contract basis with towns. He added that a noncharter county could achieve the same objective by appropriating funds for the road patrol only in towns that have entered into a contract with the county for the service.

Newly elected State Comptroller Edward Regan in 1979 appointed James Magavern, an advocate of broad powers for local governments, as counsel to the state comptroller. To cite only one example of the change in the type of opinions issued in the name of the state comptroller, Magavern reversed opinions issued over the years and advised that a municipality could use public funds to pay for free refreshments for the public at a ceremony.[78]

While most advisory opinions issued since 1979 have broadened the powers of municipal corporations in the state of New York, the state legislature retains plenary power over local governments by means of the enactment of general laws. In the next section, the amount of discretionary authority possessed by each type of local government in each of the 50 states is examined.

LOCAL DISCRETIONARY AUTHORITY

The full amount of power granted to local governments by the state constitution and statutes is not exercised for four principal reasons. First, the amount of discretionary authority granted to political subdivisions in the typical state is not expressed in explicit terms, and ambiguity often revolves around the question of whether a local government may exercise a certain regulatory power or provide a given service. Power is granted to political subdivisions by a complex mosaic of constitutional provisions, general laws, and special laws, which typically have been interpreted by the courts. As mentioned earlier, court interpretations of a constitutional grant of authority have been both broad and narrow in the same state. Even if it were possible to delimit local powers in express terms, most local officials would not be familiar with the extent of and the limitations upon these powers.

Second, local governments may lack the required finances to engage in many activities. Third, local officials may prefer not to exercise a power for a number of reasons, including the possibility of "passing the buck" on controversial issues to the state legislature.

Fourth, recent U.S. Supreme Court decisions restricting the sovereign immunity of local governments and increasing the liability of local officials for their official actions have discouraged the exercise of local discretionary authority.[79] In 1980 the Court stripped states and their political subdivisions of immunity for the actions of their public servants by an expansive interpretation of section 1983 of the Civil Rights Act of 1871,[80] a subject discussed in greater detail in Chapter 5.

Attempts have been made to measure the discretionary authority of local government by utilizing aggregate data. In 1974, for example, Professor G. Ross Stephens of the University of Missouri measured in quantitative terms the degree of state centralization of political power by employing three surrogates reflecting state powers versus local powers:

> (1) Financial responsibility, or which level pays for public goods and services; (2) determination of the level which delivers each of 15 major functional activities; and (3) distribution of public personnel between levels modified by the relative labor intensity of different services rendered by State and local governments.[81]

Stephens developed an index for 1957 and 1969 based upon U.S. Census of Government data and placed each state in a continuum of state centralization ranging from decentralized to balanced to centralized.[82] In a report five years later, Professor Stephens and Professor Gerald Olson updated the index.[83] No attempt, however, was made to measure the distribution of political power between the state and each type of local government or to measure the amount of discretionary authority exercisable by each type.

The U.S. Advisory Commission on Intergovernmental Relations in the same year released a report analyzing state-local fiscal relations and placing each state in one of three categories based upon the degree of state dominance: local dominance (9 states), strong state role (28 states), and state dominance (13 states).[84] An updated listing of states on the basis of the 1978 local share of state-local own sources of revenues was issued in 1980 by the commission.[85]

Index of Local Discretionary Authority

In 1979 and 1980, the author conducted for the U.S. Advisory Commission on Intergovernmental Relations a study of local discretionary authority involving legal research on constitutional and statutory grants of power and related court decisions and a survey of state and local officials concerning their perceptions of the amount of discretionary authority exercisable by each type of local government in their respective states.[86]

The purpose of the study was to make readily available to citizens and local, state, and federal officials an index quantifying local discretionary authority. The reader should be alerted to the limitations of the data employed to develop the indexes.

TABLE 2.1 *(continued)*

States	Structure	Functional Areas	Finance	Personnel
North Dakota	1.80	1.50	3.50	2.00
Ohio	1.00	1.50	2.50	1.50
Oklahoma	1.00	1.50	2.50	1.50
Oregon	1.00	1.50	2.00	1.50
Pennsylvania	2.00	2.00	2.50	2.00
Rhode Island	1.00	2.00	5.00	3.00
South Carolina	4.00	2.00	2.00	2.00
South Dakota	3.00	4.00	3.00	3.00
Tennessee	3.00	3.00	3.00	2.00
Texas	1.00	1.20	1.50	1.00
Utah	2.50	2.00	3.50	2.00
Vermont	5.00	2.00	5.00	3.00
Virginia	3.00	1.50	2.00	1.25
Washington	1.30	2.50	3.50	3.00
West Virginia	4.00	2.00	5.00	3.00
Wisconsin	1.00	2.00	3.00	2.00
Wyoming	1.00	3.00	3.00	2.50

While Arkansas cities possess relatively little discretionary power to change the structure of their governments, they possess relatively broad personnel powers. Georgia is unique in granting its cities no authority to alter their structure, yet granting them broad functional and personnel powers.

The broadest overall powers are granted to cities by Texas, followed by Maine. Broad powers also are granted by Alaska, California, Connecticut, and Michigan. At the other extreme, the most stringent control over cities is exercised by New Mexico, followed by Vermont.

The County Index

In general, states exercise more stringent control over county governments than over city governments, as evidenced by a comparison of Table 2.2 with Table 2.1. This finding is not surprising in view of the origin of county governments as quasi-municipal corporations serving as an arm of the state government for convenience in administration. In New Hampshire, the historical legal status of counties has not been changed and each annual county budget is adopted by the members of the House of Representatives from the county.

TABLE 2.2 Index of County Discretionary Authority by States, 1980

States	Structure	Functional Areas	Finance	Personnel
Alabama	4.50	4.00	4.75	2.25
Alaska	1.00	2.00	2.00	2.00
Arizona	4.00	4.00	4.00	4.00
Arkansas	1.00	3.00	3.00	1.50
California	3.00	3.00	3.00	3.00
Colorado	4.50	5.00	4.50	3.00
Connecticut*	—	—	—	—
Delaware	3.00	2.00	2.00	2.00
Florida	1.00	1.30	4.50	2.75
Georgia	5.00	5.00	3.00	3.00
Hawaii	1.00	3.20	4.00	3.50
Idaho	5.00	3.00	5.00	4.00
Illinois	2.10	3.30	2.80	3.80
Indiana	4.00	3.50	4.00	2.00
Iowa	4.00	2.50	4.50	3.60
Kansas	2.50	2.50	3.00	3.00
Kentucky	3.50	3.50	2.60	2.50
Louisiana	2.00	2.00	3.50	2.00
Maine	1.75	4.00	3.50	2.00
Maryland	2.60	2.33	3.20	2.20
Massachusetts	5.00	5.00	5.00	5.00
Michigan	4.50	3.50	3.50	3.50
Minnesota	3.00	3.00	3.00	2.00
Mississippi	5.00	4.00	4.00	3.00
Missouri	5.00	5.00	5.00	4.00
Montana	1.00	2.00	4.00	3.50
Nebraska	3.00	4.00	5.00	3.00
Nevada	2.00	4.00	4.00	4.00
New Hampshire	5.00	4.00	5.00	1.00
New Jersey	3.00	3.50	4.50	3.00
New Mexico	3.00	3.00	3.00	5.00
New York	1.50	3.00	4.00	4.00
North Carolina	1.00	1.25	2.50	2.50

(continued)

*There are no organized county governments in Connecticut and Rhode Island.

Note: Scale 1 to 5 with 1 indicating the greatest degree of freedom from state control and 5 indicating the smallest degree of freedom.

Source: Joseph F. Zimmerman, *Measuring Local Discretionary Authority* (Washington, D.C.: U.S. Advisory Commission on Intergovernmental Relations, 1981), pp. 54–55.

TABLE 2.2 *(continued)*

States	Structure	Functional Areas	Finance	Personnel
North Dakota	3.00	3.00	4.00	2.00
Ohio	4.00	4.00	4.00	4.50
Oklahoma	4.00	3.50	3.50	3.50
Oregon	1.00	1.50	2.00	1.50
Pennsylvania	2.00	2.00	2.00	2.00
Rhode Island*	—	—	—	—
South Carolina	4.00	3.00	2.00	2.00
South Dakota	5.00	3.00	5.00	3.00
Tennessee	5.00	3.00	5.00	2.00
Texas	5.00	4.80	4.50	2.00
Utah	3.50	3.00	3.00	1.50
Vermont	5.00	5.00	5.00	3.00
Virginia	4.00	2.50	3.00	2.25
Washington	3.00	2.80	4.00	4.50
West Virginia	5.00	3.00	5.00	3.00
Wisconsin	2.50	3.00	3.00	2.50
Wyoming	5.00	4.00	3.00	3.00

An examination of Tables 2.1 and 2.2 reveals that the most significant difference in the powers of counties and cities is in the area of structure of government, with counties in 12 states possessing no discretionary powers in this area. In Alaska and Oregon, counties and cities possess identical discretionary authority. The power of counties and cities in North Carolina is nearly identical with the exception of personnel powers.

Reforming State-Local Relations

In conducting the study of local discretionary authority for the U.S. Advisory Commission on Intergovernmental Relations, the author posted a questionnaire to the following in each state: governor, attorney general, department of community affairs, legislative research bureau, municipal association, county association, and experts on state-local relations. Each respondent was requested to rate as very desirable, desirable, or undesirable a total of 28 provisions that could be incorporated into the state constitution or statutes.[90]

Seventy-one percent of the responding governors and 85 percent of the experts on state-local relations rated a constitutional provision for an

Imperium in Imperio undesirable, but 44 percent of the attorneys general and 50 percent of the county associations rated such a provision very desirable. Since counties generally are subject to Dillon's Rule, county associations may view an *Imperium in Imperio* provision as an improvement, and attorneys general may contemplate the fewest legal problems with this approach to granting local discretionary authority.

Consistent with their relatively strong support for an enumerated power provision, attorneys general rated as undesirable by the same percentage a devolution of powers constitutional provision. On the other hand, 58 percent of the municipal associations rated the devolution of powers approach very desirable, and an additional 27 percent rated the approach desirable. A particularly interesting finding was that 69 percent of the county associations and 61 percent of the municipal associations rated the removal of local debt limits undesirable.

The most striking differences in perception according to region involved the desirability of a state law authorizing local governments to levy a sales tax. Fifty-seven percent of the respondents in the south rated such a law very desirable compared to only 10 percent of the northeastern respondents. Fifty-five percent of the latter respondents labelled a constitutional prohibition of special legislation very desirable compared to 32 percent of the respondents in the north central region of the nation.

When respondents are classified in terms of the degree of state dominance of the state-local fiscal partnership in their states, it is revealed that one-half of the respondents in strong fiscal partner states—where the state provides half to two-thirds of state-local revenue—rated as very desirable or desirable an *Imperium in Imperio* constitutional provision. Where local governments raise more than half of the state-local revenue and the state is a junior fiscal partner, 88 percent of the respondents considered the devolution of powers approach to granting local discretionary authority to be very desirable or desirable. Consequently, one is not surprised that 86 percent of these respondents view the constitutional prohibition of special legislation as very desirable or desirable.

Perhaps the most surprising finding concerning the views of respondents in states classified as junior fiscal partners was the fact that 83 percent opposed the removal of local debt limits and 71 percent opposed the removal of local tax limits. This finding may be attributable to the fact that local governments in these states rely heavily upon the states for funds and are not inhibited in the exercise of their discretionary authority by debt and tax limits.

When respondents were classified as residing in a state with a constitutional grant of power to local governments, or a statutory grant of power, or the Ultra Vires Rule, the greatest support for the *Imperium in*

Imperio approach was in Dillon's Rule states where 58 percent of the respondents rated the approach as very desirable or desirable and 42 percent rated the devolution of powers approach as undesirable. Strong support was expressed by respondents in each of the three types of states for a statutory grant of discretionary powers to political subdivisions with only 15 percent of the respondents in Dillon's Rule states rating such a grant undesirable.

Perceptions of respondents also differed according to whether the state constitution restricted the length of the legislative session. In states with legislative sessions unrestricted in length, 70 percent of the respondents expressed opposition to the *Imperium in Imperio* approach compared to only 48 percent of the respondents in states with sessions restricted in length. Only 8 percent of the former group of respondents rated the devolution of powers approach undesirable compared to 27 percent of the latter group of respondents. These two groups also held different views concerning the desirability of a constitutional prohibition of special legislation; 31 percent of the first group oppose such a prohibition, while 88 percent of the second group favor such a provision.

SUMMARY AND CONCLUSIONS

The system of substate governance followed the centralization paradigm until 1850 when the Michigan Constitution was amended to prohibit special legislation; its lead has been followed by 40 other states. The first affirmative grants of relatively broad discretionary powers to local governments took the form of constitutional or statutory provisions authorizing municipalities to draft, adopt, and amend a charter and supersede all special laws and specified general laws.

State constitutional grants of local discretionary authority have taken two forms. The original form attempted to establish a state within the state or *Imperium in Imperio*, but judicial decisions severely limited the scope of the grant of power. The devolution of powers approach has been more successful in broadening the discretionary powers of local governments. Under this approach, the state constitution delegates to specified types of general purpose local governments all powers capable of delegation but makes the devolution of powers subject to preemption by the state legislature by means of the enactment of general laws. With the exception of Oregon, no state has adopted the *Imperium in Imperio* approach since Dean Jefferson Fordham issued a report in 1953 advocating the devolution of powers approach. In 1958 Oregon adopted an *Imperium in Imperio* provision for counties. Several states, including Florida, Illinois, and New

York, have adopted hybrid constitutional provisions combining the *Imperium in Imperio* and devolution of powers approaches.

The indexes of local discretionary authority reveal that cities generally possess more discretionary powers than counties. However, there has been a trend since midcentury for states to grant additional powers to counties, and in two states counties and cities possess the same discretionary authority.

A national survey by the author revealed strong support for the devolution of powers approach to granting discretionary authority to local governments and relatively little support for the *Imperium in Imperio* approach except by attorneys general and county associations. The inescapable conclusion is that the former approach is the only one that will be employed by states amending the local government article in their constitutions in the foreseeable future.

In view of the fact that the exercise of discretionary authority to a large extent is dependent upon adequate finance, it was surprising to discover the strong opposition to the removal of state debt and tax limits on local governments. This finding supports the conclusion that the removal of such limits is improbable in the typical state.

Chapters 3 and 4 examine state and federal financial assistance to local governments. As will be seen, both of the higher levels of government have increased their financial support of local governments with the passage of time, but the support in the view of many local officials has been encumbered by expensive mandates.

NOTES

1. Nathaniel B. Shurtleff, ed., *Records of the Governor and Company of the Massachusetts Bay in New England*, vol. I (Boston: From the Press of William White, Printer to the Commonwealth, 1853), pp. 76, 79.

2. Ibid., pp. 84–85, 87, 90, 96, 120, 150, 160.

3. Ibid., p. 247.

4. *Watertown Records* (Watertown, Mass., 1894), p. 71; and *Dorchester Town Records: Fourth Report of the Records Commissioners of the City of Boston*, 2nd ed. (Boston, 1883), p. 25.

5. *City of Clinton v Cedar Rapids and Missouri Railroad Company*, 24 Iowa 455 at 461 (1868).

6. *Merriam v. Moody's Executors*, 25 Iowa 163 at 170 (1868).

7. *People v. Hurlburt*, 24 Michigan 44 (1871).

8. Thomas M. Cooley, *A Treatise on the Constitutional Limitations which Rest Upon the Legislative Power of the States of the American Union*, 7th ed. (Boston: Little Brown, 1903).

9. *Atkins v. Kansas*, 191 U.S. 207 at 220–21 (1903).

10. *City of Trenton v. New Jersey*, 262 U.S. 182 (1923).

11. *Constitution of the State of Michigan*, art. IV, § 30 (1850).

12. *Constitution of the State of New York*, art. III, § 17.

13. Frank J. Goodnow, *Municipal Home Rule* (New York: Macmillan, 1895), p. 23.

14. Ibid., p. 24.

15. *Christoph v. City of Chilton*, 205 Wis. 418, 237 N.W. 134 (1931).

16. *Stapleton v. Pinckney*, 293 N.Y. 330 (1944).

17. Farrington v. Pinckney, 1 N.Y.2d 74 (1956).

18. For an exception upholding a geographical classification, see *State ex rel. Bowker v. Wright*, 54 N.J.L. 130, 23 Atl. 116 (1891).

19. *Constitution of the State of New York*, art. XII, § 2 (1894).

20. The mayor of a first-class city, defined as a city with a population greater than 250,000, was authorized to employ the suspensory veto unless the legislature provided for the concurrent action of the city council and the mayor. In all other cities, concurrent action by the council and the mayor was required. Should the mayor and/or city council accept the act, it was sent to the governor for review and action. If rejected by the city within 15 days, the act could be repassed by the legislature and sent to the governor for action.

21. *Constitution of the State of Illinois*, art. IV, § 34 (1870).

22. *Constitution of the Commonwealth of Massachusetts*, art. LXXXIX of the articles of amendment, § 8.

23. Jefferson B. Fordham, *Model Constitutional Provisions for Municipal Home Rule* (Chicago: American Municipal Association, 1953), p. 15. The association, now the National League of Cities, has not endorsed the proposals contained in the report.

24. *Constitution of the Commonwealth of Massachusetts*, art. LXXXIX of the articles of amendment, § 8.

25. *Constitution of the State of Wisconsin*, art. XI, § 3.

26. *Thompson v. Kenosha County*, 64 Wis. 2d 673, 221 N.W.2d 845 at 852–53 (1974).

27. *Massachusetts Laws of 1915*, chap. 267; *Massachusetts General Laws*, chap. 43, § 9.

28. *Constitution of the State of New York*, art. III, § 26 (2) (1935).

29. *New York Laws of 1937*, chap. 862, § § 201–04.

30. *Chief of Police of Dracut v. Town of Dracut*, 357 Mass. 492, 258 N.E.2d 531 (1970).

31. *Massachusetts Laws of 1979*, chap. 151, § 14; *Massachusetts General Laws*, chap. 59, app. § § 1–14 (1981 supp.).

32. *Chisholm v. City Council of Lynn*, 331 N.E.2d 529 (1975). See also *Massachusetts Laws of 1970*, chap. 842; *Massachusetts Laws of 1972*, chap. 625.

33. Carl H. Chatters, "Foreword," in Jefferson B. Fordham, *Model Constitutional Provisions for Municipal Home Rule* (Chicago: American Municipal Association, 1953), p. 1.

34. *Constitution of Missouri*, art. IX, § 19 (1875). Only St. Louis met the threshold requirement of a population exceeding 100,000.

35. Joseph F. Zimmerman, *Measuring Local Government Discretionary Authority* (Washington, D.C.: U.S. Advisory Commission on Intergovernmental Relations, 1981), pp. 26–27.

36. *Constitution of the State of New York*, art. XII, § § 2–3 (1923).

37. *New York Laws of 1929*, chap. 713.

38. *Adler v. Deegan*, 251 N.Y. 467 at 473, 167 N.E. 705 at 707 (1929).

39. Ibid., 251 N.Y. 491, 167 N.E. 714 (1929).

40. Ibid., 251 N.Y. at 467, 483, 167 N.E. at 705, 711. See also *Robertson v. Zimmermann*, 268 N.Y. 52, 196 N.E. 740 (1935).

41. Frank J. Macchiarola, "Local Government Home Rule and the Judiciary," *Journal of Urban Law* 48 (1971): 338.

42. *Constitution of the State of New York*, art. IX.

43. Jon A. Baer, *Municipal Debt and Tax Limitations in New York State: A Constraint on Home Rule* (Albany: Graduate School of Public Affairs, State University of New York at Albany, April 1980), p. 11.

44. Ibid., p. 13.

45. Jefferson B. Fordham, "Local Government in the Larger Scheme of Things," *Vanderbilt Law Review* 13 (June 1955): 675.

46. Fordham, *Model Constitutional Provisions.* It should be noted that Texas has operated under the devolution of powers approach since a 1948 Texas Supreme Court decision was rendered. See *Forwood v. City of Taylor,* 147 Tex. 161 at 165, 214 S.W.2d 282 at 286 (1948).

47. Fordham, *Model Constitutional Provisions,* p. 20. The National Municipal League in 1963 amended its model state constitution to feature the devolution of powers approach and listed the *Imperium in Imperio* approach as an alternative.

48. *State Constitutional and Statutory Restrictions upon the Structural, Functional, and Personnel Powers of Local Government* (Washington, D.C.:. U.S. Advisory Commission on Intergovernmental Relations, 1962), pp. 72–74.

49. *Constitution of the State of Washington,* art. XI § 10.

50. Zimmerman, *Measuring Local Discretionary Authority,* pp. 27–28.

51. *City of West Allis v. County of Milwaukee,* 39 Wis.2d 356, 159 N.W.2d 35 at 41–42 (1968).

52. *Jefferson v. State,* 527 P.2d 37 (1974).

53. *Constitution of the State of New York,* art. IX, § 2 (2).

54. *Seattle v. Long,* 61 Wn.2d 737, 380 P2d 472 (1963).

55. *City of Beloit v. Kallas,* 76 Wis.2d 61, 250 N.W.2d 342 at 345 (1977).

56. *Constitution of the State of Oregon,* art. XI, § 2.

57. *State ex rel. Heinig v. City of Milwaukee,* 231 Ore. 473 at 481–83, 373 P2d 680 at 685 (1962).

58. Ibid., 231 Ore. at 479, 373 P2d at 683–84.

59. *Fox v. City of Racine,* 225 Wis. 542, 275 N.W. 513 (1937).

60. *Louiselle v. City of East Providence,* 116 R.I. 585, 351 Atl.2d 345 (1976); *Cummings v. Godin,* 377 Atl.2d 1071 (1977).

61. Joseph E. Coduri, "State-Local Relations in Rhode Island" in *Rhode Island Local Government: Past, Present, Future,* ed. Robert W. Sutton, Jr. (Kingston: Bureau of Government Research, University of Rhode Island, 1974), p. 58.

62. *State ex rel. Perry J. Sloane et al. v. Thomas Reidy et al.,* 152 Conn. 419, 209 Atl.2d 674 (1965).

63. *Poulos v. Caparrelli,* 25 Conn. Sup. 370, 205 Atl.2d 382 (1965).

64. *State ex rel. Brelsford v. Retirement Board,* 41 Wis.2d 77, 163 N.W.2d 153 (1968).

65. *City of West Allis v. County of Milwaukee,* 39 Wis.2d 356, 159 N.W.2d 36 at 41 (1968).

66. *Revising the Municipal Home Rule Amendment* (Boston: Massachusetts Legislative Research Council, 1972), pp. 138–40.

67. *Analysis of Special Municipal Laws* (Boston: Massachusetts Department of Community Affairs, 1975).

68. *Constitution of the Commonwealth of Massachusetts,* art. LXXXIX of the articles of amendment, § 6.

69. Letter to Richmond County District Attorney from New York State Assistant Attorney General George D. Braden dated November 21, 1979, p. 3.

70. Letter to Counsel Ralph Nappi of the North Hempstead Community Development Agency from New York State Assistant Attorney General George D. Braden dated May 14, 1980, pp. 4–5.

71. *Constitution of the State of New York,* art. IX, § 3 (d) (1).

72. Letter to Canandaigua Corporation Counsel Andrew M. Harkness from New York State Assistant Attorney General George D. Braden dated June 5, 1980, p. 2.

73. Letter to Acting Commissioner Joseph B. Goldman of the New York State Division

of Housing and Community Renewal from New York State Attorney General Robert Abrams dated August 12, 1980.

74. *New York General Municipal Law*, § § 510 (2), 557 (2).

75. Letter to Acting Commissioner Joseph B. Goldman, p. 4.

76. Ibid.

77. Letter to Monroe County Attorney John D. Doyle from New York State Assistant Attorney General George D Braden dated April 23, 1981, pp. 2–4.

78. Eric Freedman, "State: Free Goodies at Local Events OK," *The Knickerbocker News* (Albany), March 14, 1980, p. 5 A.

79. See *Owen v. City of Independence*, 100 S. Ct. 1398 (1980); *Maine v. Thiboutot*, 100 S. Ct. 2502 (1980); *City of Newport v. Fact Concerts, Incorporated*, 101 S. Ct. 2748 (1981).

80. *Civil Rights Act of 1871*, 42 U.S.C. § 1983.

81. G. Ross Stephens, "State Centralization and the Erosion of Local Autonomy," *Journal of Politics* 36 (February 1974): 46.

82. Ibid., pp. 54–66.

83. G. Ross Stephens and Gerald W. Olson, *Pass-Through Federal Aid and Interlevel Finance in the American Federal System, 1957 to 1977*, vol. 1 (Kansas City: University of Missouri-Kansas City, August 1, 1979), pp. 59–65.

84. *Local Revenue Diversification: Income, Sales Taxes and User Charges* (Washington, D.C.: U.S. Advisory Commission on Intergovernmental Relations, 1974), pp. 16–17.

85. *The State of State-Local Revenue Sharing* (Washington, D.C.: U.S. Advisory Commission on Intergovernmental Relations, 1980), pp. 60–61.

86. Zimmerman, *Measuring Local Discretionary Authority*. The material that follows is based upon data and information contained in the commission's report on pages 52–55.

87. U.S. Office of Management and Budget, *1980 Catalog of Federal Domestic Assistance* (Washington, D.C.: U.S. Government Printing Office, 1980).

88. For indexes of towns, villages, townships, and boroughs, see the Appendix or Zimmerman, *Measuring Local Discretionary Authority*, pp. 57–58.

89. *Vermont Acts of 1969*, no. 19; *Vermont Statutes Annotated*, chap. 31, § 703a (a).

90. This section is based upon data and information contained in Zimmerman, *Measuring Local Discretionary Authority*.

CHAPTER 3

State-Local Fiscal Relations

Local government is big government whether measured in terms of the number of employees (9,174,800), annual payrolls ($9,996,100,000), or annual expenditures ($225,379,000,000).[1] A distinctive feature of local government finance during recent decades has been the sharp increase in intergovernmental financial assistance with the federal government providing local governments with $20,616,000,000 in 1979 and state governments providing $74,162,000,000 in the same year.[2]

With state aid averaging one-third of local government total revenue and ranging from 9.9 percent in Hawaii to 53.1 percent in New Mexico, it is not surprising that states exhibit a great interest in and control over local government finance.[3] Operating under the Ultra Vires Rule until state constitutions were amended to authorize the exercise of local discretionary authority, the state legislature stringently controlled local finance and generally restricted local taxation to the general property tax. Because of financial abuses by numerous local governments in the nineteenth century, many state constitutions were amended to place debt and/or tax limits on these units.

General purpose local governments have historically relied upon the property tax as their major source of revenue. While declining in relative importance, this tax remains the principal source of local tax revenue. One major problem associated with this tax has been property assessment with inequitable valuations common. States have intervened to require special training for assessors and established state boards to equalize assessments statewide for the purpose of distributing state financial aid. With several state supreme courts ruling the current fractional assessment system violates the state constitution, the concerned states have been faced with the choice of assisting local governments to reassess property or seek the amendment of the state constitution to permit a fractional valuation system of assessment.

Problems with the property tax and growing need for additional revenue have prompted many local governments to seek authority from the state to levy nonproperty taxes. While states have jealously guarded the power to tax, authority has been granted to local governments in many states during recent decades to levy one or more nonproperty taxes.

The principal source of poor state-local relations is the state mandate, that is, a legal requirement—constitutional provision, statutory provision, or administrative regulation—that local governments must undertake a specified activity or provide a service meeting minimum state standards. A California official wrote to the author in 1980 that "the increase in State mandated programs and performance standards, together with statewide tax and spending limitations . . . have left local officials relatively little discretion in financing government services." As shown in Table 1.1, 85 percent of the respondents in the northeast viewed state mandates as a major problem.

While state officials concede that state mandates create a problem in state-local relations, they argue that state financial assistance to local governments more than offsets the increase in local government costs attributable to mandates, and as pointed out in a subsequent section, several states restrict the imposition of mandates and/or reimburse local units for costs attributable to mandates.

Constitutional and statutory provisions for tax and bond referendums have been common for decades in a number of states. Commencing in the 1970s, the referendums began to play a new major role when used in conjunction with the initiative to impose spending and/or tax limits on local governments.

The nature of state-local fiscal relations in a typical state is illustrated by a statement released by the Michigan Municipal League:

> . . . historically the State-local fiscal relationships . . . have been characterized by (a) repeated efforts at wholesale takeover by the State of all or portions of certain local revenue sources or State-collected, locally-shared taxes as easy methods for solving the State's periodic fiscal problems, (b) placing severe restrictions on the ability of local government to utilize local self-help tax and revenue programs, (c) imposing more and more duties and service responsibilities on local governments without providing adequate means for paying the costs of

these new responsibilities and services, and (d) weakening the local property tax base by granting more and more property tax exemptions without reimbursing local units for the revenue losses.[4]

CONSTITUTIONAL AND STATUTORY FISCAL PROVISIONS

Acting under the Ultra Vires Rule, the state legislature always had the power to control local government finance completely. A new form of state control, however, was introduced in the nineteenth century in the form of constitutional restrictions upon the taxing and debt powers of political subdivisions. New York City Chancellor of Education Frank Macchiarola offered an explanation of the reasons why state interference increased:

> The tradition of State interest developed as a result of the rapid growth of cities in newly industrializing America and the repression of them by both frightened and power-seeking legislators in the late 19th century. To this was added the fact of alarming municipal fiscal mismanagement. The turn of the century in New York State was marked by city governments indulging in various speculative enterprises and excess borrowing. Cities borrowed for ordinary expenses and let taxes become delinquent.[5]

The New York State Constitution, for example, directs the state legislature "to restrict the power of taxation, assessment, borrowing money, contracting indebtedness, and loaning the credit of counties, cities, towns and villages, so as to prevent abuses in taxation and assessments and in contracting of indebtedness by them."[6]

The U.S. Advisory Commission on Intergovernmental Relations attributes the recent increase in state control of local finance to five factors:

(1) The public demand for property tax relief;
(2) Court-mandated upgrading of assessment practices;
(3) State assumption of an increasing share of State-local responsibilities;
(4) State efforts to control the growth in school spending; and
(5) A perception by State Legislators that local officials need State-imposed restrictions on local tax and spending powers in order to withstand the pressure for additional spending in general and for employees wages and fringe benefits in particular.[7]

The controls adopted since 1970 are of a different nature than the historic property tax rate limitations. Fiscal limitations can be placed in nine classes: full valuation of property, property tax exemptions, tax and deficit limits, debt restrictions, loan of credit restrictions, state approval of municipal and county budgets, pension fund management controls, codes of ethics, and sunshine laws.

Full Valuation of Property

By constitutional or statutory provision, 27 states require local governments to assess real property at full value for purposes of property taxation.[8] The remaining states authorize fractional assessment of all or specified classes of real property.

In states with a full valuation requirement, underassessment has been a perennial problem. The Connecticut Supreme Court addressed this problem in 1957:

> Nor can we overlook a further matter in demonstrating the impropriety of pursuing a role of fractional valuation. When assessors adopt such a role, they indirectly assume a role which rightfully is not theirs. . . . The borrowing power of the municipality is affected, since its indebtedness may not exceed specified percentages of the grand list. Assessors who use fractional valuations . . . therefore, interfere . . . with a power which legally belongs to others.[9]

Because of the vagaries of assessment practices in political subdivisions, 41 states conduct assessment ratio studies, that is, the ratio between assessed value and full value of real property. Assessment is a state function in Maryland and Montana and, consequently, assessment ratio studies are not needed. Since many state aid formulas are designed to equalize the fiscal resources of local governments, assessment ratio studies are essential for the equitable distribution of the aid.

Property Tax Exemptions

State constitutions and statutes exclude all or portions of specified types of real property from the general property tax. Religious, eleemosynary, private educational, federal government, and state government property are totally excluded from property taxation. These exclusions can cause a serious fiscal problem for cities in which large amounts of these types of real property are located, for example in Cambridge, Boston, and Albany. In 1979 the value of property totally exempt from the real property tax was $35,846 million in New York and only $1,255 million in California.[10]

Partial exemptions from the general property tax are granted in a number of states for owner-occupied homes (homestead exemption), veterans of the armed forces, senior citizens, and owners of agricultural land, forests, historical buildings, and open spaces; such exemptions represented 25.6 percent of gross assessed value of real property in Louisiana, 19.2 percent in Florida, and 16.6 percent in Alabama in 1979.[11]

In Louisiana, an owner may apply to have agricultural, horticultural, marsh, or timber land valued at 10 percent of the use value assessment. Use value often is a much lower figure than the market value of the properties. In New Hampshire, a system of deferred taxation is employed for qualified farm land, flood plain land, forests, recreation land, "wild" land, and wetland. Upon the sale of such land, a tax is levied at the rate of 10 percent of the market value of the land if its use is changed to a use other than open space.

Relative to homestead exemptions, a 1980 Florida constitutional amendment increased the exemption to $15,000 in 1980, $20,000 in 1981, and $25,000 in 1982 and subsequent years. In 1975 the Ohio General Assembly extended the homestead exemption to persons totally and permanently disabled.

Tax and Deficit Limits

Arizona, Iowa, and New Jersey impose expenditure limits, 39 states limit tax rates, and 22 states impose levy limits.[12] Tax or levy limits are not applicable to all political subdivisions. In New Jersey, for example, the tax limits are applicable only to its 21 counties. Delaware is unusual in that its code establishes a specific tax rate limit only for Kent County.[13] Limits can be exceeded under specific conditions, and voter approval usually is a requirement. The Kansas State Board of Tax Appeals, however, may authorize increases in the tax rate limit.[14] Relative to deficit limits, the 1979 Rhode Island legislature restricted cumulative deficits to a maximum of 2 percent of the current tax levy.[15]

Arguments advanced in support of such limits include the need to prevent the imposition of burdensome taxes, assist elected officials to withstand exorbitant demands of public employee unions, force elected officials to examine spending proposals more carefully, and limit governmental powers and interference with the lives of citizens.

Opposition to these limits is strong and based upon the belief that they result in the neglect of the needs of the relatively powerless poor, are simplistic responses to complex public problems, and reflect a distrust in representative government.

In 1940 Professor George Spicer concluded that the tax rate limits had accomplished little and often required the curtailment of local services, while encouraging excessive borrowing and employment of devices to evade the limits.[16] A 1976 study concluded that the limits had reduced per capita public expenditures by local governments but had little impact "on total State-local expenditures, excluding Federal aid."[17] Two years later, Professor Helen Ladd concluded "the economic benefits from controls . . . are likely to be slight, while the costs, in terms of service level distortions, are potentially significant."[18]

In our judgment, the establishment of fixed tax limits in a state constitution is undesirable as illustrated by New York State experience. To assist the cities of Buffalo, Rochester, and Yonkers and 65 school districts in cities with a population under 125,000 operating at the constitutional debt limit, the 1969 state legislature authorized the units to exclude from the limit taxes collected to pay for public employee retirement costs.[19] The New York Court of Appeals, however, ordered the political subdivisions to stop the practice of excluding from the tax limit the taxes used to finance retirement expenses, thereby depriving these units of approximately $40 million in taxing authority.[20] The 1976 legislature attempted to provide fiscal relief by approving a bill authorizing these units to request state financial assistance from a special account, thereby triggering the imposition of a state real property tax at a rate sufficient to generate revenue equal to the amount requested.[21] The court of appeals held the law to be an attempt to evade a constitutional requirement and reaffirmed its original decision.[22]

Debt Restrictions

Debt restrictions are of several types and include a quantitative maximum limit, purposes for which funds may be borrowed, prescribed procedures that must be followed in borrowing funds, and types of debt obligations that may be utilized. Forty-six states have debt limits for some or all local governments; Alaska, Colorado, Florida, and Nebraska do not have debt limits, and the Tennessee restriction applies only under a special condition.[23] Voter approval of long-term borrowing is required in the 46 states with limits except in Connecticut, Hawaii, and Indiana; in Massachusetts, New Jersey, New York, Tennessee, and Washington, the restrictions apply only to specified classes of school districts.[24]

The U.S. Supreme Court's "one-person, one-vote" dictum appeared to make extramajority referendum vote requirements unconstitutional since a required two-thirds vote of approval means that one negative vote is equal to two positive votes. The West Virginia Supreme Court reached this conclusion in 1969, but two years later the U.S. Supreme Court ruled that the three-fifths voter approval requirement in the West Virginia Constitution singled out no "discrete and insular minority" for special treatment since the requirement applied to all bond issues for any purpose.[25]

Clearly, debt restrictions are not desiderata and have led to the development of devices to evade the restrictions. To avoid exceeding a legal debt limit and/or a referendum requirement, a local government may issue revenue bonds backed by tolls or other charges instead of "full faith and credit" bonds. Under the special fund legal doctrine, revenue bonds are exempt from the debt limit and referendum requirement. An undesirable consequence of debt restrictions is the resulting further fractionation of the local government system since the restrictions are often evaded by the establishment of special district governments that either are not subject to debt restrictions or have a debt limit of their own. Restrictions also can be avoided by use of a lease-purchase agreement under which a political subdivision contracts with a private firm to have a facility constructed that will be leased for a stipulated number of years by the subdivision and title to the facility transfers automatically to the local government upon expiration of the lease.

Loan of Credit and Property Restrictions

Reckless state financing of canals and railroads, including the loan of state credit and property, led in the 1840s to the incorporation in a number of state constitutions of restrictions upon such practices.[26] These restrictions, in turn, prompted railroad companies to turn to municipalities for financial assistance, including the loan of credit. In New York State, local governments sought special permission to lend funds and credit to facilitate the construction of railroads, and in 1869 the legislature responded with the Town Bonding Act granting towns blanket authority to lend public funds to railroad companies.[27]

Although the New York Court of Appeals upheld actions taken by New York City to assist the construction of the New York Rapid Transit Lines, Judge O'Brien in dissent stressed that legislative grants of broad powers of indebtedness held the danger of reviving the "abuses that grew out of the exercise by municipalities of the power to issue bonds and to use their credit and funds for the construction of railroads.[28]

Currently, the New York State Constitution contains the following restrictions:

> No county, city, town, village, or school district shall give or loan any money or property to or in aid of any individual, or private corporation or association, or private undertaking, or become directly or indirectly the owner of stock in, or bonds of, any private corporation or association; nor shall any county, city, town, village or school district give or loan its credit to or in aid of any individual, or public or private corporation or association, or private undertaking.[29]

State Approval of Budgets and Balanced Budgets

Originating as quasi-municipal corporations, county governments lacked the power to adopt budgets, and their budgets were included in the state appropriation bills. The Massachusetts General Court appropriated funds for counties until 1981. A county budget in New Hampshire is approved by the "county convention" composed of members of the House of Representatives from the county since counties lack the legislative power. Today, local governments in New Jersey, New Mexico, and North Carolina must submit budgets for approval to a state division or a state commission.

State constitutions and statutes typically require local governments to operate with balanced budgets. In New Jersey, the director of the Division of Local Government Services is authorized to disapprove a local government budget for reasons listed in law and also may disapprove revenue estimates. The latter power gives the director broad powers over the adoption of a local budget since state law mandates that budgets be balanced.

Pension Funds

With cash and investment securities totalling approximately $163 billion in 1981, state and local government retirement systems may be viewed as major financial institutions.[30] At the state capitol, the questions of contributory versus noncontributory pension systems, indexing payments to the cost-of-living index, and supplemental benefits commonly are major issues.

With 5,234 locally administered systems out of a total of 5,788 separately administered systems, it is not surprising that about four-fifths of the plans have less than 100 members.[31] The number of retirement systems ranges from one in Hawaii to 1,413 in Pennsylvania. Two-thirds of the systems are restricted to police officers and firefighters.

Reviewing state and local pension systems, the U.S. Advisory Commission on Intergovernmental Relations concluded:

> The large number of small systems complicates effective pension administration. It impedes employee mobility, promotes diseconomies of scale, discourages effective oversight, leads to benefit competition, and most importantly diffuses authority and decision-making which can promote fiscal irresponsibility. While size is not a precondition of fiscal soundness, there is reason to believe that establishing larger, consolidated systems promotes better management.[32]

A major problem with local pension systems is the use of the cash system instead of the actuarial system. The U.S. General Accounting Office surveyed 72 pension plans administered by eight states and 26 local governments within the eight states and discovered that the plans had accumulated unfunded actuarial liabilities of approximately $29 billion.[33] Local governments in recent years have been seeking state financial assistance to make their systems actuarily sound, and state legislatures have established pension review commissions to oversee local systems and make recommendations to the legislature. After experimenting with a temporary state commission, the New York legislature in 1971 established the Permanent Commission on Public Employee Pension and Retirement Systems.[34] Currently, the New York State Constitution guarantees payment of permanent pension benefits, and all retirement systems must be operated on the actuarial principle.[35]

Codes of Ethics and Sunshine Laws

The first laws in the United States dealing with ethics of public servants were conflict-of-interest laws relating to "black and white" situations in which overt unethical behavior, such as embezzlement, is recognized by the vast majority of the citizenry. As society became more complex, ethical issues became more subtle and conflict-of-interest laws could not deal effectively with such issues. In consequence, many state and local legislative bodies adopted codes of ethics containing standards and guidelines for dealing with contemplated actions by public officials falling in the "gray" area between what is clearly ethical behavior and outright unethical behavior, and providing sanctions for the violations of the standards.[36] To administer the code, a board of ethics typically is created. Codes of ethics have a restraining effect upon public employees relative to local finances and may cause delays in instituting action until the board of ethics issues an advisory opinion approving a proposed action.

Closely related to conflict of interest and codes of ethics are so-called sunshine laws, which open meetings and officials records to the public and seek to promote high ethical standards by making the action of public servants visible. While these laws have laudable purposes, including making officials more accountable to the citizenry, governmental action in the finance area tends to be slowed down.[37]

GENERAL PROPERTY TAX

The general property tax remains the principal source of locally raised tax revenue although the importance of the tax has declined in several states, as local governments have been authorized to levy nonproperty taxes and state financial assistance has increased. Commencing in the early days of the century, states began to relinquish the general property tax as a source of revenue and in 1979 received only $2.67 billion in property tax revenue or 2 percent of total revenue, a decrease from 2.4 percent in 1960.[38] In the same year, local governments received $62,876,000,000 in property taxes or 77.7 percent of total revenue, a decline from 82.8 percent in 1974 and 86 percent in 1969.[39] County property tax revenue declined from $14 to $13 billion, a 6.8 percent decrease, between 1978 and 1979 chiefly because of the impact of proposition 13 (discussed in a subsequent section) in California and property tax relief programs in several states.[40] Similarly, property tax receipts in the 75 largest metropolitan areas fell by approximately $2 billion between 1978 and 1979, reflecting the impact of California's proposition 13.[41]

As pointed out in an earlier section, full versus fractional assessment of real property is a major issue in many states, and pressures have been growing for a fractional system with residential property assessed at a lower rate than commercial and industrial property. A related issue is the question of the nature and extent of property tax relief for senior citizens.

Senior Citizen Circuit Breaker Laws

The most popular type of tax relief program is the circuit breaker property tax program for senior citizens, which originated in Wisconsin in 1964 and bases relief on the ability to pay the property tax.[42] These programs typically establish upper limits on the amount of relief or the amount of assessed value or property tax used in computing the amount to be rebated. In several states, each eligible home owner is required to pay a minimum property tax. This newer form of tax relief has not been substituted for the older homestead exemptions, and both types of relief are found in several states.

Circuit breaker programs assume three principal forms. First, the program is a local option in some states, and an individual local government is not required by the state to grant the tax relief. Second, a tax deferral program allows eligible property owners to defer part or all of the property tax due until the title to the property is transferred upon its sale. Third, relief programs assume the form of a tax freeze, holding the property tax at a specified level when the property owner reaches the age of 65. One study reached the following conclusions with regard to circuit breakers for the elderly:

> Evidence was found that the elderly rarely move for *any* reason; the role of property tax relief in influencing the decisions of those who do is presently unknown. No evidence suggesting that programs slow neighborhood decay was encountered; the relatively modest average

program benefit makes this outcome appear implausible. There may be some impact of property tax relief programs on the voting behavior of the general population on public finance questions, but the effects on elderly voters appear to be minimal.[43]

The Initiative and Referendum

State legislatures have initiated various types of action to provide relief for property owners. In 1979 the Massachusetts General Court, for example, enacted a tax and expenditure cap law limiting expenditures and property tax revenue to 104 percent increase over the previous year's base with certain exceptions; the cap may be overridden by a two-thirds vote of a city council or town meeting.[44]

In spite of legislative actions designed to provide property tax relief, citizen groups have employed the initiative and the referendum in several states to place limits on the property tax. Currently, 24 states authorize the use of the direct and/or indirect initiative.[45] Under the former type, a question is placed directly upon the referendum ballot if the requisite number of signatures of registered voters is obtained. The latter type provides that the initiative petition, upon receipt of the specified number of signatures, is sent to the legislature, which has a specified number of days to act upon the petition. Should the legislature reject or amend the petition, the question automatically is placed upon the referendum ballot. Six states allow the use of the direct and the indirect initiative, and Maine and Massachusetts permit the use only of the indirect initiative.

In an important decision, the U.S. Supreme Court in 1978 struck down a Massachusetts law restricting corporate contributions to referendum campaigns involving issues "that materially affect its business, property, or assets" by holding that a corporation under the First Amendment to the U.S. Constitution can spend funds to publicize its views in opposition to a proposed constitutional amendment authorizing the state legislature to levy a graduated income tax.[46]

Not all initiative drives are successful in convincing voters to approve propositions. In 1980 more than two-thirds of the tax reduction petitions on the ballot were rejected by the voters.[47] Although Dallas voters defeated, by a two-to-one margin, a 1981 proposal to reduce property taxes by close to 30 percent, the consensus of observers was that voters were in an antitax mood but did not favor the specific proposal on the ballot.[48]

Proposition 13

The most famous initiative and referendum proposition in recent years is California proposition 13 of 1978, which instituted a grass roots movement in many states to limit property taxes and local expenditures.[49] Proposition 13 reduced local property tax revenue by approximately $7 billion, or 60 percent, and predictions of an imminent local government financial crisis were common.

To date, proposition 13 has not caused a serious financial problem for political subdivisions because the state used its surplus of $5 billion to assist local governments. As a result, the state finances a larger share of state-local spending—80 percent instead of 50 percent of the cost of public education. A Los Angeles County official wrote the author in 1980 that "the financial effects have been minimal. A large State surplus and a continuously healthy State economy have generated sufficient revenue to permit the State to replace much of the lost property taxes, thus preventing catastrophic results of the kind predicted before proposition 13." Furthermore, local governments levied additional user fees to finance services that had been free and have deferred capital projects and maintenance. Nevertheless, local governments laid off approximately 17,000 employees during the first year proposition 13 was in effect.

The ability of the state government to assist its local units financially became more impaired when electors in 1979 approved proposition 4, which added Article XIIIB to the state constitution and limited the annual increase in tax-supported state and local government appropriations to the percentage increase in the state's population and the consumer price index. Proposition 4 also directs the state and its political subdivisions to return surplus revenues to residents within two years by revising tax rates or fee schedules and directs the state to reimburse local governments for all costs attributable to state mandates. Voters in 1980, however, defeated proposition 9, which would have lowered the state's personal income tax and indexed it to the California consumer price index, eliminated the business inventory tax, and limited the sales and use taxes to their current rates.

In presenting his fiscal 1982 budget to the legislature, Governor Edmund Brown, Jr. stated "the moment of truth is upon us" since the state will have no surplus as of June 30, 1981 and can no longer afford to fund local governments at the rate in effect since the approval of proposition 13.[50]

Proposition 2½

Massachusetts local governments are facing difficult decisions as the result of voter approval of proposition 2½, which was defeated in the House of Representatives by a vote of 146 to 5 on May 6, 1980.[51] This proposition limits property taxes to 2.5 percent of the full and fair cash value of real property in a city or town and reduced local government revenue by approximately $500 million in 1981. Local governments exceeding the limit—52 municipalities with a population over 27,000—must reduce their tax levies by 15 percent annually until the limit is reached. The proposition also reduced the motor vehicle excise tax, a major source of local revenue, by 62 percent and ended the fiscal autonomy of school committees, which previously assessed their respective cities and towns an amount to cover the cost of operating the public schools.

Proposition 2½ stipulates that the question of overriding the property tax limit by a local government could be placed on the referendum ballot only by the legislature. In 1981 the legislature enacted a law allowing a city council, town council, and town selectmen to place the override question on the ballot and requiring a simple majority instead of a two-thirds majority for approval of an override.[52]

Called the "second Boston tea party," proposition 2½ will hurt cities and towns greatly exceeding the property tax limit; Boston has a tax rate estimated to be equal to 10 percent of the full and fair cash value of real property. By the autumn of 1981, approximately 15,000 city, town, and county employees had been laid off and school districts curtailed programs.

An Assessment

In 1776 Adam Smith developed canons of a good tax that are useful in deciding which taxes are the most desirable.[53] The principle of equity holds that the tax burden should be apportioned on the basis of benefits received and the ability to pay. The convenience criterion refers to the method, place, and time of tax payment, while the certainty criterion means that taxation should not be arbitrary and a taxpayer should be able to determine his tax liability in advance of the due date. The economy canon measures the administrative cost of a tax. We add to these criteria a canon providing that a tax should not be levied at a level that will drive taxpayers from the taxpaying jurisdiction.

A major criticism of the general property tax has been the poor quality of the valuation of properties with resulting inequities. While state-mandated training programs for local assessors and some recent full valuation requirements have improved the administration of the general property tax, it still is subject to major criticism on the ground that the tax is an inequitable one not reflecting ability to pay. The circuit breaker laws for senior citizens are one response to this criticism. Other disadvantages of this tax include discouragement of modernization of buildings, encouragement of smaller buildings, creation of tax havens with low property tax rates attracting additional development, and generation of pressures for tax exemption.[54]

In spite of these criticisms, it is possible to argue that the general property tax has advantages: benefits received are correlated with the amount of the tax levied in many instances, property owners are made aware of the cost of local government and the need for an alert citizenry, and compliance costs can be low. Nevertheless, we conclude that the general property tax is not the most desirable type of local tax when measured against other possible local taxes.

LOCAL NONPROPERTY TAXING AUTHORITY

Commencing in the twentieth century, a number of states authorized specified local governments to levy one or more nonproperty taxes. The trend toward nonproperty taxes accelerated during the Great Depression of the 1930s, when many local governments found it very difficult to finance essential services. In addition to nuisance taxes, several states have authorized certain political subdivisions to levy one or both broad-based taxes, that is, the income tax and the sales tax.

The Income Tax

In 1912 Ohio voters approved a proposed constitutional amendment stipulating that "municipalities shall have authority to exercise all powers of local self-government and to adopt and enforce within their limits such local police, sanitary, and other similar regulations, as are not in conflict with general laws."[55] Courts have interpreted this broad grant of authority to include the power to levy taxes, including an income tax "in the absence of legislation by the General Assembly providing for a uniform or graduated income tax and the required apportionment thereof."[56] Seven years after this decision, the 1957 Ohio General Assembly enacted a law stipulating that a municipal income tax be levied at a uniform rate and requiring voter approval for a tax rate in excess of 1 percent.[57]

Ohio courts have invalidated municipal attempts to levy other taxes if the courts were convinced that the state had preempted the concerned field of taxation.[58] In enacting a state income tax law in 1971, the general assembly included a disclaimer of intent to preempt the field of income taxation, thereby avoiding the invalidating of municipal income taxes.[59]

Currently, a total of 4,456 local governments in 11 states levy income taxes falling within three categories.[60] The first type is a flat rate tax on earned income and is referred to as a payroll tax. The second type applies to unearned and earned income, and the third type, employed by New York

City, is a graduated tax on unearned and earned income. The Maryland authorization provides for a 20 percent state-administered supplement of the state tax liability with provision for increasing the supplement to 50 percent.

States have been reluctant to authorize local governments to levy an income tax. Of the total number of local income taxes in the United States, 3,865 are in Pennsylvania. Although New York State authorizes New York City to levy an income tax, the state has refused to extend the authorization to other jurisdictions despite the recommendations of state study commissions.[61]

In our judgment, a local income tax best meets the canons of a good tax dependent, of course, upon the specific provisions of the tax, and we urge states to authorize the levying of such a tax under carefully drafted state guidelines or provide for a local supplement to the state income tax.

The Sales Tax

First levied during the Great Depression, the sales tax has become a major source of revenue with 45 states and 5,464 local governments levying such taxes.[62] The largest number of local sales taxes is in Texas where 921 municipalities and 25 municipal transit authorities levy such taxes.

A general sales tax is a major revenue producer for local governments even if the rates are low. Currently, rates vary from .5 to 3 percent, and the taxes typically are piggybacked upon the states sales tax, thereby reducing the cost of collection. Furthermore, the sales tax usually does not generate major political opposition when levied at a low rate since the taxpayer in effect is paying the tax on the installment plan rather than in a single sum once a year.

The two major disadvantages of the local sales tax are compliance costs for merchants and the regressive nature of the tax. States and local governments use merchants as tax collectors and often require merchants to pay the tax in advance. The general sales tax is a regressive tax bearing most heavily upon low-income citizens since these citizens spend all or most of their income on taxable items whereas high-income citizens spend only a fraction of their income on such items. To lessen the regressivity of the general sales tax, 26 states exempt food purchased for human consumption from the tax, and 40 states exempt medicines.[63]

The exemptions reduce but do not eliminate the regressiveness of the sales tax. Since equity should be the principal criterion determining the best tax to levy, we strongly recommend the adoption of a local income tax in preference to a local sales tax since the former can be adjusted to be the most equitable tax.

THE MANDATE PROBLEM

The problem of state mandates is an old one, as described in Chapter 2. For purposes of analysis, it is useful to refer to the distinction, made by Professor Frank Goodnow in 1895, between an authorization under Dillon's Rule and a mandate:

> Being called upon continually to enlarge the extent of municipal powers, being at the same time obliged to exercise a central control over matters of general concern attended to by cities, and generally feeling, for the reasons adduced, little responsibility for the protection of private and local rights, the Legislature has easily confused its powers of authorization with its powers of compulsion, and has exercised the latter where it should have confined itself to the exercise of the former. It has come to regulate itself local matters, and has encroached upon the domain of municipal home rule. This encroachment upon the field of local self-government has been productive of greater evil than its attempted encroachments on the domain of the rights of private individuals. For, while the courts could protect individual private rights, they have been unable to protect the rights of local government of municipal corporations.[64]

A Montana correspondent wrote to the author in 1980 that "during the past twenty years imbeded State agencies with rule-making authority consistently have imposed obligations on local governments to the point of a deterioration of State and local relations." An Oklahoma county official in 1980 pointed out that the state has "mandated duties and responsibilities upon counties without adequate funding measures to accompany the added costs. The State Legislature has, upon several occasions, taken taxing power away from counties and left responsibilities with the County to perform the duties tied to the tax."

Of the various state-local problem areas identified in Table 1.3, the mandate problem was viewed universally as the most serious problem. We define a state mandate as a legal requirement—constitutional provision, statutory provision, or administrative regulation—requiring political subdivisions to undertake a specified activity and/or provide a service meeting minimum state standards. Mandates should be distinguished from state restraints, such as tax and debt limits, which limit the activities of local governments.

Typology of Mandates

The U.S. Advisory Commission on Intergovernmental Relations (ACIR) developed a typology by placing mandates in five major categories: rules of the game, spillover or service, interlocal equity, loss of local tax base, and personnel mandates.[65] The first type of mandate deals with such matters as local elections, form of government, designation of local officials, due process of law, and ethical standards for local officials and employees. The spillover mandates relate to services, for example, education, health, and hospitals, that benefit persons outside the jurisdiction of the local government providing the services.

The purpose of interlocal equity mandates is to prevent local governments from engaging in actions that would harm their neighbors, and these mandates relate to environmental protection, land use, and tax assessment. A loss of tax base mandate is a state law exempting property from the local property tax or food and medicine from a local general sales tax. The personnel mandates deal with pension benefits of local government employees, wages, house, personnel standards, and working conditions.

Mandates can reduce the revenues of local governments and/or increase their expenditures. Not all state mandates add to the cost of local governments since the compliance cost of a new mandate may be less than that of the old mandate, and other mandates may only change a procedural requirement relative to a traditional local government function and may not increase the cost of operations. Furthermore, a state mandate will not force a local government to raise taxes to meet the additional cost associated with the mandate if the statute authorizes the financing of the mandated service by user charges.

Rationale for Mandates

Mandates are justified by states on five grounds. First, the state may be convinced that the mandated activity is of such statewide importance that the decision to undertake the activity cannot be left to the discretion of local governments. Second, a mandate, for example, a senior citizen property tax exemption, may be justified on the ground of helping to achieve a desirable public goal, that is, tax relief for the elderly property owners. Third, the courts or the state legislature may decide that statewide uniformity in the provision of a service is essential. Fourth, tradition is advanced as support for a state mandate even though it no longer is justifiable on other grounds. Fifth, critics in California argued that the California state government in the 1970s decided to build a budget surplus by requiring local governments to provide services previously provided by the state.

Regardless of the rationale advanced in support of mandates, they are the products of interest group activity at the state capitol. Groups unable to achieve their goals on the local level often find the goals can be achieved on a statewide basis. The 1938 New York State Constitutional Convention reported that "most of the members of the Legislature who vote upon bills introduced by such groups do not represent the localities involved and are not concerned over the fact that these bills will increase the expenditure of these localities."[66]

Unenforced mandates obviously do not add to the cost of local government. While no national survey of the enforcement of mandates has been undertaken, limited evidence suggests that reliance upon voluntary implementation of mandates is common and some states lack the administrative capacity to enforce mandates. To cite one example, a 1971 New Hampshire law requires each city and town to provide a public disposal site for materials pumped from septic tanks of homes and businesses lacking connections to city or town sewer lines. A mid-1980 survey by *The Keene Sentinel* revealed that only 8 of 27 municipalities in the Monadnock region had state-approved disposal sites.[67] The New Hampshire Bureau of Solid Waste Management sent letters to town officials directing the towns to comply with the law but lacked the staff to enforce the law.

Survey of State Mandates

A national survey of 77 local government functions conducted by the author in 1976 disclosed a total of 1,762 functional mandates.[68] The southern states were the only ones where less than 54 percent of the 77 functional areas surveyed were mandated. In part, the explanation for the smaller number of mandates in these states is the constitutional limitations on the length of the legislative session.

A third major finding of the national survey was a tendency for states with a locally dominated fiscal system to have the most mandates.[69] One can speculate that the legislature in these states concluded that local governments were in the best position to finance mandates.

The number of state mandates varies from 8 in West Virginia to 60 in New York. The most common mandates in the 50 states were special education programs (45), solid waste disposal standards (45), minimum years and/or age of eligibility for normal education pension (44), minimum years and/or age for eligibility for normal police and fire pensions (43), workmen's compensation (42), minimum vesting period for education pension (41), and disability pension benefit levels for educational personnel (40).

Relatively few state mandates are levied in the area of social service for two reasons: extensive federal involvement in the form of mandates and centralization of the responsibility for public welfare on the state level in several states.

Local government officials are upset by what they consider to be unwarranted state intrusion in their affairs and the state's failure to reimburse political subdivisions completely for additional expenditures attributable to mandates. These officials argue that while a single mandate may not significantly add to the financial problems of local governments, a series of mandates may have a burdensome cumulative effect. In states with tax and expenditure cap provisions, the mandate problem can be a major one. Not surprisingly, local officials are perturbed if the state reduces the amount of financial support provided to local governments to finance mandated activities.

The survey revealed that some local government officials oppose mandates under any circumstance, but other officials hold that certain mandates have worthy goals yet the standard for the initiation of a state mandate should be local desuetude; that is, the failure of local governments to act in critical areas will lead to state mandates or preemption of functional responsibility.

Mandates are viewed in a different light by state officials, who maintain that there is a tendency by local officials to perceive the fiscal implications of mandates only in terms of their numbers and costs, completely overlooking the fact the state is meeting its obligations to its political subdivisions through revenue sharing and/or grants-in-aid. One prominent New York State official informed the author that local officials in certain instances want a state mandate to enable them to provide a service they favor that may be politically unpopular, and they want to shift the blame or criticism related to the service to the state. One local official informed a state official that "we are not going to do this voluntarily, but we will do it if you mandate that all local governments must do it." A second New York State official indicated he favors the use of mandates because it is politically difficult for local elected officials voluntarily to make a decision that currently is mandated by the state.

Fiscal Notes

Local government officials have attributed mandates in part to members of the state legislature who are unaware of the cost to local governments of state mandates. For several decades, legislatures in a number of states have required that all bills with spending implications must have a fiscal note or impact attached indicating the impact of the bills upon state finances in the future. The use of such notes on local bills is a relatively new development.

A 1977 survey by ACIR revealed that fiscal notes were employed in 22 states: by both houses of the legislature in 19 states, by the senate in Alabama, and by the governor's office in Minnesota and Washington.[70] Survey respondents indicated that the fiscal note requirement usually does not apply to administrative rules and regulations, the cost estimates are generally accurate, and no major effort has been made to repeal the requirement.

More recently, Maine and New Hampshire adopted fiscal impact statements, and local governments in the latter state may delay the effective date of a mandate if the fiscal impact is greater than a specified maximum.[71] And an executive order issued by the Massachusetts governor requires consultation with local governments by state agencies prior to issuing regulations to implement state-mandated programs.

State Reimbursement of Mandated Costs

Many local government officials contend that effective local discretionary authority will not be achieved until a constitutional amendment is adopted forbidding the legislature to mandate local spending without compensating state financial assistance. To deal effectively with the mandate problem, Jefferson Fordham in 1953 included the following in his model constitutional provisions for municipal home rule:

> State legislation requiring increased municipal expenditures may not become effective in a municipal corporation until approved by ordinance enacted by the legislative body of the municipal corporation, unless the legislation is enacted by two-thirds vote of all the members elected to each house of the legislature or funds sufficient to meet the increased municipal expenditure are granted to the municipal corporations by the legislation or separate legislation enacted at the same session of the legislature.[72]

Fordham justified the model provision by stressing "that it is generally undesirable for the decision to be taken finally at the state level without heed to the local situation and, particularly, the financial burden involved."[73]

Only the constitutions of Alaska, California, Louisiana, Massachusetts, Pennsylvania, and Tennessee restrict the power of the legislature to mandate costs upon local governments. The Alaska Constitution stipulates that special acts necessitating appropriations by a local government do not become effective unless approved by a voter referendum.[74] Proposition 4, approved by California voters in 1979, added Article XIIIB to the state constitution and directs the state to reimburse local governments for all costs attributable to state mandates. The Louisiana Constitution restricts the power of the legislature by stipulating that a special law requiring increased expenditures for wages and employee fringe benefits does not become effective until approved by the local governing body or the legislature appropriates funds for the purpose of the special law.[75]

In 1980 Massachusetts voters approved a constitutional amendment forbidding the general court to impose mandates on local governments unless the associated costs are funded completely by the commonwealth.[76] The Pennsylvania Constitution allows the legislature to grant exemptions from local taxes only if the legislature reimburses the local governments for the revenue losses resulting from the exemptions.[77] The Tennessee Constitution stipulates "no law of general application shall impose increased expenditure requirements on cities or counties unless the General Assembly shall provide that the State share in the cost."[78]

The principal argument in favor of a constitutional prohibition of state mandates without state compensation is based upon the proposition that the unit mandating a public expenditure should be responsible for financing the expenditure. Proponents also object to mandates on the ground that political subdivisions lose control over a significant part of their budgets and are deprived of funds needed to implement programs capable of being carried out under their discretionary authority.

Such a constitutional provision is opposed by those stressing the dangers associated with introducing rigid constitutional provisions relating to state-local relations and local government finance in an age when swift and decisive action is essential if the needs of the public are to be met. In addition, they argue that the financial problems associated with mandates can be solved by means of reform of the state's tax structure and revision of state aid programs.

A middle position in this controversy has been adopted by individuals favoring a constitutional provision of the type recommended by Jefferson Fordham. Such a provision is in conformity with provisions in several state constitutions allowing the legislature to enact a special law by a two-thirds vote of the legislature provided the governor has recommended passage of the law.

Currently, 13 states have mandate reimbursement laws. The best known reimbursement law is the California Property Tax Reform Act of 1972, which establishes property tax limits and provides for state reimbursement of all types of mandated costs.[79] The major criticism directed at the reimbursement law until 1979 was the use of disclaimers by the legislature, which makes provisions mandating local spending nonreimbursable.[80] Furthermore, the 1972 law is a statement of intent, and the legislature is not bound to reimburse local governments for added costs. As pointed out in a preceding section, the 1979 voter-initiated proposition 4 directs the state to reimburse local governments for all costs attributable to state mandates.

STATE FINANCIAL ASSISTANCE

Local government finance must be viewed within the perspective of state government finance since the state legislature, unless limited by the state constitution, possesses plenary authority in the area of finance. In 1974 ACIR issued a report placing the financial system of each state in one of three categories: state junior partner role (9 states), strong state role (28 states), and state dominance (13 states).[81] As pointed out earlier, the most mandates are found in states with a fiscal system dominated by local governments. Conversely, the fewest mandates are found in states where local governments are the junior partners.

ACIR in 1977 classified state-local fiscal systems by both expenditure and financing responsibilities: 10 states were classified as high state financing/high state expenditure, 8 as low state financing/low state expenditure, and 32 as falling between the first two categories.[82]

In view of the fact that the exercise of local discretionary authority is dependent to a great extent upon the adequacy of local financial resources and is partially reflected in patterns of expenditures, ACIR's categories may be viewed as approximate measures of the degree of political power centralization in each state.

The governor is a major intergovernmental actor and may harbor presidential ambition. In states with a large central city that has experienced financial distress, the governor may encounter serious political problems with the mayor who also may have presidential aspirations. The mayor constantly is seeking additional state financial assistance and may blame the governor and the legislature for failing to provide sufficient aid. This struggle may be part of a larger geographical political struggle between "upstate" and "downstate" areas as in Illinois and New York.

Six major reasons are advanced in support of state financial assistance. First, the state possesses a superior fund-raising capacity. Second, basic local services are in need of state support, or they will have to be curtailed. Third, state funding is essential for the expansion of existing or institution of new services. Fourth, states have an obligation to fund state-mandated costs. Fifth, property tax relief can be provided only with state assistance. Sixth, indirect state support in the form of technical assistance and equipment is needed if local governments are to meet their responsibilities in the most effective and efficient manner. Opponents of revenue sharing argue that governmental accountability is dependent upon the government raising funds being responsible for spending the funds. The Louisiana Association of Business and Industry maintains that the state has been providing an exceptionally large proportion of local revenues and will not be able to continue to do so as oil and gas production decline. The association thus recommends an orderly transition to greater local government self-sufficiency.[83]

States provide financial assistance to political subdivisions through revenue sharing, categorical grants-in-aid, and assumption of responsibility for a local government function. The latter is viewed by some as centralization.

State Revenue Sharing

State revenue sharing is similar to federal revenue sharing in that relatively few conditions are attached to the funds. Currently, 49 states have revenue-sharing programs; 13 percent of the state funds were distributed by revenue origin, 27 percent as reimbursement for state-authorized property tax exemptions, 21 percent by population, and 23 percent by relatively complex need formulas.[84]

The approximately $7 billion shared by states with their local governments annually represents a sharp increase compared to 1958 when the total involved was approximately three-quarters of a billion dollars.[85] In terms of importance, state revenue sharing outranked federal revenue sharing in 1980 as indicated by the following examples: $495 million in state funds and $196 million in federal funds in Michigan and $474 million in state funds and $107 in federal funds in Wisconsin.[86]

The major deficiencies in the New York State aid system have been identified as the following:

> (1) County units were unfairly excluded; (2) jurisdictional classification is not an accurate indicator of fiscal need, capacity, or effort, and therefore, it should be replaced as the major determinant of individual aid shares; (3) the formula treats jurisdictions with extensive resources the same as municipalities with little resources; and (4) fixed per capita amounts for the various jurisdictions do little to further the goal of long-term stabilization at the local level.[87]

Although several study groups over recent decades diagnosed the same deficiencies, the basic formulas remain unchanged because of the political strength in the legislature of local units benefiting from the current system.

To reduce the need for state revenue sharing, Governor Hugh Carey of New York in 1979 proposed the establishment of a local government expenditure review board composed of the lieutenant governor as chairperson, the director of the state division of the budget, and the secretary of state.[88] The proposed board would be charged with annually developing voluntary guidelines for local expenditures and would be authorized to make grants for the development and implementation of cost-reduction programs. Viewing the proposal as an attempt at state centralization, local governments attacked the proposal vigorously and were able to generate sufficient opposition in the legislature that the proposal failed to be reported out of committee in either house.

The following year, Governor Carey in his budget message to the legislature stressed that "singlehandedly the State cannot fight pressures to expand spending because 60 per cent of total State revenues are spent by local governments." He proposed the establishment of a local government expenditure and finance commission, including state and local representatives, which would be responsible for recommending "voluntary expenditure guidelines to serve as budget targets for local officials" and spearheading "State-local efforts to identify and eliminate unnecessary mandates, whether in statute or regulations."[89] The provision for local representation on the proposed commission did not overcome the fears of substate officials who lobbied effectively to kill the proposal.

Changing his tactics in 1981, Governor Carey recommended the establishment of "a spending cap for localities" with local spending "held to the same level of growth as the State's."[90] As a tradeoff, the governor urged the legislature to provide for the phased state assumption of the cost of Medicaid and "a fiscal impact statement for all legislation having local fiscal and administrative implications before they are reported out of committee."[91]

Since the Medicaid proposal would only directly benefit counties, representatives of other local governments demanded that the state require counties to share the savings resulting from the state takeover with local governments. Reacting to the demands, the governor proposed that counties share 75 percent of the savings with local governments until 1985 when the percentage would be increased to 90.[92]

State Grants-in-Aid

In common with the national government, states provide their local governments conditional grants-in-aid; the total amount increased from approximately $5.9 billion in 1955 to $70.8 billion in 1979, a 1,100 percent increase.[93] The largest amount of state aid (60.4 percent) is for public education and totaled approximately $37 billion in 1977.[94] The three other functions receiving the most state aid were public welfare (14.4 percent), general local government support (10.7 percent), and highways (5.9 percent).[95]

According to a study by Thomas Dye and Thomas Hurley, state grants-in-aid are directed more toward the needs of central cities in metropolitan areas than federal grants-in-aid. They noted:

State grants-in-aid were more closely associated with size, growth rate, density, age of city, and segregation than federal grants-in-aid. Finally, State grants-in-aid were negatively associated with resource measures, more so than federal grants-in-aid, suggesting that State grants were more redistributive in their impact among cities than federal grants.[96]

As in the case of state revenue sharing, an effort by the state to reduce the amount of categorical assistance or change the formulas for the distribution of such assistance precipitates a major political struggle. To close a projected state budget deficit of $50 million, Governor William O'Neill of Connecticut in 1981 proposed that $23.8 million in aid to cities and towns be cancelled.[97] A strong protest by the Connecticut Conference of Municipalities resulted in party lines breaking down in the senate and induced the general assembly to accept a compromise under which cities and towns will receive one-half of the amount they were scheduled to receive under the urban aid program.[98]

Part of the game of politics played by a number of mayors for increased state aid involved painting a bleak picture of the city's finances. While mayors should be proud of achieving sound finances for their cities, claiming too much credit for the achievement of a balanced budget may jeopardize prospects of receiving additional state aid. In presenting in 1981 what he labelled "the second genuinely balanced budget in the city's recent history," New York City Mayor Edward Koch was careful to point out "this does not mean that the days of wine and roses have returned or that fiscal discipline can be relaxed," the state assumption of the costs of medicaid "is the most significant action taken in recent years to restructure city and state finances," and "Governor Carey has demonstrated his leadership in promoting fiscal reform."[99]

State Grants for Education

Major battles involving state grants-in-aid typically revolve around the formulas for the distribution of financial assistance for public education because of the size of such grants and pressures, including court orders, for equalizing of educational opportunities throughout the state. Only Hawaii, by having state-administered public schools, avoids the struggle over state aid for public education.

State education grants-in-aid designed to help equalize educational opportunities throughout a state totalled approximately $19.5 billion in 1977, while nonequalizing grants totaled $12.3 billion.[100] During the fiscal year 1978, state aid for education on a per capita basis varied from $45 in New Hampshire and $75 in Nebraska to $292 in New Mexico and $477 in Alaska, which suffers from severe inflation.[101]

In the typical state, there is a large gap in expenditures between the poorest and the wealthiest school districts because of the great disparity in the value of real property in the districts and reliance upon property tax as a major source of revenue for school finance. In 1978 the wealthiest school district in New York State had real property values totalling $488,451 supporting each pupil in public school and allowed an expenditure of $6,093 per pupil, whereas the poorest district could expend only $2,343 for each pupil on the basis of $30,000 in real property supporting each student in Levittown.[102]

Courts in many states commencing in the 1970s began to rule unconstitutional the system of financing public education. The California Supreme Court in 1971 ruled that heavy reliance upon the general property tax to finance public education produced substantial disparities among school districts in terms of revenue raised per student and thereby violates the California Constitution and the equal protection of the laws clause of the Fourteenth Amendment to the U.S. Constitution.[103] Although a three-judge U.S. District Court held that reliance upon the property tax to finance public education in Texas violated the equal protection of laws clause of the Fourteenth Amendment to the U.S. Constitution, the U.S. Supreme Court in 1973 held that the educational system guaranteed a basic education for each student and did not violate the equal protection of laws clause.[104]

In 1974 the Connecticut Superior Court ruled that there was a constitutional requirement for equity in education and directed the state legislature to use equalized school tax rates as measures of ability to pay and to provide educational services of equal quality throughout the state.[105] The Connecticut Public Expenditure Council reported in 1980 that the legislature at each session subsequent to the court decision altered the formula for distributing state aid for public schools, "but with virtually no assurance that the money will be used to meet Court-recognized equity standards."[106]

The Connecticut experience in revising educational aid formulas is not unique. In general, a revision of aid formulas will benefit the older central city school districts and rural school districts, both of which frequently lack the political power in the state legislature that wealthy suburban school districts possess.

The experience of New York parallels the Connecticut experience. In 1978 Justice Kingsley Smith of the New York Supreme Court, a general trial court, declared the New York public school finance system unconstitutional yet did not establish a deadline for the adoption of a new system.[107] In addition to study commissions that recommended changes in system of public educational finance over the years, the governor, the state board of regents, the New York State Educational Conference (composed of the School Boards Association, United Teachers, and other groups) advanced recommendations to improve the system of public school finance. Not surprisingly, the recommendation of the various groups differed and did not satisfy the majority in the state legislature. Wide disparities in spending by school districts continue, with the wealthiest district spending approximately six times the amount spent by the poorest district even though state aid to 27 categories of education increased from $2.8 billion in 1975 to $4 billion in 1980.

In his fiscal 1982 executive budget, Governor Carey proposed state aid totalling $4.2 billion for public education, a 6.2 percent increase over the previous year.[108] Reacting with cries of anguish, many legislators decried the governor's proposal. Senator Joseph Pisani, a Republican from suburban Westchester County, declared: "The Governor's defenders sometimes portray him as a modern-day educational Robin Hood who robs rich school districts to aid the poor ones. In fact, even a superficial glance at our suburban districts will confirm that he is functioning more like a random mugger who can't tell the rich from the working class."[109] In 1980 the governor recommended a $188 million increase in state aid to public education, but the legislature increased the amount to $350 million, reflecting in part the fact that 1980 was an election year for the legislature. To the surprise of most observers, the New York Court of Appeals, in 1982, reversed Justice Smith's decision by holding that the current system of financing public education is constitutional.[110]

Limited to a maximum of two terms by the New Jersey Constitution, Democratic Governor Brendan Byrne balanced his last executive budget in 1981 by eliminating $64 million in aid to 234 of the 611 school districts.[111] This proposal created a serious political problem for Democratic members of the state legislature from wealthy suburban districts, who experience difficulty in winning elections under normal conditions. Democrat Charles Yates, chairman of the Joint Appropriations Committee, described the governor's proposal as "a devastating blow to Democrats and an amazing opportunity for any Republican who wants to run this year." [112]

Acute Fiscal Distress

Numerous local governments in the nineteenth century and during the Great Depression of the 1930s experienced acute fiscal distress, including bankruptcy. In the most serious cases, the state legislature provided for substitute administration by state officials until the subdivision's finances were restored to a sound basis. To facilitate the fiscal recovery of bankrupt local governments, Congress enacted the Municipal Bankruptcy Act in 1934 and amended the act in 1937.[113]

Movements of industry, commercial firms, and middle-class citizens to the suburbs since 1945, coupled with an influx of low-income citizens, caused serious fiscal problems for many of the older central cities in the east and the midwest. While these cities may be able to balance their budgets, the cities are not necessarily financially healthy. State constitutions and state laws often require local governments to operate with balanced budgets, and such budgets are essential if the units wish to borrow money in the credit market.

A 1979 report by the U.S. Department of Housing and Urban Development concluded that "the urban fiscal crisis is not over" and cited the following as evidence:

> Throughout the country, cities and counties with older physical plants, higher proportions of the poor and elderly, and higher crime rates are still experiencing economic decline. The loss of population and jobs is not random. The poor and the low-skilled remain in the urban core, while the richer, upwardly-mobile part of the population continues to move to the suburbs. Attempts by local government to cut services or raise taxes in a fiscal crisis lead to further deterioration of the business climate and an increased impetus for the mobile part of the population to move out. It also places an increasing burden on low-income households who cannot afford to move and who are most likely to be dependent on public services.[114]

The list of local governments experiencing acute financial distress or bankruptcy grew during the 1970s and included Cleveland; East St. Louis, Illinois; Gary, Indiana; Dayton; Detroit; New York City; Yonkers, New York; and Wayne County, Michigan. In each instance, the state initiated action to help the distressed unit. The reduction in federal grants-in-aid during the Reagan administration also has made the fiscal distress of the cities more acute.

Targeting Assistance

A December 1980 report issued by the U.S. Advisory Commission on Intergovernmental Relations revealed that the gap in per capita taxes during the past two decades had been narrowed between central cities and suburbs, and "the growing difference between expenditures and taxes was bridged mainly by the increased responsiveness of state and federal aid to central city needs."[115] Nevertheless, a number of cities continue to suffer acute financial distress.

New York City verged on bankruptcy in 1975 and necessitated a major rescue operation by New York State, including the establishment of the Emergency Financial Control Board and the Municipal Assistance Corporation to help restore the finances of the city.[116] The board and the city were mandated to develop a financial plan for the city, and the former was empowered to approve or disapprove city contracts and borrowing by the city. In 1979 Florida enacted a law providing for the establishment of a similar board whenever the governor determines one or more specified conditions exists.[117]

The New York State Municipal Assistance Corporation, governed by a nine-member board appointed by the governor with senate approval, was authorized to issue bonds and notes up to a maximum of $3 billion and to use the proceeds, secured by the city's sales tax receipts, to pay off the city's notes as they mature.

Other actions taken by the legislature included a $250 million appropriation to the city from the Local Assistance Fund as an advance and an additional $500 million from the fund as an advance to the Municipal Assistance Corporation. During the period 1975–78, the state advanced $3.3 billion to the city and in fiscal year 1978 granted the city $3.16 billion, a 34 percent increase compared to four years earlier.

Simultaneously with New York City, the city of Yonkers suffered a financial emergency and the legislature created the Emergency Financial Control Board of the City consisting of the state comptroller, the mayor, city manager, secretary of state, and three others appointed by the governor with the approval of the senate.[118] The board was dissolved at the end of 1978 as the city's financial health was restored.

A 1979 staff report of the National Academy of Public Administration and the U.S. Advisory Commission on Intergovernmental Relations reported the following state actions taken to help fiscally distressed local governments:

- Forty-four States have authorized State efforts to provide home finance assistance to lower-income households. . . .
- Nineteen States have introduced an element of geographic targeting into their home rehabilitation efforts. . . .
- In seventeen States, a targeted tax incentive program has been adopted to encourage upgrading in designated geographic areas. . . .
- Thirty States have enacted fair housing statutes designed to eliminate discrimination in the sale or leasing of housing on the basis of race, color, creed, national origin, or ancestry. . . .
- Fifteen States attempt to target site development efforts to underdeveloped communities. . . .
- Eleven States have attempted to promote the creation of commercial or manufacturing facilities in distressed communities. . . .
- Twelve States offer tax credits calculated to stimulate industrial facilities development, rehabilitation, or job creation within designated unemployment or redevelopment areas. . . .
- Eight States have tied small business aid programs to the problems of community distress and redevelopment. . . .

— Twenty-three States have initiated customized job training efforts in conjunction with industrial recruitment activities. . . .

— Forty-eight States have enabled their local jurisdictions to create local redevelopment or renewal agencies. . . .

— Eighteen States provide targeted State-local assistance for community development activities. . . .

— Only four States have instituted preferential siting programs to locate State facilities in jurisdictions requiring redevelopment assistance. . . .

— Twenty-one States have enacted targeted State-local tax sharing and revenue sharing programs. . . .

— During the period 1970–1977, 25 States enacted school equalization finance plans. Within-state disparities in per-pupil expenditures declined in 17 States over the period. . . .

— Thirty States have assumed 90% or more of local public welfare expenditures. . . .

— Thirty-six States now permit their local jurisdictions to levy either sales taxes or income taxes, a reform which can significantly reduce local reliance on property tax levies. . . .

— Sixteen States have enacted programs to reimburse local governments for mandated activities. . . .

— Minnesota remains the only State which has authorized a local tax base sharing effort. . . . [119]

Available evidence suggests that a number of the older central cities and suburbs in the northeast and midwest will continue to experience acute fiscal distress in spite of the actions taken by states to relieve the distress and restore the fiscal health of these units. The experience of the past supports the conclusion that states in general will continue to attack the problems of these political subdivisions on an ad hoc basis and will not institute major changes in the system of state-local fiscal relations on a statewide basis. Furthermore, not all states possess the fiscal resources to bail out their financially distressed subdivisions.

Fiscal Resource Equalization

Data presented concerning the disparities in the wealth of school districts in New York State are indicative of the types of fiscal disparities found in most states. Recognizing the "need-fiscal resources mismatch" problem, most states have made attempts to reduce the mismatch through categorical grants-in-aid and revenue sharing. Because of the political strength of the wealthier suburban local governments in the typical state legislature, the grant and revenue-sharing programs commonly provide resources to these units as well as to the fiscally distressed units.

In a metropolitan area, there is a benefit overspill from the central city to the suburbs resulting from the provision of major services by the city. To assist the cities fiscally and improve the equity in the financing of these services, 13 state legislatures have authorized one or more local governments to levy a withholding income or payroll tax and more than 4,400 local governments currently levy such a tax.[120]

A withholding income or payroll tax, while generating additional revenue for the city immediately, may injure the city in the long term if the tax discourages commercial firms and industrial firms from expanding or locating in the city.

An innovative approach to reducing fiscal disparities was initiated in 1971 by the Minnesota legislature, which authorized the partial sharing of the growth in the commercial-industrial property tax base by local governments within the seven-county Twin Cities metropolitan area.[121] The purpose of the tax base sharing law is to reduce gross fiscal disparities among political subdivisions by directing that the revenue produced by 40 percent of new nonresidential construction be deposited in the municipal equity account in the state treasury and distributed to local governments according to a need and population formula.

Metropolitan Financing District

Failing to approve several proposals to establish a multipurpose state authority or a metropolitan county in eastern Massachusetts, the general court (legislature) in 1975 directed the Legislature Research Council to study the feasibility of creating a metropolitan services financing district with authority to levy taxes to raise revenue to pay all or part of the cost of metropolitan services currently financed by the general property tax.[122] Under the proposal, no units of local government would be consolidated or lose any of their functions.

In its report, the council identified 64 regional entities—6 counties, 56 special purpose regional districts, and 2 state authorities—providing regional services.[123] The council sought the views of the chief executives of the 101 cities and towns in the metropolitan area concerning the desirability of creating a financing district. Nine local government executives expressed opposition, 16 expressed no views, and 31 essentially were noncommittal pending receipt of further information on the proposed district.[124] To date, the general court has taken no further action relative to the proposed creation of a metropolitan financing district.

SUMMARY AND CONCLUSIONS

The state legislature has complete authority over the system of state-local finance except as limited by provisions of the state constitution. Major constitutional provisions in many states require the full valuation of property; grant property tax exemptions; establish tax, deficit, and debt limits; and restrict the loan of the credit and property of political subdivisions. Taken together, these restrictions and similar statutory restrictions have created serious fiscal problems for a number of older and declining cities.

The principal source of locally raised tax revenue is the general property tax, but its relative importance has been declining because of the relatively sharp increase in recent years in federal and state fiscal assistance. Citizen-initiated propositions placing limits on the general property tax and similar actions by state legislatures are forcing states to assume greater responsibility for financing local government services.

State mandates continue to be the major irritant in state-local relations and have produced an organized reaction by local governments in several states. This has led to the enactment of laws providing for state reimbursement of added local government costs resulting from the mandates of the adoption of fiscal note requirements to ensure that legislators are aware of the fiscal burden that will be placed upon local governments by a proposed mandate.

A number of state mandates are the product of increasing federal partial preemption and the establishment of minimum standards that must be met by the states if they desire to continue to be responsible for certain regulatory functions. The federal government also has been supplying an increasing amount of fiscal assistance to local governments, a subject examined in Chapter 5.

States respond to local problems in a variety of ways, including financial assistance to local governments. In Chapter 4, the state response to local problems is analyzed by examining the three roles played by states.

NOTES

1. *State and Local Government Employment Payrolls* (Washington, D.C.: U.S. Bureau of Labor Statistics, October 1981), p. 1; *Governmental Finances in 1979–80* (Washington, D.C.: U.S. Bureau of the Census, 1981), p. 31.

2. *Governmental Finances in 1978–79*, p. 17.

3. *Significant Features of Fiscal Federalism: 1979–80 Edition* (Washington, D.C.: U.S. Advisory Commission on Intergovernmental Relations, 1980), p. 78. The low percentage for Hawaii is deceptive since most government functions are performed by the state. The New Hampshire percentage of 15.8 is the realistic low figure.

4. "State-Local Fiscal Relations," *Michigan Municipal Review* 70 (August 1977): 160.

5. Frank J. Macchiarola, "Constitutional, Statutory and Judicial Restraints on Local Finance in New York State," *New York Law Forum* 15 (Winter 1969): 853.

6. *Constitution of the State of New York*, art. XIII, § 12.

7. *State Limitations on Local Taxes & Expenditures* (Washington, D.C.: U.S. Advisory Commission on Intergovernmental Relations, 1977), pp. 1–2.

8. *State and Local Ratio Studies, Property Tax Assessment, and Transfer Taxes* (Washington, D.C.: U.S. Bureau of the Census, 1980), pp. 45–47.

9. *Ingraham Company v. City of Bristol*, 144 Conn. 374, 132 A2d 563 at 566 (1957).

10. *Property Values Subject to Local General Property Taxation in the United States: 1979* (Washington, D.C.: U.S. Bureau of the Census, 1980), p. 8.

11. Ibid., p. 9.

12. *Property Tax Limits* (Chicago: International Association of Assessing Officers, 1978), pp. 14–28; *Significant Features of Fiscal Federalism: 1976–77 Edition*, vol. II (Washington, D.C.: U.S. Advisory Commission on Intergovernmental Relations, 1977), pp. 83–91. Massachusetts voters in 1980 approved an initiative petition limiting the property tax rate. In 1978 California voters approved initiative proposition 13, thereby reducing property taxes by more than 50 percent.

13. *Delaware Code*, § 8002 (b) (1975).

14. *Kansas Statutes*, § 79-1964a (1978).

15. *Rhode Island Laws of 1979*, chap. 298; *General Laws of Rhode Island*, § 45-12-9 (1980).

16. George W. Spicer, "Fiscal Aspects of State-Local Relations," *The Annals* 207 (January 1940): 154.

17. John Shannon, Michael Bell, and Ronald Fisher, "Recent State Experience with Local Tax and Expenditure Controls," *National Tax Journal* 29 (September 1976): 278.

18. Helen F. Ladd, "An Economic Evaluation of State Limitations on Local Taxing and Spending Powers," *National Tax Journal* 31 (March 1978): 15.

19. *New York Laws of 1969*, chap. 1105.

20. *Hurd v. City of Buffalo*, 34 N.Y.2d 628 (1974).

21. *New York Laws of 1976*, chaps. 349, 485.

22. *Bethlehem Steel Corporation v. Board of Education*, 44 N.Y.2d 831 (1978).

23. *Significant Features of Fiscal Federalism: 1976–77 Edition*, pp. 83–91.

24. Ibid., pp. 92–93.

25. *Lance v. Board of Education*, 170 S.E.2d 783 (1969); *Gordon v. Lance*, 91 S. Ct. 1889 (1971).

26. For an example, see *Constitution of New York*, art. VIII, § 11 (1846).

27. *Town Bonding Act, New York Laws of 1869*, chap. 907.

28. *Sun Printing & Publishing Association v. Mayor*, 152 N.Y. 257 at 273, 46 N.E. 499 at 503 (1897).

29. *Constitution of New York*, art. VIII, § 1.

30. *Finances of Selected Public Employee Retirement Systems* (Washington, D.C.: U.S. Bureau of the Census, March 1981), p. 1.

31. Committee on Education and Labor, U.S. House of Representatives, *Task Force Report on Public Employee Retirement Systems* (Washington, D.C.: U.S. Government Printing Office, 1978), pp. 51–59.

32. *State and Local Government Pension Reforms* (Washington, D.C.: U.S. Advisory Commission on Intergovernmental Relations, 1979), p. 2.

33. *Funding of State and Local Government Pension Plans: A National Problem* (Washington, D.C.: U.S. General Accounting Office, 1979), p. i.

34. *New York Laws of 1971*, chap. 733; *New York Executive Law*, § § 800–2 (McKinney 1972).

35. *Constitution of New York*, art. V, § 7; *New York Retirement and Social Security Law*, § § 11, 311; *New York Education Law*, § 517; *Administrative Code of the City of New York*, § § B3.11.0, B18-18.0, B19-7.61.

36. The New York State legislature has required all local governments to adopt a code of ethics. See *New York Laws of 1969*, chap. 646; *New York General Municipal Law*, art. 18, § 806 (1) (McKinney 1981 supp.).

37. For additional information, see Joseph F. Zimmerman, "Ethics in Local Government," *Management Information Service Report* 8 (August 1976): entire issue.

38. *State and Local Ratio Studies, Property Tax Assessment, and Transfer Taxes* (Washington, D.C.: U.S. Bureau of the Census, 1980), p. 1.

39. Ibid.

40. *County Government Finances in 1978–79* (Washington, D.C.: U.S. Bureau of the Census, 1980), p. 1.

41. *Local Government Finances in Selected Metropolitan Areas and Large Counties: 1978–79* (Washington, D.C.: U.S. Bureau of the Census, 1981).

42. For details, see Abt Associates, *Property Tax Relief Programs for the Elderly: Final Report* (Washington, D.C.: U.S. Department of Housing and Urban Development, 1975).

43. Ibid., p. 4.

44. *Massachusetts Laws of 1979*, chap. 151.

45. *The Book of the States: 1980–1981* (Lexington, Ky.: Council of State Governments, 1980), p. 26.

46. *First National Bank of Boston et al. v. Bellotti*, 435 U.S. 765 (1978).

47. "Tax Reduction Proposals Lose," *National Civic Review* 70 (January 1981): 46–47.

48. "Dallas Rejects Bid for a 30% Tax Cut," *New York Times*, January 19, 1981, p. A18.

49. In California, there may be a proposition with the same number in more than one year since the propositions are listed numerically on the ballot each year.

50. Wallace Turner, "1978 Coast Tax Initiative Now Spurs Budget Crisis," *New York Times*, January 10, 1981, p. A8.

51. *Proposition 2½: Estimated Impacts* (Boston: Massachusetts Executive Office of Communities and Development, 1980), p. 1. The initiated limit is printed as an appendix to Chapter 59 of the *Massachusetts General Laws Annotated* (1980 supp.).

52. *Massachusetts Laws of 1981*, chap. 782.

53. Adam Smith, *An Inquiry into the Nature and Causes of the Wealth of Nations*, vol. 2 (Oxford: Clarendon Press, 1976), pp. 825–26.

54. For additional details, see C. Lowell Harriss, "Property Taxation: What's Good and What's Bad About It," *The American Journal of Economics and Sociology* 33 (January 1974): 89–102.

55. *Constitution of the State of Ohio*, art. VIII, § 3.

56. *Angell v. Toledo*, 153 Ohio St. 179 at 184, 91 N.E.2d 250 at 253 (1950).

57. *Ohio Revised Code Annotated*, § 718.01 (Page 1976).

58. *East Ohio Gas Company v. Akron*, 7 Ohio St.2d 73 at 76, 218 N.E.2d 608 at 610 (1966).

59. *Ohio Revised Code Annotated*, chap. 5747 (Page 1973).

60. *Significant Features of Fiscal Federalism: 1979–80 Edition*, p. 108.

61. See *Report of the Temporary State Commission on the Powers of Local Governments*, pt. II (New York, 1973), p. 78; and *Final Report* (Albany: Temporary State Commission on Constitutional Tax Limitations, 1975), p. 94.

62. *Significant Features of Fiscal Federalism: 1979–80 Edition*, pp. 96, 108.

63. Ibid., p. 100. In Idaho, food, medicine, and medical appliances are taxed at 3 rather than 4 percent. Kansas grants a $20 food sales tax refund to elderly and disabled persons.

64. Frank J. Goodnow, *Municipal Home Rule* (New York: Macmillan, 1895), pp. 54–55.

65. *State Mandating of Local Expenditures* (Washington, D.C.: U.S. Advisory Commission on Intergovernmental Relations, 1978), pp. 5–6.

66. *Problems Relating to Taxation and Finance* (Albany: New York State Constitutional Convention, 1938), pp. 273–74.

67. Stephen Gordon, "Most Towns Still Lack Septage Disposal Sites," *The Keene Sentinel* (Keene, N.H.), June 27, 1980, pp. 1, 6.

68. *State Mandating of Local Expenditures*, p. 40.

69. A locally dominated fiscal system is defined as one in which local governments raise more than half of the total state-local tax revenue.

70. *State Mandating of Local Expenditures*, p. 32.

71. Eva M. Ennis, "State Actions Affecting Local Affairs," in *The Book of the States: 1980–1981* (Lexington, Ky.: Council of State Governments, 1980), p. 617.

72. Jefferson B. Fordham, *Model Constitutional Provisions for Municipal Home Rule* (Chicago: American Municipal Association, 1953), pp. 23–24.

73. Ibid., p. 24.

74. *Constitution of the State of Alaska*, art. II, § 19.

75. *Constitution of the State of Louisiana*, art. IV, § 14.

76. *Constitution of the Commonwealth of Massachusetts*, art. CXV of the articles of amendment.

77. *Constitution of the Commonwealth of Pennsylvania*, art. VIII, § 2 (b).

78. *Constitution of the State of Tennessee*, art. II, § 24.

79. *California Laws of 1972*, chap. 1406.

80. For additional details, see *State Mandating of Local Expenditures*, pp. 22–27.

81. *Local Revenue Diversification: Income, Sales Taxes & User Charges* (Washington, D.C.: U.S. Advisory Commission on Intergovernmental Relations, 1974), pp. 16–17.

82. *Federal Grants: Their Effects on State-Local Expenditures, Employment Levels, Wage Rates* (Washington, D.C.: U.S. Advisory Commission on Intergovernmental Relations, 1977), p. 19.

83. *A Sane Fiscal Policy for Louisiana* (Baton Rouge: Louisiana Association of Business and Industry, 1977).

84. *The State of State-Local Revenue Sharing* (Washington, D.C.: U.S. Advisory Commission on Intergovernmental Relations, 1980), pp. 5, 8.

85. Ibid., p. 2.

86. Ibid.

87. *State Revenue Sharing* (Albany: Temporary State Commission on State and Local Finances, 1975), p. 20.

88. *State of New York Executive Budget, Submitted by Hugh L. Carey, Governor, to the New York State Legislature* (Albany: Executive Chamber, 1979), p. m36.

89. Hugh L. Carey, *State of New York Annual Budget Message, 1980–1981* (Albany: Executive Chamber, 1980), pp. m19–m20.

90. *State of New York Executive Budget for the Fiscal Year April 1, 1981 to March 31, 1982* (Albany: Executive Chamber, 1981), p. m37.

91. Ibid., pp. m37–m38.

92. Robin Herman, "Carey Alters Medicaid Plan to Calm Mayors' Criticism," *New York Times*, February 20, 1981, p. B3.

93. *Significant Features of Fiscal Federalism: 1979–80 Edition*, p. 165.

94. Ibid., p. 170.

95. Ibid.

96. Thomas R. Dye and Thomas L. Hurley, "The Responsiveness of Federal and State Governments to Urban Problems," *Journal of Politics* 40 (February 1978): 204.

97. Joel Cogen, "Gov. O'Neill's Wrong Plan to Hold Down Connecticut Spending," *New York Times*, January 14, 1981, p. A22.

98. Richard L. Madden, "Connecticut's Budget," *New York Times*, February 6, 1981, p. B2; "Keeping Connecticut Solvent: Round Two," *New York Times*, February 12, 1981, p. A26.

99. "Text of Letter from Mayor Koch Accompanying Proposed Budget for Fiscal '82," *New York Times*, January 17, 1981, p. 28.

100. *Significant Features of Fiscal Federalism: 1979–80 Edition*, p. 170.

101. *Book of the States: 1980–81*, p. 626.

102. *The Fleischmann Report on the Quality, Cost and Financing of Elementary and Secondary Education in New York State*, vol. I (New York: Viking Press, 1973), pp. 62–63.

103. *Serrano v. Priest*, 5 Cal.3d 584, 487 P.2d 1241 (1971). See also *Constitution of the State of California*, art. I, § § 11, 21.

104. *San Antonio Independent School District v. Rodriguez*, 337 F.Supp. 280 (1971); *San Antonio Independent School District v. Rodriguez*, 93 S. Ct. 1278 (1972).

105. *Horton v. Meskill*, 31 Conn. 377, 332 A.2d 813 (1974); *Horton v. Meskill* 172 Conn. 592, 376 A2d 359 (1977).

106. "Connecticut's New School Finance Plan is Much More Costly and Still Inequitable," *CPEC News and Views* 93 (August 1980): 1.

107. *Board of Education v. Nyquist*, 95 Misc.2d 466 (1978).

108. *State of New York Executive Budget for the Fiscal Year April 1, 1981 to March 31, 1982*, p. m39.

109. Robin Herman, "State School Aid Sought by Carey Called Too Small," *New York Times*, January 21, 1981, p. B10.

110. E.J. Dionne, Jr., "Financing Method for Schools Ruled Valid in New York," *New York Times*, June 24, 1982, pp. 1 and B7. Also, *Board of Education v. Nyquist*, 57 NY2d 27 (1982).

111. Joseph F. Sullivan, "Byrne Budget: Thorny Adieu," *New York Times*, February 3, 1981, p. B3.

112. Ibid.

113. *Municipal Bankruptcy Act*, 48 STAT. 798, 50 STAT. 653, 11 U.S.C. § § 401–3.

114. *The Urban Fiscal Crisis: Fact or Fantasy?* (Washington, D.C.: U.S. Department of Housing and Urban Development, 1979), p. 4.

115. *Central City-Suburban Fiscal Disparity & City Distress, 1977* (Washington, D.C.: U.S. Advisory Commission on Intergovernmental Relations, 1980), p. 11.

116. *New York Laws of 1975*, chaps. 868–70; *New York Laws of 1974*, chaps. 168–69; *New York Public Authorities Law*, § 3033 (McKinney 1981 supp.).

117. *Florida Laws of 1979*, chaps. 79–183; *West's Florida Statutes Annotated*, § 218.503 (1981 supp.).

118. *New York Laws of 1975*, chap. 871. See also *New York Laws of 1976*, chaps. 488–89; *New York Laws of 1977*, chap. 445.

119. *The States and Distressed Communities: Indicators of Significant Actions* (Washington, D.C.: National Academy of Public Administration and U.S. Advisory Commission on Intergovernmental Relations, 1979), pp. 8–34.

120. *Significant Features of Fiscal Federalism: 1979–80 Edition*, p. 126.

121. "Metropolitan Revenue Distribution Act," *Minnesota Statutes*, chap. 473F (1971).

122. *Massachusetts House of Representatives, Resolution Number 6398 of 1975*.

123. *Report Relative to Establishing a Metropolitan Services Financing District in the Boston Metropolitan Area* (Boston: Massachusetts Legislative Research Council, 1976), p. 13.

124. Ibid., p. 18.

CHAPTER 4

State Response to Local Problems

Local governments in rural, suburban, and urban areas, as the primary direct providers of services to citizens, have experienced major and minor problems throughout their history. The industrial revolution and concomitant urbanization in the nineteenth century posed serious problems for rapidly expanding cities. Additional problems were created by the mechanization of agriculture in the twentieth century, which drastically reduced the demand for farm labor and resulted in the migration of millions of relatively unskilled workers from farms to the central cities of the midwest and the east.

The nature of urban problems in metropolitan areas changed dramatically after World War II since a great suburban movement developed that drained many of the older central cities of the midwest and east of a substantial portion of their middle-class residents, commercial businesses, and manufacturing companies. Compounding the problems of many of these central cities, which were unable to expand their territorial boundaries through annexation, was an influx of low-income citizens resulting in a resource-needs mismatch and deterioration of buildings and physical facilities.[1]

Rural areas did not escape the forces underlying the economic and population changes. The continued decline in population increased the difficulty of providing many basic public services—water supply, refuse disposal, highway maintenance—by rural governments possessing limited financial resources. Suburban areas also experienced difficult problems in accommodating the demands for services from their rapidly growing populations.

Writing in 1965, Professor Roscoe Martin concluded that the states were gripped by three major deficiencies that inhibited their ability to respond to urban problems:

> The first is in orientation—most States are governed in accordance with the rural traditions of an earlier day. The second is in timeliness— the governments of most States are anachronistic; they lack relevance to the urgencies of the modern world. The third is in leadership—state leaders are by profession cautious and tradition-bound, which ill equips them for the tasks of modern government. Governors are less subject to this charge than are legislators, for they represent larger constituencies and therefore are in position to adopt broader views.[2]

Martin wrote before state legislatures had been reapportioned in conformance with the U.S. Supreme Court's "one-person, one-vote" dictum. The legislature or one of its houses in a number of states was controlled by members from rural areas prior to the reapportionment revolution, and many observers had anticipated that urban areas would greatly benefit from the ending of rural domination of the legislature. Experience, however, has indicated that power has tended to shift to members from suburban areas who often find they have more in common with rural members than with members from the central cities.

In general, the governor in urban states has been more responsive to the problems of large cities than the legislature. The role of the governor in some instances has been motivated by a desire to become president of the United States. The governor's role as a major intergovernmental actor has been challenged on more than one occasion by the mayor of a large city harboring presidential ambitions. The best known example of competition in solving urban problems involved Governor Nelson Rockefeller of New York State and Mayor John Lindsay of New York City in the period 1966 to 1973.

Numerous organizations and study groups during the past three decades have called upon the state to "unshackle" local governments and play a positive role in solving areawide problems. In 1956 the Council of State Governments issued a report describing the states as "the key to solving the complex difficulties that make up the general metropolitan problems."[3] In 1961 the U.S. Advisory Commission on Intergovernmental Relations called for vigorous action by the states, including a constitutional provision granting local discretionary authority but reserving to the legislature sufficient authority to cope with metropolitan problems. The provision also gave authorization for municipal annexation of unincorporated areas without the consent of the areas proposed for annexation, and for interlocal contracting and joint enterprises, creation of functional authorities, voluntary transfers of functions between municipalities and counties, and creation of metropolitan area study commissions and metropolitan area planning bodies.[4] The commission also recommended direct state action in the form of the establishment of a state agency for metropolitan area affairs and a state program of financial and technical assistance to the areas, control of new incorporations, financial and regulatory action to secure and preserve open space, and action to resolve disputes among local governments in metropolitan areas.[5]

In 1967 David Walker described what the role of the state should be:

> The States have ample potential to play a triple-threat role in urban affairs: as "unshacklers" of local governments; as leaders in encouraging and pointing the way to new forms of urban government and intergovernmental cooperation; and as coordinators and direct providers of funds with emphasis on mitigating economic and social disparities among local units in metropolitan areas. If States are to retain their claims as positive partners in the federal systems, they must fulfill this triple-threat potential.[6]

Chapter 2 described the broadening of the discretionary authority of many local governments in recent decades, and Chapter 3 examined the intervention of the state in traditional local affairs in the form of state mandates. The focus of this chapter is upon the states response to urban and metropolitan problems. Three roles—inhibitor, facilitator, and initiator—have been played, often simultaneously, by the state because of political pressures and pragmatic considerations.

THE STATE AS INHIBITOR

Historically, Dillon's Rule limited the ability of local governments to solve problems through innovations since they would violate the Ultra Vires Rule unless special permission was obtained from the legislature. General replacement of Dillon's Rule in many functional areas by constitutional and statutory devolution of powers upon certain types of political subdivisions has facilitated problem solving. Nevertheless, local governments in the typical state are encumbered by constitutional and statutory restrictions.

Corruption and financial irregularities in many cities in the nineteenth century induced a public response in the form of constitutional and statutory restrictions upon the financial powers of political subdivisions. While local government responsibilities have mushroomed during the past 35 years, restrictions on their powers generally have not been removed, and units are hampered unduly in their problem-solving efforts. These restrictions, among other things, promoted the formation of special districts by the state to evade the constitutional restrictions on the state and its political subdivisions, thereby further fragmenting the local government system and creating problems of accountability, coordination, and duplication.

Areawide Government

The development of metropolitan areas has produced problems overspilling local government boundaries, yet no government below the state level typically exists that possesses sufficient authority and resources to solve these problems. As a result, problems either are not solved effectively, or their solution depends upon interlocal cooperation or direct state action.

With the exceptions of Connecticut and Rhode Island, a unit of government, the county, exists that often possesses sufficient areal jurisdiction to deal with problems overspilling municipal boundaries. Yet the county usually lacks sufficient authority and resources to attack areawide problems, and constitutional provisions may make the strengthening of county government exceedingly difficult.

The constitutions of three states contain specific provisions inhibiting the development of county governments as major areawide governments. In New York State, the constitution does not allow a city or town function to be transferred to the county unless town voters as one unit and city voters as a second unit give their approval in a referendum.[7] Should a village function be involved, a triple concurrent majority vote of approval is required—town voters as a unit, city voters as a second unit, and village voters as a third unit. Each village voter may vote twice, once as a village voter and once as a town voter since all villages are located within towns.

The Ohio Constitution contains a similar provision stipulating no charter or amendment vesting any municipal powers in the county shall become effective unless:

> ... it shall have been approved by a majority of those voting thereon (1) in the county, (2) in the largest municipality, (3) in the county outside of such municipality, and (4) in counties having a population based upon the latest preceding federal decennial census of 500,000 or less, in each of a majority of the combined total of municipalities and townships in the county (not including within any township any part of its area lying within a municipality).[8]

The Tennessee Constitution permits the consolidation of municipal and county functions provided that municipal voters as one unit and voters outside municipalities as a second unit approve the merger of the functions.[9]

A number of observers were convinced that the U.S. Supreme Court's "one-person, one-vote" dictum would be employed to strike down, as violating the U.S. Constitution, provisions in state constitutions requiring a concurrent affirmative vote to transfer functions. The U.S. Supreme Court in 1977, however, ruled that the New York State mandatory referendum requirement does not violate the Court's dictum or the equal protection of the laws clause of the Fourteenth Amendment to the U.S. Constitution.[10]

Fiscal Restraints

It is a truism that the vigorous exercise of local discretionary authority depends heavily upon the availability of adequate revenue. Currently, the following state fiscal restrictions limit local governments: expenditure limits in Arizona, Iowa, and New Jersey; property assessment limits in California, Idaho, Minnesota, and New Mexico; tax rate limits in 39 states; levy limits in 22 states; and debt limits in 46 states.[11]

Expenditure lids are expressed either as a fixed percentage of the previous year's expenditures (for example 10 percent in Arizona) or as a variable percentage dependent upon the increase in the state's personal income. In New Jersey, local budgets do not become effective until approved by the director of the State Division of Local Government Services who may disapprove a budget only for reasons specifically listed in law. According to the Municipal Finance Officers Association, "the Director may, however, disallow revenue estimates made by localities. This power, coupled with the stipulation for balanced budgets, gives the State their wherewithal to force local governments to follow sound overall spending policies."[12] The property assessment limits, which freeze assessments or allow limited change over time, do not by themselves significantly restrict local governments since the property tax rate can be raised unless there is a tax rate limit. In California and Idaho, property may be reassessed only upon new construction or a change in ownership.

Property tax rate limits are established as a percentage of the assessed value of property and may be overall (13 states) or specific limits (31 states). The former specifies a maximum tax rate that may be levied by any local government authorized to tax the same property. A specific tax rate limit restricts only one type of political subdivision, such as a city or town. Occasionally, a state statute restricts only one named unit; Kent County in Delaware specifically is limited to a five-mills rate.[13]

Tax rate limits can be exceeded under specific conditions, and voter approval typically is required. In Kansas increases in the rate limit may be authorized by the state board of tax appeals.[14]

Constitutional real estate tax limits can be troublesome for local governments. The New York State Constitution sets the limits in a range of 1.5 to 2 percent of "average full valuation" for political subdivisions other than New York City, which is limited to 2.5 percent but also provides exceptions.[15] To assist Buffalo, Rochester, Yonkers, and 65 school districts solve their financial problems, the state legislature allowed these units to exclude from the limit taxes collected to pay for public employee retirement costs.[16] In 1974 the court of appeals ruled the exclusion unconstitutional.[17]

Alaska, Colorado, Florida, and Nebraska are the only states that do not limit the authority of local governments to contract long-term debts, and the Tennessee restriction applies only under a special condition.[18] All states with debt limits, except Connecticut, Hawaii, and Indiana, have constitutional or statutory requirements for voter approval of long-term borrowing, but five of these states—Massachusetts, New Jersey, New York, Tennessee, and Washington—have restrictions applying only to specified classes of school districts.[19] The complexity of constitutional debt limits is illustrated by the New York State provisions. The limits vary from 7 percent for a city, town, or village with a population under 125,000 to 9 percent for cities exceeding a population of 125,000, with the exceptions of New York City and Nassau County, which have 10 percent limits.[20] Exceptions from the limits are provided for Buffalo, New York City, Rochester, and Syracuse.

Debt limits can be evaded in a number of states by the issuance of debt instruments not backed by a pledge of full faith and credit of the issuing government, establishment of special districts exempt from the debt limits, and entering into a lease-purchase agreement under which the leasee political subdivision purchases a facility on the installment plan and acquires full title at the expiration of the agreement.[21] Lease-purchase agreements as well as borrowing for long-term purposes by municipalities in some states are also not subject to a popular referendum.

Tax and debt limitations have not prevented the bankruptcy or the near bankruptcy of cities, and the argument can be advanced that voters of each local government should possess an unrestricted right to tax and borrow. Nevertheless, the survey of municipal and county associations, described in Chapter 2, reveals there is strong support among local governments for these restrictions.

THE STATE AS FACILITATOR

State legislatures have facilitated the solution of substate problems by: (1) establishing or authorizing the establishment of local government study commissions, regional planning commissions, and state agencies for local affairs; (2) passing enabling legislation for the creation of single and multipurpose areawide governments; (3) authorizing local governments to enter into contracts with other governments and private firms for the provision of services; (4) permitting the transfer of functional responsibilities between levels of government; (5) establishing municipal bond agencies and insurance and investment pools for local governments; and (6) authorizing the levy of nonproperty taxes to reduce overreliance on the property tax.

Commissions and Local Affairs Agencies

Interest in the study commission approach to solving substate problems peaked in the 1950s. Of the 112 surveys initiated between 1923 and 1957, 79 were launched between 1948 and 1957, compared to 1 or 2 per year from 1923 to 1948.[22]

The number and nature of studies underwent a significant change in the 1960s, primarily as the result of conditions attached to various federal grant-in-aid programs. There was a sharp rise in comprehensive land use and transportation studies, while the number of studies concerned with governmental organization declined from 40 in 1960 to 34 in 1966 and 29 in 1967. In 1968, 36 such studies were launched.[23] A national survey of study commissions has not been conducted since 1968, yet it is apparent that the number of commissions concerned with reorganization of the local government system in metropolitan areas is small today.

In a chapter entitled "The Twilight of Metropolitan Study Commissions," Schmandt and Standing offered an explanation for the failure of most study commissions to achieve their goals:

> Advocates of metropolitan surveys have long insisted on study commissions of high ranking citizens drawn largely from business and industrial circles. Conceiving the structure of power as monolithic, they have assumed that key civic decisions are made by a select group of individuals of upper socio-economic status who stand at the top of a stable power hierarchy.[24]

State legislatures also attempt to facilitate the resolution of areawide problems by enacting legislation for the creation of metropolitan and regional planning commissions; some were organized as councils of governments (COGs) and are composed of local elected officials only. The early commissions were created on an ad hoc basis; but by 1970, 40 states had established statewide regional planning systems.[25]

The effectiveness of the commissions and COGs in solving areawide problems has been adversely affected by the voluntary nature of the organizations, which possess only advisory powers and suffer all the disadvantages of the United Nations approach to resolving world problems. COGs and commissions have been heavily dependent on the national government for funding, and the curtailment of such funding by the Reagan administration will weaken COGs and commissions.

The early state agencies for local affairs, dating back to 1919 in Pennsylvania, primarily were control agencies that exercised oversight over political subdivisions. The first noncontrolling agency was the New York State Office for Local Government, created in 1959. The functions of these agencies, which vary greatly from state to state, may be grouped into eight categories: advice and information, research, publication, planning and area development, promotion of interlocal cooperation, training programs, coordination of state services and federal grants, and control functions. The last function is performed only by the North Carolina, Pennsylvania, and New Mexico agencies. The other agencies are noncoercive ones providing advice and technical assistance to local governments at their request and have not acted as catalysts for a major reorganization of the governance system in any area.[26] By statute, 15 states have established state advisory commissions on intergovernmental relations, which function in a manner similar to their national counterpart—the U.S. Advisory Commission on Intergovernmental Relations.

Single and Multipurpose Special Districts

To facilitate the solution of particular local and areawide problems, state legislatures have enacted laws authorizing voters to decide in a referendum whether to form a single or a multipurpose special district. Currently, there are 900 areawide special districts.

In some instances, special districts have been created to evade constitutional tax and/or debt limits on general purpose local governments and civil service requirements. As a general rule, special districts are subject to fewer state restraints than municipalities but are opposed by individuals who object to the further fragmentation of the local governance system and raise questions of accountability since most governing bodies are appointed rather than elected. Critics also contend that these districts have not solved preexisting areawide problems and have created other problems. State-controlled special districts are discussed in a subsequent section.

Service Agreements and Functional Transfers

Forty-two states have sought to facilitate the resolution of regional problems by enacting statutes authorizing (and in some cases encouraging with grants-in-aid) intergovernmental agreements for the provision of services. In 29 of these states, local governments may cooperate with neighboring units in other states. Unfortunately, a power in 31 states can be exercised jointly by two political subdivisions only if each possesses the power. Furthermore, the general interlocal cooperation law in 13 states does not supersede individual statutes authorizing cooperation in specific fields, and many of these statutes are encumbered with detailed procedural requirements.

The first national survey of intergovernmental service agreements, conducted in 1972, revealed that 63 percent of the responding municipalities had entered into agreements during the previous ten years with other governments and/or private firms for the provision of services to their citizens.[27] Larger units generally had a greater tendency to enter into agreements than smaller units, and three-fourths of the respondents reported active state encouragement of the intergovernmental provision of services.

Ten states have constitutional or statutory provisions authorizing general purpose local governments to transfer responsibility for a governmental function or functional component. Voter approval is required for a transfer in Florida, New York, Ohio, Pennsylvania, and Vermont. A referendum is not required for a transfer in Alaska, California, Illinois, Michigan, and Virginia. The state government also has mandated the statewide transfer of functions, such as the shift of responsibility for property tax administration to the county level in Florida and welfare to the county level in New York.[28]

Thirty-one percent of the 3,319 municipalities responding to a 1975 national survey reported they had transferred responsibility for one or more functions or functional components during the previous decade to another municipality, the county, the state, special districts, and councils of governments. Although 608 municipalities transferred responsibility for only one function, 38 municipalities shifted responsibility for five or more functions.[29] The tendency to transfer functional responsibility was directly correlated with the size of the municipality. The number of functions transferred averaged 4.2 for municipalities with a population over 500,000 and 1.5 for municipalities with a population under 25,000. Functions most commonly transferred by cities with a population over 500,000 were law enforcement and public health in contrast to municipalities with a population below 10,000, which transferred solid waste collection and disposal most often.

Bond Banks and Insurance and Investment Pools

To assist local governments financially, a number of states have established municipal bond banks as well as investment and insurance pools for local governments. These mechanisms are based upon what can be considered a market discount for larger quantities.

Municipal Bond Banks

Vermont (1970), Maine (1972), New York (1972), Alaska (1975), North Dakota (1975), and New Hampshire (1975) established state municipal bond banks to make it easier for local governments to borrow funds and at lower transaction and premium costs.[30] Participation in a municipal bond bank is voluntary, with smaller municipalities the primary participants because they have a lower credit rating than the bank's rating and conventional borrowing is expensive. No local government in New York State has participated in the bank.

A municipality has to meet all the usual constitutional and statutory requirements for the issuance of debt instruments before the unit may participate in the bank. The municipal bond bank collects information on political subdivisions desiring to issue general obligation bonds and, after an examination of relevant data, notifies the units that have been accepted for participation in a forthcoming bank issue of bonds. A municipality is excluded from participation if the bank determines that such participation would lower the credit rating on the issue and increase the cost of borrowing.

The minimum issue of bonds by a municipal bond bank to date has been $6 million plus a reserve fund, equal to about 10 percent of the issue, to cover the annual debt service. The bank uses the funds obtained from its bond issue to purchase the participating units' general obligation bonds and invests the balance in U.S. Treasury securities. To date, the premium paid by the winning bidder and interest from the Treasury securities have covered the operating costs of the banks.

Investment Pools

Thirteen States—California, Connecticut, Florida, Georgia, Illinois, Massachusetts, Montana, New Jersey, Oregon, Utah, Virginia, West Virginia, and Wisconsin—have created state investment pools for local governments. Proponents cite six advantages of such pools: professional management of idle local funds, a higher yield on the invested funds, improved liquidity with the ability of a local government to withdraw funds on a daily basis, greater diversification of the investment portfolio, scale economies in administration, and a reduction in the cash management activities of participating units.

Investment pools are managed by the state treasurer who is also responsible for the investment of idle state funds. In addition, a state investment board provides policy guidance and issues rules governing the operation of the pool and its investment portfolio. Several states also created an advisory council of local government officials. State law typically restricts the type of investments that may be made by local governments. State investment pools, however, are authorized to invest in other obligations in addition to the ones municipalities may invest in.

Participating local governments may make transactions with the investment pool on a daily basis by personal visits of local officials, mail, or wire. Interest is earned on deposited funds from the day of deposit to the day of withdrawal, and administrative costs are financed by earnings from investments.

Local bankers oppose a state investment pool for municipalities because funds are removed from the economy of the area of each participating unit, thereby reducing the availability of funds to finance local projects. Opponents of the pools object to the inability of a pool to guarantee a fixed rate of return and the possibility of the loss of capital funds. Proponents of pools maintain that the benefits to participating units outweigh any loss associated with a reduction in the availability of funds for local projects; they suggest that a minimum rate of return can be guaranteed and argue that professional management minimize the possibility of the loss of capital funds.

Although not publicly stated, a major reason for nonparticipation by local governments in state investment pools is the fact that decisions on the deposits of idle municipal funds are made on a political basis, with the political party controlling the municipality rewarding certain banks with deposits.

Municipal Insurance Pools

A total of 21 states have created or authorized the establishment of municipal insurance pools since Texas established the first one in 1973. In California two or more local governments may form insurance pools under the joint exercise of powers statute. These pools are particularly important since courts in 37 states have terminated general governmental immunity from suit for municipalities.

By pooling, local governments benefit from group risk protection and achieve savings in premium costs. Each participating unit is responsible for a deductible loss minimum, usually $1,000, and the remainder of a loss is covered by the pool up to a maximum amount. To protect against catastrophic losses, commercial insurance is purchased. With a few exceptions, pools originally were established to provide workers' compen-

sation benefits but have been broadened to provide participating municipalities with personal injury liability and general liability insurance. The
Texas Municipal League's Workmen's Compensation Joint Insurance
Fund provides coverage that is 25 percent cheaper than commercial
insurance coverage and also annually returns a 4 percent dividend on
premiums to municipalities.

THE STATE AS INITIATOR

Whenever political subdivisions became bankrupt or verged on bankruptcy, the state initiated action to solve the financial problems. In a
number of instances, substitute administration was employed with the
state directly administering the local governments. In other instances, the
state targeted financial assistance to units experiencing acute fiscal
distress. These actions were described and analyzed in Chapter 3.

In the nineteenth century, Massachusetts and New York State each
acted to enable its largest city to cope with problems caused by urbanization spilling over the city's boundaries. Numerous towns were annexed to
the city of Boston by mandate of the general court, and New York City was
formed in 1898 by a legislatively directed amalgamation of all local
governments within a five-county area. Despite the precedent of direct
state action, no other major consolidation of local governments was ordered
by a state legislature without provision for a referendum until the Indiana
legislature enacted in 1969 a law merging Indianapolis and Marion
County.[31] The governmental system within the county, however, remains a
federated one since two small cities, a town, 16 townships, school
corporations, Marion County Health and Hospital Corporation, and
Indianapolis Airport Authority were excluded from the consolidation.

This merger must be viewed as an isolated one resulting from special
circumstances in a state operating under a Dillon's Rule philosophy. It is
highly improbable that a state legislature will mandate another major city-
county consolidation within the foreseeable future. The state, however, will
continue to play a role in solving local government problems through the
initiation of direct action via state-controlled instrumentalities, annexation
and incorporation statutes, and standard setting.

State Controlled Public Authorities

A belief that only the state government possesses sufficient authority and
resources to solve major areawide problems is an old one and was
responsible for the resort to extragovernmental devices, including the

creation of single-purpose state authorities on a regional basis in the late nineteenth century. Authorities are not-for-profit corporations authorized by the state legislature to operate outside the regular state government structure and controls. Members usually are appointed by the governor with senate approval, although the enabling statutes sometimes stipulate that named officials will serve as ex officio members. The principal method of financing employed by authorities involves the issuance of revenue bonds supported by charges and fees levied for the use of facilities and services provided.

Metropolitan District Commission

Massachusetts recognized the need to handle sewage disposal, parks, and water supply in the Boston area on a regional basis by organizing the Metropolitan Sewage Commission in 1889, the Metropolitan Parks Commission in 1893, and the Metropolitan Water Commission in 1895; each was a unifunctional state authority.[32] The sewage commission was merged in 1901 with the water commission to form the Metropolitan Water and Sewage Board, which in turn was merged in 1919 with the parks commission to form the Metropolitan District Commission (MDC), one of the very few multifunctional state authorities in the United States.[33] The governor appoints the commissioner and four associate commissioners of MDC for a term coterminous with the governor's own.

MDC administers a park district composed of four cities and 37 towns, a sewage district composed of four cities and 43 towns, and a water district composed of three cities and 32 towns. MDC's 650-member police force is the third largest force in New England. The Commission's budget is part of the executive budget submitted annually by the governor to the general court (legislature).

A report by three faculty members of the Maxwell Graduate School of Syracuse University concluded:

> The Massachusetts experience with the MDC should be capitalized rather than abandoned. It is a metropolitan jurisdiction, providing metropolitan services, and having a sound political base. It is our judgment that the route for Massachusetts to take is to build on the experience of the MDC, adjust it to fit the contemporary world of greater citizen participation, and employ that example for the establishment of a statewide system of regional governments.[34]

New York State Authorities

The Massachusetts approach to solving metropolitan problems in the greater Boston area was not followed by another state until New York, under Governor Nelson Rockefeller, decided in the 1960s to use its plenary authority to solve areawide problems directly and adopted the authority approach to deal with problems in multicounty areas. The state has used the authority device since 1921, when the Port Authority of New York and New Jersey was created by an interstate compact.[35]

In the 1962 Godkin lectures at Harvard University, Governor Rockefeller concluded:

> The problems of urbanism outrun individual local government boundaries, legal powers, and fiscal resources. And the national government is too remote to sense and to act responsively on the widely varying local or regional concerns and aspirations. The states—through their relations with local governments, their greater resources and powers, and their closeness to the people and the problems—can and should serve as the leaders in planning, and the catalysts in developing, cooperative action at local-state-federal levels.[36]

Both statewide and regional authorities—quasi-public corporations—have been created in New York State for special purposes: Urban Development Corporation (UDC), Environmental Facilities Corporation (EFC),[37] Job Development Authority (JDA), five regional transportation authorities, and 34 others. The Port Authority of New York and New Jersey and the Lake Champlain Bridge Authority were created by interstate compacts, and the Buffalo and Fort Erie Public Bridge Authority is based on an international agreement. Many public authorities are popular with their state legislature because they are self-financing by means of user charges and revenue bonds.

The Washington State Supreme Court in 1895 ruled that revenue bonds issued by authorities were not debt that was subject to the restrictions contained in the state constitution.[38] In 1935 the New York State Court of Appeals rejected Buffalo's argument that the creation of the Buffalo Sewer Authority by a special act of the legislature "violates the provisions of article 8, section 10, of the Constitution of the State in that it attempts by indirection to permit the bonded indebtedness of the properties of the City of Buffalo to exceed 10 per cent of the assessed valuation thereof."[39] The Court held that the act did not offend the constitution as the Buffalo Sewer Authority was powerless to pledge the credit of the city. By the end of the Rockefeller era in December 1973, the outstanding bonds and notes of public authorities totalled $12.1 billion.[40]

The early New York State public authorities were created to finance, construct, and operate facilities, such as bridges, roads, and tunnels, on a self-sustaining basis. In 1960 the State Housing Finance Agency was created to finance middle-income housing.[41] The agency later was made responsible for helping to finance the construction of mental hygiene and state university facilities, which the state had been financing directly. Commencing in 1967, state-controlled authorities were established to operate deficit-producing transit systems formerly operated by private enterprise and to finance urban development, including low-income housing and new towns.

Professor Joan Aron noted a major change in the method of financing "new style" authorities in New York State:

> With the advent of the recent authorities, particularly those in mass transit and housing, a new frame of reference has been introduced. Stubborn and intractable public problems, rooted in cost structures which provide no hope in the foreseeable future of generating anything but large deficits, have been spilled into public authorities. It is known, *ab initio*, that the public treasury will be required on an annual basis to provide an important portion of the total costs in a manner very little different, in effect, from the usual state operation of public services.[42]

The Urban Development Corporation, created in 1968, attracted national attention because of the extraordinary powers granted to it by the state legislature, including the power to override all municipal codes by a two-thirds vote of the corporation's nine-member board of directors.[43] This power was repealed by the 1973 legislature.[44]

UDC's board consists of four ex officio members and five others appointed by the governor with the advice and consent of the senate. The interlocking directorate device is employed since the UDC board also serves as the ex officio board of the Corporation for Urban Development and Research of New York and the Urban Development Guarantee Fund of New York.[45]

Concerning the former power of the UDC board to override a municipality's disapproval or modification of a UDC-proposed project, UDC reported in 1971:

> It is interesting that while this provision has been used several times, in only one instance has there been a local objection, and in that case the objections of the affected local government were quite restrained. On the other hand, UDC has frequently had the experience of having support (usually muted) for the use of the override powers from local governments impatient for progress on long-stalled projects.[46]

The Environmental Facilities Corporation is empowered to contract with municipalities and state agencies for the construction and operation of sewage treatment works, sewage collection systems, solid waste disposal facilities, air pollution control facilities, water management facilities, and storm water collection systems. EFC also may own, operate, and maintain these facilities on behalf of municipalities and state agencies.

EFC is tied closely to state agencies in that its board of directors consists of the commissioner of environmental conservation, commissioner of health, and four directors appointed by the governor with the advice and consent of the senate. The chairman is the commissioner of environmental conservation.

The rationale for the creation of state authorities in New York State is a simple one: only the state has the power and financial resources to solve critical metropolitan problems. Other reasons for the use of authorities include their relative ease of organization, autonomy in operations permitting the use of the flexible managerial controls employed by private industry to improve efficiency, and a desire to circumvent the constitutional debt limit and civil service and to remove items from the state budget and annual appropriation processes.

The New York State Temporary State Commission on the Powers of Local Governments reported:

> The use of public authorities by New York State has enabled the State to move rapidly and effectively in situations where regional action was demanded. Because of their relative freedom from bureaucratic restraints, they can act with flexibility and attract expert personnel with salaries and other benefits which a regular government agency can not offer for comparable positions.[47]

Former UDC President Edward Logue expressed a similar viewpoint:

> An important but overlooked reason for the failure of promising new approaches to the urban problem has been the quickness with which they succumb to the bureaucratic straight-jacket. We like to think that UDC remains relatively free to devise new administrative and organizational solutions as experience and opportunities indicate.[48]

Since 1846 the state of New York has been required to secure the approval of voters in a statewide referendum prior to issuing "full faith and credit" bonds.[49] This requirement, according to a special committee of the Association of the Bar of the City of New York, is a major reason for the creation of public authorities.

> It appears that the creation of many public authorities has been undertaken primarily to finance and operate projects which it was felt the people would not approve at a referendum and which the State could not undertake for other constitutional reasons such as the

prohibition of the gift or loan of money or credit of the State to private undertakings. By using a public authority as an intermediary between the State and the non-public recipient of state funds or credit, the gift and loan prohibitions and the referendum and other requirements are circumvented.[50]

The "moral obligation" doctrine, however, allows the legislature to appropriate funds to pay the interest on and retire bonds issued by state-controlled public authorities.[51] This doctrine suggests that authority debt in effect is "full faith and credit" debt of New York State even though the authority bonds usually carry a higher rate of interest than regular state bonds.

In 1970 *Business Week* optimistically wrote "right on schedule, New York's Urban Development corporation is emerging as the most powerful state agency in the country for coping with urban growth."[52] In 1975 UDC had completed or started construction on 189 commercial and residential projects valued at $1.6 billion.[53] UDC had sold $1,075 million in bonds when it encountered difficulties in selling additional "moral obligation" bonds in the autumn of 1974. The attitude of the investment community toward such bonds changed in 1974 with the advent of high interest rates, a recession, and curtailment of federal housing grants.

Senior officers of two large banks at a public hearing of the Assembly Ways and Means Committee in early 1975 implied that the investment community no longer would purchase UDC bonds unless they were backed by the full faith and credit of the state.[54] To help alleviate a cash shortage problem faced by UDC, Governor Hugh Carey recommended that the 1975 legislature approve a $178 million emergency appropriation for UDC.[55] The legislature responded by appropriating $90 million and creating the New York State Project Finance Agency to purchase certain UDC assets and make loans to UDC secured by other assets.[56] After protracted negotiations, commercial and savings banks agreed to provide the funds needed by UDC to complete its projects.

In a 1972 report, New York State Comptroller Arthur Levitt wrote that state-controlled public authorities

> ... have been operating on a scale so massive that, in some instances, they overshadow the fiscal operations of the State itself. Moreover, authorities now perform many public benefit activities once accomplished within the regular framework of State government. Since authority operations are not subject to the same degree of public scrutiny to which regular State activities are subjected, this trend tends to obscure the overall scope of public activities, as well as the fiscal impact of public sector services within the State.[57]

The state comptroller also strongly criticized as "back-door financing" the use of authorities to raise revenue through the issuance of bonds that dangerously extended the state's credit responsibilities and circumvented the constitution's prohibition of debt financing without the voters' approval.[58] On January 21, 1973, Comptroller Levitt sent a letter to the legislature revealing that as of June 30, 1972 the state was committed to long-term capital construction "financing schemes" totaling $5.6 billion "in derogation of the right of the people to vote upon indebtedness of the State of New York."[59]

On February 6, 1975, Levitt sent a letter to Governor Carey and legislative leaders proposing a series of bills relating to moral obligation bonds." [60] Bills in the first group would eliminate the moral commitment clause from the statutes creating the seven authorities that have not made use of the clause. Bills in the second group apply to nine authorities and place a ceiling on the amount of debt service reserve funds secured by the moral commitment that is equal to the amount of outstanding debt and the estimated debt that will be generated by projects in process. The third group of bills places limits on the bonds issued by the Dormitory Authority for health facilities and on the bonds issued by the Housing Finance Agency for state university construction. This group also reduces the authorized indebtedness of the Urban Development Corporation and the Housing Finance Agency for mental hygiene facilities. The legislature, however, failed to act on these bills.

Maryland Environmental Service

To help solve local problems, the 1970 Maryland General Assembly created the Maryland Environmental Service and endowed it with authority to supply water and dispose of liquid and solid waste.[61] The three officers of the service—a director, a secretary, and a treasurer—are appointed by the secretary of natural resources with the approval of the governor. Although the service possesses the power of eminent domain, it is forbidden to construct a solid waste disposal facility within "the boundaries of a municipality without the express consent of the governing body of the municipality." [62]

In the event a municipality fails "to comply with an order of the Secretary of Health and Mental Hygiene to provide a sewerage system or refuse disposal work," the secretary is authorized to direct the service to install and operate the necessary facilities.[63] Similarly, if a municipality fails to correct deficiencies in "the operation of sewerage systems or refuse disposal works," the secretary may direct the service to operate the systems or works." [64] Currently, the service operates more than 100 water supply, waste water treatment plants, and solid waste facilities for state and local governmental agencies and private firms. It also operates a major sludge-composting project at Beltsville and a 750-ton-per-day resource recovery plant in Baltimore County.

New Jersey Water Supply Authority

Serious water supply problems prompted the 1981 New Jersey legislature to establish the New Jersey Water Supply Authority and to transfer to it all state-owned or -operated water supply facilities.[65] The authority can issue bonds, which are not backed by the state, to raise revenue for acquiring, constructing, and operating water systems throughout the state.

The water supply authority consists of the commissioner of environmental protection serving ex officio as chairman and six other members appointed by the governor with the advice and consent of the senate for three-year terms. Authority projects must conform to the standards contained in the New Jersey Water Supply Master Plan. Prior to their issuance, bond issues must be approved by the governor and state treasurer or comptroller of the treasury. The governor also possesses the power to veto actions of the water supply authority within ten days of an action.

An Assessment

One major problem associated with the use of state authorities flows from their creation on an ad hoc basis. Fractionalization of responsibility on the regional level results in nearly total neglect of essential coordination since the authorities are independent of each other and of local governments in terms of planning, financing, and programming.

The fractionalization problem within a given metropolitan area resulting from the ad hoc creation of authorities can be reduced to some extent by the consolidation of authorities. In 1946, for example, the New York State legislature formed the Triborough Bridge and Tunnel Authority by consolidating the New York City Parkway Authority, the Triborough Bridge Authority, and the New York City Tunnel Authority.[66]

The amalgamation of public authorities is blocked if they have nonrecallable bonds outstanding since a provision in the U.S. Constitution forbids states to impair the obligation of contract.[67] To achieve the same objective without merging authorities, New York State has employed the corporate device of the interlocking directorate in the New York City area to coordinate the activities of certain authorities. In 1939 the commissioners of Long Island State Park Commission were made the board of directors of the Jones Beach State Parkway Authority and the Bethpage Park Authority.[68] An interlocking directorate has also been utilized since 1968 to coordinate transportation authorities and develop policy within a framework of unified fiscal and operational planning and programming.

A second major problem associated with the use of state authorities flows from the lack of voter control of the authorities. Members have been referred to as "the untouchables" since they are appointed by the governor with senate approval for long and often overlapping terms.[69] Commencing in 1967, the New York State legislature has provided that some members of new regional transportation authorities will be appointed by the governor with senate approval from lists of nominees submitted by local government officials. The intent of this appointment policy is to facilitate cooperation and coordination between the authorities and local officials.

A common charge directed against authorities is that they are autonomous bodies responsible to no one. Although this charge is not entirely fair, many concerned citizens believe that they have no direct control over the authorities and have no one to appeal to other than a remote governor since the boards tend to have little public visibility. According to Jerome Shestack:

> The merits and demerits of the state and local authority must also be evaluated in the area of political philosophy. It is a tenet, if not an axiom, of democratic society that government be politically responsible to the electorate. If we are to divorce a governmental body from direct control of politically responsible officers, it seems fair to ask that the reasons for such divorcement be compelling ones.[70]

Plural-headed authorities make the fixation of responsibility particularly difficult. The U.S. Advisory Commission on Intergovernmental Relations in 1961 recommended that state legislatures authorize local governments in metropolitan areas to establish multifunctional metropolitan service authorities with taxing and borrowing powers subject to the approval of the voters. Each authority would be governed by an ex officio board composed of mayors, city councillors, and county commissioners to help ensure public accountability since "poor performance of the corporation would carry the possibility of retribution at the polls for its board of directors." [71]

While public authorities often possess the capacity to deal effectively with problems found within a state or a region, this advantage is outweighed by the disadvantages flowing from fractionalization of responsibility on the state and regional level, lack of voter control, and the higher cost of borrowing often related to the issuance of moral obligation bonds. Authorities operating on a statewide basis could be integrated into the regular structure of the state government, and regional authorities could be converted into popularly controlled multifunctional areawide governments.

If states wish to abolish public authorities, the requirement of voter approval for the issuance of "full faith and credit" bonds by the state should be deleted from the state constitution. This restriction is based upon the invalid assumption that the voters possess sufficient information to make an intelligent decision on highly complex issues and has had the unfortunate effect of contributing to political fragmentation by fostering the creation of public authorities.

Twin Cities Metropolitan Council

The most important state-initiated organizational response to growing areawide problems during the past two decades is the Metropolitan Council established for the seven-county Twin Cities area in 1967 by the Minnesota legislature without a referendum.[72] The council was structured in a way that would reduce much of the political opposition typically generated when the creation of a metropolitan government is proposed. The council's chairperson, who serves at the pleasure of the governor, and 16 other members are appointed by the governor for overlapping six-year terms with the advice and consent of the senate.

The Twin Cities model of metropolitan governance is a federated one with powers divided between the Metropolitan Council, counties, municipalities, and metropolitan special districts. The council assumed the functions of the Metropolitan Planning Commission, which was abolished, and was granted authority to review and indefinitely suspend plans of each metropolitan special district in conflict with the council's development guide. A district may appeal the suspension of its plans to the legislature. The council is authorized to review and suspend for up to one year proposed projects of local governments. The Metropolitan Land Planning Act of 1976 required each local government in the Twin Cities to develop comprehensive plans consistent with the regional airports, parks, sewers, and transportation plans developed by the council.[73] The act set July 1, 1980 as the deadline for the preparation of the local plans but also authorized the council to grant extensions. As of January 1, 1981, the council had completed its review of 21 of 194 city, county, and township plans, 60 additional plans were under review, 96 local governments were granted time extensions, and 10 units had not submitted plans or requested a time extension. The council has required only one local government to modify its comprehensive plan.

The council acts as a housing authority, appoints one of its members as a nonvoting member of the boards of metropolitan special districts, conducts research, operates a data center, and intervenes before the Minnesota Municipal Commission in annexation and incorporation proceedings.

Shortly after the council's formation, it signed contracts with the State Highway Department and Metropolitan Transit Commission, thereby assuming responsibility for transportation planning in the area. The council also has been designated as the criminal justice planning agency by the governor's crime commission. Furthermore, the council appoints and provides guidance to a health board responsible for coordination of planning for health facilities, manpower, and services. To finance its activities, the council is authorized to levy a tax not exceeding "seven tenths of one mill on each dollar as assessed valuation of all taxable property."

The council was designed to be a policy-forming rather than an operating agency. However, it assumed responsibility in 1969 for overseeing the performance of two service functions. Acting upon the council's request, the 1969 legislature created two 7-member functional service boards and provided for their appointment by the council. The Metropolitan Sewer Board[74] and the Metropolitan Park Reserve Board[75] were designed to be operating agencies executing policies in their respective areas developed by the council. The Park Reserve Board's role as an operating service body was terminated in 1970 by a Minnesota Supreme Court ruling invalidating laws passed by the one hundred twenty-first day (one day past the constitutional limit) of the 1969 legislative session.[76] The council retained the board—renamed the Metropolitan Parks and Open Spaces Commission—as an advisory body, but reenactment of the original park reserve bill has been blocked by opposition from the Inter-County Council and the Hennipin County Park Reserve District. Regional parks and waste disposal facilities are operated by the counties.

A distinguishing characteristic of the Twin Cities model is the separation of policy execution from policy making with the council determining metropolitan policies to be carried into execution by service boards appointed by the council. In theory, it can devote its full attention to broad policy making for the region. Routine administrative problems in many governmental units preempt the attention and energy of the governing body, leaving little time for the study of major problems and the development of a long-range program to solve the problems.

Glowing accounts of the Twin Cities Metropolitan Council were published shortly after its creation. Stanley Baldinger concluded that "the Twin Cities area has developed the most promising and innovative means yet to plan and govern major metropolises."[77] He added that "the Council... plans, coordinates, and controls the comprehensive development of an urban region containing 1.9 million people, seven counties, two large central cities, and some 300 units of local government."[78] Writing in the *New York Times*, John Herbers concluded that the Metropolitan Council "is unique in that it has taxing authority and the power to coordinate the overall social, physical, and economic development in the 3,000-square mile area."[79]

The highly favorable published accounts of the Twin Cities regional governmental system tend to obscure the fact the system is still a fragmented one in which many units of government—the Metropolitan Council, regular state departments, Metropolitan Airport Commission, Metropolitan Transit Commission, Mosquito Control Commission, Waste Control Commission, counties, and municipalities—share governmental powers and responsibilities.

The umbrella concept underlying the Metropolitan Council appears to have considerable merit, yet the legislature has demonstrated a marked reluctance to grant strong powers to the council. In fact, the legislature specifically rejected the council's proposals that a seven-member zoo board be established and placed under the council's control and that the Metropolitan Airport Commission be reorganized as a service board under the council. The legislature also created the Metropolitan Transit Commission in the same year as the Metropolitan Council and in 1969 specifically rejected a proposal to authorize the council to appoint the members of the commission.[80] The 1974 legislature, however, authorized the council to appoint the members of the Metropolitan Transit Commission. Furthermore, the legislature has refused to reestablish the Park Reserve Board as an operating board under the council following the 1970 State Supreme Court ruling invalidating the act creating the board.

Is the legislature opposed to the establishment in the Twin Cities area of a strong, popularly elected regional governing body because it might play a dominant role in Minnesota politics? Stanley Baldinger maintained that "the rural and conservative legislators felt they had a substantial stake and role to play in the future of the Twin Cities area. The Legislature, therefore, sought to maximize the State's role in the operation of the Council by making it an appointed rather than an elected body. A more local (elected) Council might not be as responsive to the needs of the rest of the State or to the wishes of the Legislature."[81] It also has been argued that the caliber of the council's members will be higher if they are appointed rather than elected because many highly qualified individuals will not seek an elective post but would accept an appointive one.

Ted Kolderie wrote that the popular election of the council was advocated by many citizens, local officials, and legislators at the time the council was created "partly as a counter to the system of gubernatorial appointment which seemed to establish the council as a state agency. Their original fervor has cooled somewhat, as they have watched the Council work as a local agency and move with some genuine competence, determination, and courage on major area-wide issues . . . and the cry for election has increasingly been taken up by opponents of the Council who see this, now, as the way to temper its aggressiveness."[82]

In 1980 Arthur Naftalin and John Brandl emphasized the centrality of the legislature:

> Its relationship with the Legislature makes the Twin Cities program unusual among regional strategies. It is not dependent on the voluntary cooperation of autonomous local governments, as are the councils of government. It draws its vitality and power from the state by way of the Legislature. As a result, it moves ahead with its planning and coordinating and returns, as needed, to the Legislature for new authority or additional resources.[83]

Council Weaknesses

Operationally, the Twin Cities model suffers from three major weaknesses. First, the most important problems generally are being attacked on a piecemeal basis, and the legislature continues to play a major role as referee between competing regional bodies and interests. This situation is not the most desirable one since a coordinated attack on regional problems will be difficult to launch, and representatives and senators elected outside the Twin Cities area will continue to play an important role in the governance of the region.

Political fragmentation on the regional level is responsible for a second and related weakness of the model—deadlocks arising between various regional entities as they fail to operate on the basis of comity. An example of this problem involves the selection of a site for a new jetport. The Metropolitan Council twice exercised its power to veto indefinitely a new jetport site proposed by the Metropolitan Airport Commission, yet the council lacks the power to order the commission to construct the jetport at a site selected by the council. Consequently, a continuing deadlock between these two regional entities may block the development of a facility that both bodies agree is needed. The dispute may have to be settled by the legislature. The commission is authorized to bring the dispute to the legislature for resolution but has not yet chosen to do so. Hein, Keys, and Robbins wrote in 1974:

> While the Council has more powers than the Metropolitan Planning Commission that was its predecessor, the Legislature prefers a Council with limited powers that refers most controversies to the Legislature for final decision. The Legislature's preference is reinforced by the demands of the local governments for limitations on the powers and activities of the Council. Thus, like its predecessor the Council must rely heavily on its ability to educate and persuade citizens and local and state officials.[84]

Writing in 1980, Naftalin and Brandl referred to the ambivalence of the legislature toward the council and the opposition of some legislators to an elective council:

> The ambivalence is intensified by the constant controversy over Council decisions, which almost always adversely affect some interest. The result is that legislators often receive complaints about Council actions. Since the Legislature began to hold annual sessions, individual legislators are spending more time at the capitol, becoming more accessible to complaining metropolitan residents. . . . It is perhaps a measure of this ambivalence that each session sees the introduction of one or more proposals to either eliminate the Council or reduce its power, and each session the proposals are given no serious attention.[85]

Despite the indications that the legislature does not prefer a strong Metropolitan Council, the 1974 legislature strengthened the control of the council by authorizing it to appoint members other than the chairperson of each regional commission with the exception of the Metropolitan Airport Commission. Chairpersons of commissions, except the Parks and Open Spaces Commission, will be selected by the governor. The council is required to prepare and adopt policy plans for the commissions, and each commission must prepare a development program to implement the policy plans subject to council approval. Parts of the commissions' budgets relating to capital improvements also are subject to council approval.

The possibility of disputes between the council and its service boards is a third and inherent defect of the Twin Cities model. The council and the Metropolitan Sewer Board (now the Metropolitan Waste Control Commission) engaged in a major dispute related to the board's 1971 construction program.

In terms of political support for the council, Dennis Farney reported in 1974 that "some members of the Minnesota Legislature, which created the Council, now mutter it has grown too big for its britches. Some other units of area government with which the Council must deal now charge it with high-handedness. Meanwhile, even Council supporters agree that it remains rather remote to the lives of the 1.9 million people it is trying to serve."[86]

Ted Kolderie summarized the political position of the Council in the following terms:

> The problems of the Metropolitan Council is the problem of every general government which must make choices among conflicting values. On any given issue its opponents will be specific and vociferous; its supporters probably distant and perhaps unaware they have been benefited. Much will depend on the Council's ability, issue by issue, to call into existence . . . the interests of those served by its decisions, to weigh against the displeasure of those offended.[87]

Property Tax Base Sharing

The discussion of the Twin Cities governance system is concluded with a description of an innovative action taken by the 1971 Minnesota legislature to reduce metropolitan fiscal disparities. Accepting the recommendation of the Metropolitan Council, the legislature enacted the Metropolitan Revenue Distribution Act authorizing a partial sharing of the revenue produced by the growth in the commercial-industrial property tax base in the seven-county area.[88] The purpose of the act is to reduce gross fiscal disparities among municipalities by providing that the revenue produced by 40 percent of new nonresidential construction be deposited in the Municipal Equity Account in the state treasury and distributed to municipalities according to a need and population formula. In other words, the pooled areawide revenue is distributed to municipalities in direct proportion to need and in inverse proportion to fiscal capacity. In 1974 the Minnesota Supreme Court upheld the constitutionality of the act.[89] Whether the act will reduce or eliminate fiscal zoning[90] remains to be seen since each municipality retains 60 percent of its new nonresidential tax base, and the retained revenue may provide a sufficient incentive for municipalities to employ fiscal zoning. Naftalin and Brandl in 1980 concluded the tax base sharing program "holds enormous promise over the long term for providing a solid revenue base for the Region."[91]

Incorporation and Boundary Changes

Metropolitan problems can be attributed to the jurisdictional morass resulting from the failure of the typical state legislature to facilitate the annexation of unincorporated land by central cities and to restrict the incorporation of new units of local government in metropolitan areas.

The U.S. Advisory Commission on Intergovernmental Relations in 1961 urged states "to tighten up dramatically the standards and criteria for the incorporation of new units of government."[92] The commission recommended that "the standards generally should specify minimums of total population and population density for new incorporations, with higher standards being imposed within a designated distance of larger cities."[93] The commission also urged states to authorize the annexation of unincorporated areas without the consent of the residents.[94]

Six years later, the commission strengthened its recommendation by calling upon state legislatures to authorize "a state agency—or a local formation commission—to (a) order the dissolution or consolidation of local units of government within metropolitan areas and (b) enjoin the use of an interlocal contract within the metropolitan area when it is found to promote fractionalization of the tax base without overriding compensating advantages."[95]

In December 1960, a California commission issued a report calling for the liberalization of annexation laws and the establishment of a gubernatorially appointed state metropolitan areas commission with power to review and approve "proposals for the incorporation of, or annexations to, cities, and for the creation of, annexations to, consolidations of, or dissolution of special districts."[96] The proposed commission also would be charged with responsibility to recommend changes in state laws governing boundary changes, advise the governor on metropolitan problems and solutions, delineate areas for multipurpose metropolitan districts, submit to the voters proposals for the consolidation of cities, and "prepare for a vote of the electorate a proposal for a federated form of metropolitan government for those specific metropolitan areas which by January 1, 1964, have not produced such a plan and submitted it to the voters."[97]

Instead of creating a state board or commission with authority to control new incorporations, the Maryland legislature in 1955 authorized boards of county commissioners to approve or disapprove a petition for the incorporation of a new municipality.[98]

Currently, boundary review commissions in five states—Alaska, New Mexico, Oregon, Texas, and Washington—are state controlled, commissions in California and Nevada are controlled locally, and commissions in Michigan and Minnesota are under joint state-local control. The determinations of the commissions in California, Oregon, and Texas are final. Although a commission in Nevada has the power of review—to approve, modify, or disapprove an annexation proposal—it must disapprove a proposal if protests are made by a majority of real property owners in the proposed annexation area. Certain annexation proposals in Michigan, Minnesota, New Mexico, and Washington are subject to a popular referendum.

Minnesota

One of the earliest actions taken to control the proliferation of units of local government was the creation by the 1957 Minnesota legislature of the Commission on Municipal Annexation and Consolidation "to study the laws relating to the incorporation of cities and villages and the laws granting special powers to so-called urban towns" and to report on "the need for administrative review by an impartial agency of the public interest in proposed incorporations of cities and villages."[99] Acting on the recommendation of the commission, the 1959 legislature created the Minnesota Municipal Commission and empowered it to approve, disapprove, or modify proposals for the incorporation of municipalities in metropolitan areas, annexation of unincorporated territory, consolidation of municipalities, and detachment of territory from a municipality.[100] The commission also may order annexations after a hearing.

In 1969 the law was changed to allow a city bordering 60 percent of an area to annex the area by ordinance if the affected town board does not register an objection with the commission.[101] The 1973 legislature amended the law to provide that in cases where the proceeding for annexation was not initiated by a majority of the property owners in the proposed annexation area a commission order for annexation must fix a date 20 to 90 days in the future for a referendum by voters in the proposed annexation area; the order becomes effective only if approved by an affirmative majority vote.[102] The 1975 legislature changed the name of the commission to the Minnesota Municipal Board.[103]

Three members of the board, one of whom must be "learned in law," are appointed by the governor for six-year terms, and two county commissioners serve as ex officio members of the state commission whenever it considers a proposal for incorporation of a village, consolidation of a municipality with one or more towns, or annexation of unincorporated territory to a municipality located in the county commissioners' county.[104]

The board has laid down guidelines on incorporations in metropolitan areas. Approval of a new municipality will not be given until there is reasonable proof that the proposed incorporated area "has an adequate tax base, a reasonable prospect of providing necessary services when it is completely organized, is not part of a larger entity which can more adequately sustain municipal responsibilities, and would not be better served by annexation." There must be a better reason for incorporation, states the commission, than avoidance of annexation or protection of special interests such as land use and liquor licensing. The board has ruled that unincorporated areas in metropolitan areas should be annexed to cities and villages as the need for municipal services arises.

In 1969 provision was made for an orderly annexation process initiated by a joint resolution of a municipality and a township designating an area as in need of orderly annexation and conferring jurisdiction on the board to order annexations as land is developed.[105] According to the board, the orderly annexation process has several advantages:

> It eliminates the expensive and bitter annexation hearings. Instead of generating division, it forces cooperation and long range mutual planning. Boundaries are adjusted gradually in an orderly fashion. Farmers or others who do not want to develop their property remain in the township and are not forced to pay city taxes or assessments. No property can be annexed unless the city has available and is capable of providing full municipal services. Taxes in areas annexed are increased gradually over a three to five year period, from the town mill rate to the city mill rate. Planning and zoning in orderly annexation areas are done

jointly by the city, county, and township. Unless otherwise agreed, the
municipality is authorized to regulate subdivisions in the areas.[106]

Has the Minnesota Municipal Board been successful in preventing the
incorporation of small, economically unviable municipalities? The answer is
yes. During the nine years preceding its establishment, 62 municipalities
with an average size of only 7.6 square miles were incorporated, and one had
only 43 residents compared to 5 municipalities with an average size of 31.13
square miles incorporated in the first nine years subsequent to the creation
of the board.[107]

Alaska

The 1959 Alaskan Constitution directed the legislature to establish a local
boundary commission with authority to propose boundary changes to the
legislature during the first ten days of a regular session.[108] A proposed
change becomes "effective forty-five days after presentation or at the end
of the session, whichever is earlier, unless disapproved by a resolution
concurred in by a majority of the members of each house."[109] The five-
member Alaska Local Boundary Commission, appointed by the governor
for overlapping five-year terms, has functioned since 1959 and also
possesses the power to establish procedures whereby boundaries may be
changed by local action.[110]

Wisconsin

In 1959 Wisconsin provided for state review of incorporation and annexation proceedings.[111] A petition for the incorporation of a city or village,
signed by 50 or more voters, must be filed with the circuit court of the
county, which transmits the petition to the head of the planning function in
the State Department of Local Affairs and Development. Applying
standards specified by law, the head of the planning function determines
whether the petition should be rejected. If the head determines that the
petition should be dismissed, the circuit court must issue an order
dismissing the petition. If the head grants the petition, the circuit court
must order an incorporation referendum.

In counties with a population over 50,000 (21 out of 73), the head of
the planning function reviews proposed annexations. The annexing municipality must review the reasons advanced by the head of the planning
function should the head oppose the proposed annexation.

California

Rapid population growth in California during a period when incorporation
statutes were highly permissive resulted in a complex local government

system. Special interest incorporations, designed to provide tax benefits for residents of unincorporated areas, and defensive incorporations, designed to prevent annexation by a contiguous city, occurred with relative frequency. Special districts benefiting developers and other special interest groups were formed with the same degree of ease as new cities. The Santa Clara County Agency Formation Commission reports that sprawl "has taken the form of indiscriminate, unplanning, opportunistic, premature annexation and urbanization. This practice has resulted in annexation wars and in the formation of new cities just for the purpose of protection from another city."[112]

Although the governor's Commission on Metropolitan Area Problems in 1960 had called for the liberalization of annexation laws and the establishment of a gubernatorially appointed state metropolitan areas commission to control boundary changes and new incorporations,[113] strong political opposition led to a 1965 compromise providing for the establishment of boundary commissions on the county level.[114] The five-member Local Agency Formation Commission (LAFCO) was formed in each county with the exception of the city and county of San Francisco. The county board of supervisors appoints two of its members to the LAFCO, a city selection committee appoints two city officials, and a fifth member representing the general public is appointed by the other four members.[115] Members serve for four years. A commission is authorized to review and approve, reject, or modify all proposals for the incorporation or disincorporation of a city, annexation of territory to a city, detachment of territory from a city, and creation of special districts.[116] The District Reorganization Act of 1965 strengthened LAFCOs by increasing their powers over the reorganization of special districts, including the abolition of districts.[117]

Richard Legates wrote in 1970 that "the fact that most changes now taking place in California are incremental annexation to existing special districts indicates that a state-level review board alone would be too remote from the local scene to be really effective."[118] Legates reports that commissions tend to approve annexation proposals and reject petitions for the formation of special districts.[119]

In 1977 John Eels reported that "California is left with a dichotomy between agencies having the standard land use planning tools, but no mandate to promote orderly development, and LAFCO's which have the mandate but none of the planning tools."[120] One possible solution to this problem would be to transfer complete responsibility for planning to the LAFCOs, but such a transfer would be strongly opposed by cities, which have only two members representing all cities on a commission. Eels favors granting each LAFCO "(1) the power to initiate detachment proposals for special districts, (2) control over district latent powers, and (3) the power to initiate deannexation proposals for cities."[121]

Eels is convinced that the decision to establish a county level boundary control body was sound but favors the creation of "a State Review Commission to handle those cases which (a) cross county boundaries or (b) are of sufficient import or complexity to warrant state review."[122] Another function of such a body would be providing guidance to the joint city-county planning process and solving disputes.

Colorado

In 1965 the Colorado legislature established a new procedure for the formation of special districts.[123] A petition for the creation of a special district must be filed with the board of county commissioners and must include a service plan consisting "of a financial survey and a preliminary engineering or architectural survey showing how the proposed services are to be provided and financed."[124] Following a public hearing, the board may disapprove or approve with or without modification the plan. If approved, the petition and service plan are submitted to a district court, which must approve the creation of the district unless a determination is made "that the decision of the board of county commissioners was arbitrary, capricious, or unreasonable."[125] If the board disapproves a petition, the court may approve the formation of the special district if the board's action is determined to be arbitrary, capricious, or unreasonable. Data have been collected only for three years on approvals of the creation of special districts by boards of county commissioners; 30 were approved in 1972, 25 in 1973, and 18 in 1974.

In 1974 Colorado voters ratified a constitutional amendment stipulating that a proposed annexation or consolidation of local governments in the city and county of Denver is subject to approval of the six-member Boundary Control Commission composed of one commissioner from each of Adams, Arapahoe, and Jefferson counties and three elected officials of the city and county of Denver appointed by the mayor.[126] This constitutional amendment has not yet been employed.

New Mexico

The three-member, gubernatorially appointed New Mexico Municipal Boundary Commission, established in 1965,[127] may approve or reject annexation petitions anywhere in the state with the exception of the Albuquerque metropolitan area, where such petitions are under the jurisdiction of the five-member gubernatorially appointed Metropolitan Boundary Commission, created in 1967.[128] A referendum must be held on the approval of an annexation petition by the latter commission if the petition is signed by 15 percent of the real property owners in the affected area and "filed with the clerk of the municipality within thirty days of the filing of the final order of the Commission."[129] An attempt by the city of Albuquerque to consummate a "shoe string" annexation precipitated the formation of the Metropolitan Boundary Commission. Less than six annexations have occurred under provisions of the 1965 law, and no annexation petition has been processed by the Metropolitan Boundary Commission.

Washington

Eleven-member boundary review boards were created by the 1967 Washington legislature in class AA (population of 500,000 or more) and class A (population of 210,000–500,000) counties, and other counties were authorized to establish five-member boards; 14 counties have established boards. Each board is appointed by the governor and is authorized to approve, modify, or reject petitions for (1) annexation of territory, (2) incorporation, consolidation, or dissolution of municipalities and nonschool districts, (3) "assumption by a city or town of all or part of the assets, facilities, or indebtedness of a special district which lies partially within such city or town," and (4) extraterritorial extension of sewer or water service by a city, town, or special district.[130]

If the area proposed for annexation by a city or town is less than ten acres and $200,000 in assessed valuation, the review board chairman may issue a written statement declaring that review of the proposed annexation by the board is not necessary to protect the interest of concerned parties.[131] Negative decisions of the board are final. If the board approves a petition, "it shall be presented under the appropriate statute for approval by a public body and, if required, a vote of the people."[132]

Michigan

The incorporation of cities in Michigan was supervised by the secretary of state and to a limited extent by county boards of supervisors until 1968, when the legislature created the State Boundary Commission.[133] The governor appoints three commission members for three-year terms with the advice and consent of the senate, and the presiding probate judge in each county is directed to appoint two members—one from a city and one from a township—to serve on the commission whenever it considers an incorporation or consolidation petition from that county. Located in the State Department of the Treasury, the commission is authorized to review petitions for the annexation of territory, incorporation of new cities and villages, and consolidation of two or more cities, villages, or townships as a new city.

After reviewing an incorporation or consolidation petition, the commission may approve or reject the petition. During its review, the

commission may revise the boundaries of the area proposed for incorporation or consolidation. Rejection of a petition by the commission is final.
Approval of an incorporation petition with or without a boundary revision is
final 45 days after the date of the order unless a petition for a referendum
signed by 5 percent of the registered voters residing in the proposed
incorporation or consolidation area is filed with the commission. If a
referendum is held, the decision on incorporation is made by a majority vote
of the electors in the proposed incorporation area. If a consolidation
referendum is held, the decision is made by a separate majority vote in each
affected municipality.

Nevada

Whereas the 1967 Nevada legislature granted relatively broad annexation
powers to cities located in counties with a population exceeding 200,000,
the City Annexation Commission (CAC) was established in each county in
the 100,000 to 200,000 population range.[134] Each commission is composed
of the chairperson and one other member of the board of county commissioners as well as one member of the governing body of each city.[135]
Members serve for a two-year term and have the power to review and
approve, modify, or disapprove annexation proposals. Annexations must be
disapproved if protests are made in writing or at a public hearing by a
majority of the real property owners in the proposed annexation area or by
"owners of real property whose combined value is greater than fifty per cent
of the total value of real property in the territory proposed to be annexed, as
determined by assessment for taxation."[136] A protest, however, may be
overriden if the proposed annexation territory is completely surrounded by
the city, does not exceed 40 acres, and is subdivided for residential,
commercial, or industrial purposes, or if provision of public services is
necessary to protect public health, safety, convenience, or welfare.

Oregon

The 1969 Oregon legislature created a local government boundary commission in each of the state's three metropolitan areas, effective July 1,
1969, to guide the establishment and growth of cities and special districts,
prevent illogical extension of local government boundaries, and assure the
provision of adequate public services and the financial integrity of each
local government.[137] A commission may be established in other areas by
resolution of the county board of each county within the jurisdiction of each
proposed commission.[138] A commission has eleven members if its jurisdiction includes a population exceeding 500,000 and seven members in all
other cases; members are appointed by the governor with senate approval
for four-year terms.

In contrast to California's LAFCOs, no appointed or elected local official may serve on an Oregon local government boundary commission. A five-member advisory committee composed of local elected officials, however, must be appointed by each boundary commission.[139] A commission has the power to review, approve, modify, or reject all proposed changes in the boundaries of cities and nonschool special districts within its jurisdiction without a referendum. The extraterritorial extension of sewer or water services by a city or special district as well as the creation of private sewer and water firms require commission approval. In addition, a single-purpose special district desiring to provide an additional service must obtain the commission's approval prior to assuming responsibility for a new service.

The Lane County Local Government Boundary Commission adopted three important policy statements. The commission will:

— not approve the expansion of the boundaries of any city in Lane County until such city furnishes the Boundary Commission with a plan identifying its sphere of influence or urban boundary and its priorities for annexation.
— not expand any single purpose district within the metropolitan Eugene-Springfield Urban Service Area . . . without a concurrent solution for all urban services, except where existing water supplies are inadequate.
— review requests for the extension of services outside municipal boundaries based on the following criteria:
  a. Extension of water service only to vacant land is not in the long term interests of the public;
  b. Extension of water service only to an existing structure will correct or alleviate a public health hazard which presently exists and for which no other practical solution is available; and
  c. No extension should be made to property in an area which should logically be annexed to a water district or city until such property has been annexed to either a water district or city, or contract for annexation to a city has been signed and approved by that city or the Boundary Commission.[140]

Each commission initially was funded by the state, but the base budget was not increased from 1974 to 1979. Consequently, the commissions were only able to react to requests and were unable to conduct in-depth studies of problems in their areas. A controversy over the commissions in the 1979 legislature centered on the charge they duplicated the work of the State Land Conservation and Development Commission, which approved a program requiring each city and county to draft and adopt a comprehensive land use plan conforming to the 19 statewide planning goals adopted by the commission in 1975. Legislators, influenced heavily by local government officials, concluded that adoption of local comprehensive plans would obviate the need for the boundary commissions since the plans would resolve existing and potential boundary conflicts. As a result, state funding for the commissions was reduced sharply.

Whereas the Lane County Local Government Boundary Commission and the Portland Metropolitan Area Boundary Commission were able to raise sufficient funds to continue operations, the Marion-Polk County Local Government Boundary Commission failed to raise needed funds and was dissolved. Threats of additional reductions in state funding suggest that the future role of the two remaining commissions may be limited.

Texas

Although Texas lacks a general law regulating all proposed boundary changes, the 1971 legislature enacted a law granting the Texas Water Rights Commission the authority to approve or reject petitions for the creation of a municipal utility district responsible for control and distribution of water, reclamation and irrigation of arid or semi-arid land, drainage of overflowed land, development of water and hydroelectric power, navigation on inland and coastal waters, and protection and restoration of the purity of water.[141] Land within the corporate limits or extraterritorial jurisdiction of a city may not be included in a district unless the city council enacts a resolution or ordinance granting the city's consent for the inclusion of its land within the district.[142]

Evaluation

Writing in 1968, Ronald Cease concluded: "All operating boundary review boards have been successful; that is, they have significantly reduced the proliferation of local governments. The Canadian review boards are the most successful; they have broader powers than the boards in the United States and they do not appear to have financial and staffing problems."[143]

The U.S. Advisory Commission on Intergovernmental Relations in 1973 reported that the Local Government Boundary Commission in the Portland, Oregon area reduced the number of special districts over a two-year period from 303 to 198 chiefly by providing for the absorption of highway lighting districts into a county service district.[144]

In 1974 the California Task Force on Local Government Reform reported that LAFCOs had performed satisfactorily "in resolving annexation disputes and in providing advisory information to citizen groups interested in changing their governmental arrangements."[145] The task force accused LAFCOs of thwarting local level decentralization and of favoring "larger agencies over smaller ones, annexation over incorporation, general purpose agencies over special purpose agencies, and county controlled districts over independent ones."[146] It is important to realize that the task force had a polynucleated bias and accused LAFCOs of achieving the purposes of the enabling legislation. One should also bear in mind that a boundary commission's potential is limited in most cases to the prevention of further fragmentation since the commission usually lacks authority to correct problems resulting from past sins of commission or omission.

Standard Setting and State Appeals Committee

As the superior government, the state always has possessed the authority to establish minimum standards for the performance of functions by local governments as well as the authority to require local governments to perform or not perform specified functions.

As legally inferior units, local governments must be obsequious to the will of the state as expressed in general legislation, special legislation if not prohibited by the state constitution, and state administrative rules and regulations. In every state, there are extensive bodies of general legislation applying to local units and dealing with such subjects as the civil service, finance, public safety, public welfare, and standards of official performance. These and other local activities are supervised by state administrative agencies. The extent of supervision varies from advice and investigation in some states to close control in other states.

Standard Setting

State standards and administrative supervision are most common in the areas of finance and personnel. Concerning the former area, a number of states specify the type of accounting system local governments must utilize, require periodic financial reports, prescribe procedures for local budgeting, and supervise local taxation, including the assessment of property.[147] During the Great Depression, many states in effect placed certain local governments in administrative receivership by providing for substitute state administration of the units. More recently, the state of New York engaged in a special effort to rescue New York City from municipal bankruptcy by creating the state-controlled Municipal Assistance Corporation and the Emergency Financial Control Board, which were described in Chapter 3.

With respect to local government personnel, the constitution or statutes of many states require that most employees be selected by a merit system, statutes or administrative regulations prescribe minimum standards for employees, and statutes require mandatory state training for police officers, firefighters, and/or assessors. One of the most controversial personnel issues is the question of whether public employees should have the right to strike. State laws currently forbid strikes by public employees and provide penalties for striking.

Unionization of local government employees has become more common in recent decades, and states have enacted laws governing collective bargaining by public employee unions.[148] In a number of industrial states, for example, Massachusetts, New York, Pennsylvania, the legislature enacted a compulsory binding arbitration law for the settlement of impasses involving police officers and firefighters.[149]

The ultimate form of state administrative supervision of local government personnel involves their removal from office by the governor for malfeasance, nonfeasance, and/or misfeasance.

Environmental problems, which do not respect local jurisdictional lines, are among the most serious metropolitan problems. Local governments were the early leaders in environmental protection programs dating back to smoke control ordinances enacted by Chicago and Cincinnati in 1881.[150] In recent years, state governments either completely preempted responsibility for protecting aspects of the environment or partially preempted responsibility by establishing minimum standards for environmental protection. Rhode Island, for example, has forbidden cities and towns to enact air pollution control ordinances and bylaws.[151] Delaware, on the other hand, allows local governments to establish higher standards than those established by the state air pollution control agency.[152]

The Florida Environmental Land and Water Management Act of 1972 empowers the State Planning Agency to recommend to the Administration Commission—defined as the governor and the cabinet—specific areas of critical state concern.[153] If a local government fails to transmit to the State Planning Agency within 120 days land use regulations in conformance "with the principle for guiding development set out in the rule designating the area of critical state concern," the agency may institute judicial proceedings to enforce the land development regulations. In New York State, the 1973 legislature created a state agency to regulate land use in the large Adirondack Park Reserve.[154] As pointed out in an earlier section, the 1970 Maryland legislature initiated an interesting approach to ensuring that certain environmental services meeting state minimum standards are provided on the municipal level by creating the Maryland Environmental Service.

State Appeals Committee

In 1969 the Massachusetts General Court (legislature) decided to attack the problem of suburban municipalities blocking the construction of low-income housing by creating a committee in the State Department of Community Affairs with power to overturn decisions of city and town boards of appeal denying the issuance of a zoning variance or special permit for the construction of such housing.[155]

In 1973 the constitutionality of the act was upheld by the Massachusetts Supreme Judicial Court. It ruled that the act was a proper exercise of the general court's zoning powers even though the decisions of the committee would affect individual cities and towns and the commonwealth's constitution forbids the general court to enact municipal laws other than those applying to all cities and towns or to a class of not fewer than two cities or towns.[156]

Evidence to date indicates that this act has not had a significant impact on the housing patterns of the commonwealth's metropolitan areas since only 1,243 units of low-income housing authorized by the committee were constructed during the first six years the act was in effect.[157] Housing was constructed in only 28 communities during the first ten years of the law. In 16 of the communities, it was restricted to the elderly; and in 5 other communities, the housing was for both families and the elderly.[158] Of the 45 applications for comprehensive permits denied by local appeals boards and appealed to the state board, the local decision was reversed in 24 cases, the local decision was upheld in 3 cases, 8 applications were withdrawn, other action was taken in 6 cases, and 4 cases were pending in 1979.[159]

Political Decentralization of Education

Strong support for transferring political responsibility down to the neighborhood level for functions most directly affecting citizens developed in the late 1960s as a new breed of urban reformer advanced forceful arguments for the establishment of a system of community control of many facilities and services in large cities.[160] Resistance to this movement by municipal officials was strong, and reformers succeeded partially in achieving their goals in the area of education in two cities—New York and Detroit.

New York City Community School Districts

The declining quality of the New York City public schools after 1950 promoted movements to change the system and led in 1961 to the state legislature abolishing the city's board of education and replacing it with a new one directed to appoint 25 local school boards possessing advisory powers.[161] These boards did not satisfy supporters of neighborhood control of schools who continued to work for the political decentralization of public education to the community level.

The growing proportion of blacks enrolled in public schools convinced a number of black leaders in 1967 that integration could not be achieved within the city and that black control of schools was essential if quality education was to be provided for black students. Turning their attention to the state legislature, proponents of school decentralization were successful in 1969 in achieving a federated school system with 31 (later increased to 32) popularly elected school boards controlling education below the senior high school level.[162] The city board of education, however, may suspend, supersede, or remove a community school board or one or more members of such a board, and it also possesses broad financial and personnel powers over the community boards.

One of the major arguments for community control of schools was based upon the fact that blacks and Puerto Ricans were not adequately represented on the city board of education or the city council. In 1970 blacks exceeded 20 percent of the city's population, yet there were only two blacks and no Puerto Ricans on the 37-member council. In the 1970 community school boards election, the use of proportional representation as the electoral system resulted in 77 (28 percent) of the 279 community school board members elected being black and Puerto Rican.

Although relations between the city board of education and some of the community school boards have not been good and several boards have been suspended or superseded, the State Charter Commission for New York City in 1974 issued a generally favorable report on school decentralization.[163] In the same year, Professor Diane Ravitch of Columbia University concluded that decentralization was working well, blacks and Puerto Rican employees had been promoted to supervisory positions, and reading scores had increased slightly during the previous year.[164]

School decentralization in New York City has had mixed results so far with some improvements in standardized test scores and increased citizen participation in the school system. Absenteeism and crime, however, continue to be major problems in the schools.

Detroit Regional School Boards

Agitation for community control of schools occurred in Detroit at the same time as in New York City, and the issue was also taken to the state legislature, which in 1969 enacted a law directing the city's board of education to establish 7 to 11 "regional" school districts.[165]

This limited decentralization law was not endorsed by the Detroit Board of Education and blacks favoring community control of public schools. Continued agitation led the 1970 state legislature to replace the 1969 law with an act providing for eight regional school districts, allowing students to transfer from racially integrated schools, and prohibiting changes in school district boundaries.[166] The new law was supported by a coalition with blacks giving up integration for community control, white conservatives opposing integration, and white liberals fearing the 1969 law would result in racial confrontation and riots.

Until the repeal of the decentralization law in 1981, the city board of education was responsible for allocating capital funds, central purchasing, contract negotiations, payrolls, property management, special education programs, preparation of guidelines for regional boards, and nominating candidates for the position of superintendent of schools in each region with the regional board making the appointment.

A decentralization study committee jointly appointed by Governor William Milliken and Mayor Coleman Young reported in 1978 that a decentralized school system was necessary in Detroit, a strong commitment was needed to improve the quality of education, and evidence of improved pupil achievement existed in some of the regional school districts in the period 1975 to 1978.[167] Nevertheless, Detroit voters in a 1981 referendum authorized by the state legislature decided to end the regional school system effective January 1, 1983.[168] The system originally was designed to give blacks a greater voice in establishing educational policy. In 1981 voters apparently decided that this reason no longer applied since blacks held a majority of the seats on the citywide board of education.

SUMMARY AND CONCLUSIONS

The states have played one or more of three roles—inhibitor, facilitator, and initiator—relative to the solution of local government problems. Through constitutional restrictions, the state has acted as an inhibitor of the creation of general purpose metropolitan governments and solution of areawide problems in a number of states. However, many states have taken action to facilitate the formation of metropolitan governments by authorizing the creation of study commissions and by placing the question of creating an areawide government on the referendum ballot. States also have acted as facilitators of the solution of areawide problems by empowering local governments to enter into intergovernmental agreements designed to solve the problems and by providing technical and financial assistance to local governments desiring to enter into cooperative agreements. To the extent state encouragement of cooperation is successful, pressures for a restructuring of the local governmental system will be abated.

In the nineteenth century, Massachusetts and New York acted as initiators of the formation of metropolitan governments. In the twentieth century, only Indiana, by merging Indianapolis and Marion County, has ordered the creation of a general purpose areawide government and not allowed voters in a referendum to have the final decision. This amalgamation is an isolated one, and evidence suggesting that a state legislature will mandate another major city-county consolidation in the next decade is lacking.

Massachusetts relies heavily upon state-controlled public authorities to provide services in the greater Boston area, and New York State has placed increasing reliance upon state-controlled public authorities since 1959. A number of the New York authorities operate on a statewide basis and others operate on a regional basis. Our analysis reveals that many public authorities have dealt effectively with areawide problems. However, we are convinced that the use of the authority device is undesirable since the creation of several authorities in a given metropolitan area increases fragmentation of governmental responsibility and the cost of borrowing when moral obligation bonds are issued by the authorities. Furthermore, the lack of direct voter control of such major actors in the metropolitan governance system is disturbing.

The politics of a metropolitan area with several single-purpose public authorities differs considerably from areas lacking authorities since the governor and the state legislature play a greater and more direct role in the metropolitan governance system. In many areas, the suburban legislators outnumber the central city legislators, which may make a significant difference in the nature of the governmental system.

Although still in an evolutionary stage, the Twin Cities approach—involving the development of policies by the Metropolitan Council and their implementation by council-appointed service boards—has potential for producing more orderly development and raising service levels. Complementing the council's powers is the Metropolitan Revenue Distribution Act, which authorizes a partial sharing of the revenue produced by the growth in the commercial-industrial property tax base of the area. The act, along with council policies, should help to reduce gross fiscal disparities among municipalities.

The tightening of incorporation standards, liberalization of annexation statutes, and creation of boundary review boards have been important developments in several states during the past two decades. A related development is the increasing use of preemptive powers by the state legislature. In some instances, complete responsibility for a function is shifted from the local level to the state level. In other instances, partial preemption is employed through the establishment of regulatory and service provision standards that must be met by local governments.

The urbanized states undoubtedly will become more deeply involved in solving metropolitan problems through direct state action and standard setting during the next decade. The enlarged state role, as discussed in

Chapter 5, will be attributable in part to prodding by the federal government as it continues to rely upon the states to develop and implement programs meeting federal environmental standards.

NOTES

1. For up-to-date information on the financial problems of cities, see Joint Economic Committee, *Trends in the Fiscal Conditions of Cities: 1978–1980* (Washington, D.C.: U.S. Government Printing Office, 1980).

2. Roscoe C. Martin, *The Cities and the Federal System* (New York: Atherton Press, 1965), p. 79.

3. *The States and the Metropolitan Problem* (Chicago: Council of State Governments, 1956), p. 132.

4. *Governmental Structure, Organization, and Planning in Metropolitan Areas* (Washington, D.C.: U.S. Advisory Commission on Intergovernmental Relations, 1961), pp. 19–35.

5. Ibid., pp. 35–42.

6. David B. Walker, "The States' Role in Meeting the Urban Crisis: Positive or Negative," *Metropolitan Viewpoints*, May 1967, p. 4.

7. *Constitution of the State of New York*, art. IX, § 1 (h) (1).

8. *Constitution of the State of Ohio*, art. X, § 3.

9. *Constitution of the State of Tennessee*, art. XI, § 9.

10. *Town of Lockport v. Citizens for Community Action at the Local Level*, 423 U.S. 808 (1977).

11. *Property Tax Limits* (Chicago: International Association of Assessing Officers, 1978), pp. 14–28; *Significant Features of Fiscal Federalism: 1976–77 Edition*, vol. II (Washington, D.C.: U.S. Advisory Commission on Intergovernmental Relations, 1977), pp. 83–91. Massachusetts voters in 1980 approved an initiative petition limiting the property tax rate. In 1978 California voters approved initiative proposition 13, thereby reducing property taxes by more than 50 percent. For information on the initiative, see *The Book of the States: 1980–81* (Lexington, Ky.: Council of State Governments, 1980), p. 26.

12. John E. Petersen, Wayne Stallings, and Catherine L. Spain, *State Roles in Local Government Financial Management: Nine Case Studies* (Washington, D.C.: Municipal Finance Officers Association, 1980), p. 50.

13. *Delaware Code*, § 9-8002 (1975).

14. *Kansas Statutes*, § 79-1964a (1978).

15. *Constitution of the State of New York*, art. VIII, § § 10, 10a, 11.

16. *New York Laws of 1969*, chap. 1105.

17. *Hurd v. City of Buffalo*, 34 N.Y.2d 628 (1974).

18. *Significant Features of Fiscal Federalism: 1976–77 Edition*, pp. 83–91.

19. Ibid., pp. 92–93.

20. *Constitution of the State of New York*, art. VIII, § § 4, 6–7, 7a.

21. Joseph F. Zimmerman, "Lease-Purchase Fails," *National Civic Review* 48 (May 1959): 241–45.

22. Daniel R. Grant, "General Metropolitan Surveys: A Summary" in *Metropolitan Surveys: A Digest* (Chicago: Public Administration Service, 1958), p. 3.

23. Joseph F. Zimmerman, ed., *Metropolitan Surveys* (Albany: Graduate School of Public Affairs, State University of New York at Albany, 1966–68).

24. Henry J. Schmandt and William H. Standing, *The Milwaukee Metropolitan Study Commission* (Bloomington: Indiana University Press, 1965), p. 266.

25. *Substate Regionalism and the Federal System*, vol. I: *Regional Decision Making: New Strategies for Substate Districts* (Washington, D.C.: U.S. Advisory Commission on Intergovernmental Relations, 1973), p. 222.

26. For further details, see Joseph F. Zimmerman, "A Growing Trend," *National Civic Review* 58 (November 1969): 462–68.

27. Joseph F. Zimmerman, "Intergovernmental Service Agreements and Transfer of Functions" in *Substate Regionalism and the Federal System*, vol. III: *Challenge of Local Government Reorganization* (Washington, D.C.: U.S. Advisory Commission on Intergovernmental Relations, 1974), p. 35.

28. *Florida Laws of 1970*, chap. 243; *West's Florida Statutes Annotated*, chap. 195; *New York Laws of 1972*, chap. 28.

29. Joseph F. Zimmerman, *Pragmatic Federalism: The Reassignment of Functional Responsibility* (Washington, D.C.: U.S. Advisory Commission on Intergovernmental Relations, 1976), p. 26.

30. For examples of enabling legislation, see *Vermont Acts of 1970*, no. 216; *Vermont Statutes Annotated*, chap. 93; *New York Laws of 1972*, chap. 902; *New York Public Authorities Law*, § § 2430–454 (1981). See also Martin T. Katzman, "Measuring the Savings from State Municipal Bond Banking," *Governmental Finance* 9 (March 1980): 19–25.

31. *Indiana Acts of 1969*, chap. 173. *Burn's Indiana Statutes Annotated*, tit. 18, art. 4, § § 1-1 through 15-2 (1974). See also Joseph F. Zimmerman, "Indianapolis Consolidates," *The American City*, January 1970, p. 76.

32. *Massachusetts Acts of 1889*, chap. 439; *Massachusetts Acts of 1893*, chap. 407; *Massachusetts Acts of 1895*, chap. 488.

33. *Massachusetts Acts of 1901*, chap. 168; *Massachusetts Acts of 1919*, chap. 350.

34. Guthrie S. Birkhead, Alan K. Campbell, and Marsha Weissman, *Massachusetts Substate Government: A Report to the Secretary of Environmental Affairs* (Syracuse, N.Y.: Metropolitan Studies Program, Maxwell Graduate School, Syracuse University, August 15, 1972), p. 83.

35. *New York Laws of 1921*, chap. 154; *New Jersey Laws of 1921*, chap. 151. The compact is reprinted in Joseph F. Zimmerman, ed., *Metropolitan Charters* (Albany: Graduate School of Public Affairs, State University of New York at Albany, 1967), pp. 181–84.

36. Nelson A. Rockefeller, *The Future of Federalism* (New York: Atheneum, 1964), p. 47.

37. Chapter 744 of the *New York Laws of 1970* amended the Public Authorities Law and the Local Finance Law and reconstituted the Pure Water Authority as the Environmental Facilities Corporation. See *New York Public Authorities Law*, § § 2180–289 (McKinney 1981).

38. *Winston v. Spokane*, 12 Wash. 524, 41 Pac. 888 (1895).

39. *Robertson v. Zimmermann*, 268 N.Y. 52, 196 N.E. 743 (1935).

40. *1974 Annual Report of the Comptroller, Part I: Narrative* (Albany: Office of the State Comptroller, 1974), p. 25.

41. *New York Laws of 1960*, chap. 671; *New York Housing Finance Law*, § § 40–58; *New York Finance Law*, § § 53, 94, 98, 105 (2), 139 (McKinney 1973).

42. Joan Aron, "New York Public Authorities: Changing Form and Function," *National Civic Review* 64 (June 1974): 300.

43. *New York State Urban Development Corporation Act, New York Laws of 1968*, chap. 174. *New York Unconsolidated Laws*, § § 6251 et seq. (McKinney 1968). For details on the origin of the corporation, see Robert S. Amdursky, "A Public-Private Partnership for Urban Progress," *Journal of Urban Law* 46 (1969): 199–215.

44. *New York Laws of 1973*, chap. 446, § 3 (5) (McKinney 1973).

45. New York State Urban Development and Research Corporation Act, *New York Laws of 1968*, chap. 173 (McKinney 1968); Urban Development Guarantee Fund of New York Act, *New York Laws of 1968*, chap. 175 (McKinney 1968).

46. Edward J. Logue, *Goals, Guidelines, Concerns of the New York State Urban Development Corporation* (New York: Urban Development Corporation, 1971), p. 2.

47. *Strengthening Local Government in New York*, pt. 2: *Services, Structure & Finance* (New York: Temporary State Commission on the Powers of Local Government, 1973), p. 84.

48. Logue, *Goals, Guidelines, Concerns*, p. 3.

49. *Constitution of the State of New York*, art. VII, § 12 (1846). The New York State Constitution currently stipulates that no debt can be contracted by the state—other than short-term notes in anticipation of taxes and debt contracted on account of invasion, insurrection, war, and forest fires—without the approval of a majority of the voters. See *Constitution of the State of New York*, art. VII, § § 9–11.

50. Special Committee on the Constitutional Convention, *State Finance, Taxation, and Housing and Community Development* (New York: Association of the Bar of the City of New York, April 1967), p. 8.

51. *Williamsburg Savings Bank v. State*, 243 N.Y. 231 (1926).

52. *Business Week*, March 7, 1970, p. 96.

53. "Carey Asks $178 Million in Loan for Urban Unit," *New York Times*, January 24, 1975, p. 53.

54. Linda Greenhouse, "U.D.C. Head Seeks Banks' Guarantee," *New York Times*, February 4, 1975, p. 11.

55. Hugh L. Carey, *Message to the Legislature* (Albany: Executive Chamber, January 8, 1975), p. 24.

56. *New York Laws of 1975*, chaps. 7, 11 (McKinney 1975).

57. *Statewide Public Authorities: A Fourth Branch of Government?* (Albany: Office of the State Comptroller, 1972), p. 1.

58. Francis X. Clines, "Wilson to Study Bond-Curb Plans," *New York Times*, March 15, 1974, p. 39.

59. William E. Farrell, "State 'Financing Schemes' are Questioned by Levitt," *New York Times*, January 22, 1973, p. 59.

60. *New York State Senate Bills 4059–069* (1975).

61. *Annotated Code of Maryland*, § § 3-101 through 3-201.

62. Ibid., § 3-104 (u).

63. Ibid., § 3-110 (a).

64. Ibid., § 3-110 (c).

65. *New Jersey Laws of 1981*, chap. 293; *New Jersey Statutes Annotated*, chap. 58:1B-1 et seq.

66. *New York Laws of 1946*, chap. 954; *New York Public Authorities Law*, § § 550–76 (McKinney 1973).

67. *U.S. Constitution*, art. I, § 10. A bond indenture is a legally binding contract.

68. *New York Laws of 1939*, chap. 870; *New York Public Authorities Law*, § § 152, 202 (McKinney 1973).

69. *Governmental Structure, Organization, and Planning*, p. 28.

70. Jerome J. Shestack, "The Public Authority," *The Univesity of Pennsylvania Law Review* 105 (February 1957): 568.

71. *Governmental Structure, Organization, and Planning*, pp. 26, 29.

72. *Minnesota Statutes*, chap. 473B (1978).

73. "Metropolitan Land Planning Act," *Minnesota Statutes*, § § 473.851–473.872 (1978).

74. *Minnesota Statutes*, chap. 473C.

75. Ibid., chap. 473E.

76. *Knapp v. O'Brien*, 179 N.W. 2d 88 (1970).

77. Stanley Baldinger, *Planning and Governing the Metropolis: The Twin Cities Experience* (New York: Praeger, 1971), p. 215. See also "Twin Cities Metropolitan Council Anticipates and Supplies Orderly Growth," *Urban Action Clearinghouse*, Case Study No. 20 (Washington, D.C.: Chamber of Commerce of the United States, 1971). For an early enthusiastic account of the council, see John Fischer, "The Minnesota Experiment: How to Make a Big City Fit to Live In," *Harper's Magazine* 250 (April 1969): 12, 17–18, 20, 24, 26, 28, 30, 32.

78. Baldinger, *Planning and Governing the Metropolis*, p. 3.

79. John Herbers, "Minneapolis Area Council is Emerging as a Pioneer in Strong Regional Government," *New York Times*, February 2, 1971, p. 62.

80. Ted Kolderie, "Minnesota Legislature Aids Metropolitan Setup," *National Civic Review* 58 (July 1969): 321.

81. Baldinger, *Planning and Governing the Metropolis*, p. 222.

82. Ted Kolderie, "Regionalism in the Twin Cities of Minnesota," in *The Regionalist Papers*, ed. Kent Mathewson (Detroit: Metropolitan Fund, 1974), p. 116.

83. Arthur Naftalin and John Brandl, *The Twin Cities Regional Strategy* (St. Paul: Metropolitan Council of the Twin Cities Area, 1980), p. 23.

84. C. J. Hein, Joyce M. Keys, and G. M. Robbins, *Regional Governmental Arrangements in Metropolitan Areas: Nine Case Studies* (Washington, D.C.: U.S. Government Printing Office, 1974), p. 33.

85. Naftalin and Brandl, *Twin Cities Regional Strategy*, p. 25.

86. Dennis Farney, "The Twin City Experiment," *Wall Street Journal*, March 21, 1974, p. 1.

87. Kolderie, "Regionalism in the Twin Cities," p. 117.

88. *Minnesota Statutes*, chap. 473F (1971).

89. *Village of Burnsville v. Onischuk*, 222 N.W.2d 523 (1974).

90. Fiscal zoning is often loosely defined. It is used here to refer to the adoption by a municipality of zoning and other codes designed to keep low-income persons from becoming residents and to encourage certain types of commercial and industrial development requiring relatively few municipal services and producing substantial property tax revenue.

91. Naftalin and Brandl, *Twin Cities Regional Strategy*, p. 67.

92. *Governmental Structure, Organization, and Planning*, p. 39.

93. Ibid.

94. Ibid., pp. 21–24.

95. *Fiscal Balance in the American Federal System*, vol. 2: *Metropolitan Fiscal Disparities* (Washington, D.C.: U.S. Advisory Commission on Intergovernmental Relations, October 1967), p. 14.

96. *Meeting Metropolitan Problems* (Sacramento: Governor's Commission on Metropolitan Area Problems, December 1960), pp. 16–17, 20.

97. Ibid., p. 20.

98. *Maryland Laws of 1955*, chap. 423; *Annotated Code of Maryland*, art. 23A, § 21.

99. *Minnesota Laws of 1957*, chap. 833.

100. *Minnesota Laws of 1959*, chap. 414; *Minnesota Statutes*, chap. 414.02–414.06 (1978).

101. *Minnesota Laws of 1969*, chap. 1146, § 12; *Minnesota Statutes*, chap. 414.033 (3) (1978).

102. Minnesota Laws of 1973, chap. 621, § 11; *Minnesota Statutes*, chap. 414.031 (5).

103. *Minnesota Laws of 1975*, chap. 271; *Minnesota Statutes*, § 5.012 (1978).

104. *Minnesota Statutes*, chap. 414.01 (2) (1978).

105. *Minnesota Laws of 1969*, chap. 1146; *Minnesota Statutes*, chap. 414.032 (1) (1978).

106. *1974 Annual Report* (St. Paul: Minnesota Municipal Commission, n.d.), p. 5.

107. Ibid., p. 13.

108. *The Constitution of the State of Alaska*, art. X, § 12.

109. Ibid.

110. *Alaska Laws of 1959*, chap. 64, § 7; *Alaska Statutes*, § § 44.19.250 et seq.

111. *Wisconsin Laws of 1959*, chap. 261; *Wisconsin Municipal Law*, § § 66.013 et seq. (1973).

112. *Guidelines* (San Jose: Santa Clara County Local Agency Formation Commission, 1970), p. 1.

113. *Meeting Metropolitan Problems*, pp. 16–17, 20.

114. *California Laws of 1965*, chap. 587; *California Government Code*, § § 54773–4799.

115. *California Government Code*, § § 54780–4784.

116. Ibid., § 54790.

117. *California Acts of 1965*, chap. 2043; *California Government Code*, § 56250.

118. Richard T. Legates, *California Local Agency Formation Commissions* (Berkeley: Institute of Governmental Studies, University of California, 1970), p. 58.

119. Ibid.

120. John M. Eels, *LAFCO Spheres of Influence: Effective Planning for the Urban Fringe?* (Berkeley: Institute of Governmental Studies, University of California, 1977), p. 110.

121. Ibid., p. 135. Latent powers refer to powers granted to special districts that have not been exercised. A water district, for example, may be empowered to provide fire protection and sewer service.

122. Ibid., p. 130.

123. *Colorado Revised Statutes*, § § 89-18-1 through 89-18-10.

124. Ibid., § 89-18-4.

125. Ibid., § 89-18-9 (1).

126. *Constitution of Colorado*, art. XX, § 1.

127. *New Mexico Laws of 1965*, chap. 300; *New Mexico Statutes Annotated*, § § 14-7-11 through 14-7-16 (1974 supp.).

128. *New Mexico Laws of 1967*, chap. 248, § 9; *New Mexico Statutes Annotated*, § § 14-58-1 through 14-58-14 (1974 supp.).

129. *New Mexico Laws of 1967*, chap. 248, § 13; *New Mexico Statutes Annotated*, § 14-58-13 (1974 supp.).

130. *Washington Laws of 1967*, chap. 189; *Revised Code of Washington Annotated*, chap. 36.93.010-920 (1973 supp.).

131. *Revised Code of Washington Annotated*, chap. 36.93.110 (1973 supp.).

132. Ibid., chap. 36.93.150 (5).

133. *Michigan Public Act Number 191 of 1968*; *Michigan Compiled Laws Annotated*, § § 123.1001–123.1020 (1974 supp.).

134. *Nevada Revised Statutes*, § § 268.570–268.670 (1973).

135. Ibid., § 268.626.

136. Ibid., § 268.660.

137. *Oregon Laws of 1969*, chap. 494; *Oregon Revised Statutes*, § § 199.410–199.514 (1973).

138. *Oregon Revised Statutes*, § 199.430.

139. Ibid., § 199.450.

140. *Report of the Lane County Local Government Boundary Commission: 1969–1973*

(Eugene, Oreg.: Lane County Local Government Boundary Commission, January 1974), pp. 5–7.

141. *Texas Laws of 1971*, chap. 84; *Vernon's Texas Code Annotated*, chap. 54 (1974 supp.)

142. *Vernon's Texas Code Annotated*, chap. 54.016.

143. Ronald C. Cease, *A Report on State and Provincial Boundary Review Boards* (Portland, Oreg.: Portland State College, August 1968), p. 32.

144. U.S. Advisory Commission on Intergovernmental Relations, *Regional Decision Making: New Strategies for Substate Districts*, p. 26.

145. *Local Government Reform* (Sacramento: California Task Force on Local Government Reform, 1974), p. 42.

146. Ibid.

147. For details, see *State-Local Relations* (Chicago: Council of State Governments, 1946), pp. 11–55. Although dated, the volume contains the most comprehensive treatment of the subject of state administrative supervision of local governments.

148. *New York Laws of 1967*, chap. 392; *New York Civil Service Law*, § § 200–14 (McKinney 1973 and 1979 supp.).

149. *Pennsylvania Acts of 1968*, Act No. 111; *Pennsylvania Statutes*, § § 217.1 et seq. See also Jane L. Stein et al., eds. *The Effects of Public Safety Employee Bargaining* (Lexington, Mass.: D. C. Heath, 1975).

150. Joseph F. Zimmerman, "The Municipal Stake in Environmental Protection," *The Municipal Year Book: 1972* (Washington D.C.: International City Management Association, 1972), pp. 105–09.

151. *Rhode Island General Laws Annotated*, § 23-25-19 (1968).

152. *Delaware Code Annotated*, tit. 7, § 6207 (1968 supp.).

153. *Florida Laws of 1972*, chap. 72-317; *West's Florida Statutes Annotated*, tit. 26, chap. 380, § § 380.012–380.10 (1973).

154. *New York Laws of 1973*, chap. 348; *New York Executive Law*, art. 27, § § 810–17 (McKinney 1973).

155. "Low and Moderate Income Housing Act," *Massachusetts General Laws Annotated*, chap. 40B, § § 202–23.

156. *Board of Appeals of Hanover v. Housing Appeals Committee in the Department of Community Affairs*, 294 N.E.2d 393 (1973). See also the *Constitution of the Commonwealth of Massachusetts*, art. LXXXIX of the articles of amendment, § 8. This amendment annulled and replaced Article II of the articles of amendment.

157. David T. Rowell, "Massachusetts Law Spurs Subsidized Housing," *National Civic Review* 65 (September 1976): 406–07, 432.

158. Elisabeth A. Ruben and Constance Williams, *Comprehensive Permits for Housing Lower Income Households in Massachusetts* (Boston: Citizens Housing and Planning Association, 1979), p. 5.

159. Ibid., p. 8.

160. For additional information on this movement, see Joseph F. Zimmerman, *The Federated City: Community Control in Large Cities* (New York: St. Martin's Press, 1972), pp. 1–27.

161. *New York Laws of 1961*, chap. 971.

162. *New York Laws of 1969*, chap. 330; *New York Education Law*, art. 52 A (McKinney 1970 and 1980 supp.).

163. *Impact of School Decentralization in New York City on Municipal Decentralization* (New York: State Charter Commission for New York City, 1974).

164. Diane Ravitch, "School Decentralization, and What It has Come To," *New York Times*, June 30, 1974, sec. 4, p. E5.

165. *Michigan Public Act 244 of 1969*; *Michigan Compiled Laws*, § § 388.174 et seq.

166. *Michigan Public Act 48 of 1970* ; *Michigan Compiled Laws*, § § 388.174 et seq. The history and politics of the law are described in William R. Grant, "Community Control vs. School Integration—The Case of Detroit," *The Public Interest* (Summer 1971): 62–79.

167. *Final Report of the Decentralization Study Committee, Detroit Public Schools* (Detroit, January 1, 1978), pp. 21–22, 27.

168. *Michigan Public Act 96 of 1981.*

CHAPTER 5

The Federal Influence

Fluidity has been a key characteristic of federalism in the United States with the distribution of formal political powers changing with the passage of time. The founding fathers recognized the undesirability of a static distribution of political power between Congress and the states and provided for partial and total federal preemption of responsibility for various governmental functions. However, it is inconceivable that they could have foreseen the extensive growth of federal powers to the point that the national government today, via informal and formal preemptory actions, determines to a significant extent the nature of numerous state and local government services and regulatory activities.[1]

Of the external factors affecting state-local relations, the federal government has the greatest impact. The U.S. Constitution contains no reference to local governments and the U.S. Supreme Court ruled that municipalities are "creatures" of the state possessing only expressly delegated and necessarily implied powers.[2] Nevertheless, the federal government started to exercise increasing influence over local governments during the Great Depression. The federal involvement, however, did not have a major impact upon state-local relations and local governments until the 1950s.

Roscoe Martin, writing in 1965, referred to "the demonstrated incapacity of the States to play an effective role in the war on urban problems" and added:

> In the circumstances it is not strange that the cities sought, and where opportunity offered, embraced new arrangements. Their recourse was

to appeal direct to the federal government for assistance. The narrow and crooked paths of other years were broadened and straightened into expressways connecting the city halls and the national Capitol. Direct relations between Washington and the cities, long existent but as long submerged, were brought to the surface and recognized openly for what they were. The chief instrument by which this transformation was effected was the grant-in-aid.[3]

In the conclusion of his study, Martin wrote: "it may be argued persuasively that the national government is more sensitive to public needs in the beginning and more subject to popular control in the end than are either state or local governments."[4] He concluded that the federal government is "the most democratic government in the United States."[5]

While one can argue that the federal government has been responsive to the needs of urban local governments, it must not be overlooked that federal policies largely have been responsible for population movements and developmental patterns that caused the present area-fiscal resources mismatch between local governments in metropolitan areas. During the past 35 years, federal highway, mortgage insurance, sewage disposal, and water supply grant-in-aid programs promoted the development of "spread city" with its debilitating effect on the economic health of the central city in the typical metropolitan area. Furthermore, federal attempts to facilitate the solution of regional problems created additional governance problems. Convinced of the importance of areawide planning, the federal government made such planning a condition for local government receipt of federal funds for many purposes. Unfortunately, the federal requirements produced fragmented unifunctional planning on the regional level, thereby making the development and implementation of comprehensive plans more difficult.

EXPANSION OF NATIONAL POWERS

The broad accretion of power on the national level is attributable to constitutional amendments, statutory elaboration of powers delegated to Congress, and judicial interpretation. Public and private interest groups, including local governments, played important roles in this power expansion.

Constitutional Amendments

The first constitutional amendment to limit the powers of state and local governments directly was the Fourteenth Amendment with its due process of law, equal protection of the laws, and privileges and immunities clauses. Numerous federal court decisions struck down state and local actions as violative of one of the amendment's three clauses. Among other things, the federal courts have interpreted the privileges and immunities clause to include the First Amendment's guarantees.

Several states and numerous local governments currently are subject to the Federal Voting Rights Act of 1965 as amended, which is based upon the Fifteenth and Fourteenth Amendments. The Fifteenth Amendment prohibits the abridgement of the right to vote "because of race, color, or previous condition of servitude" and serves as the principal constitutional basis for the Voting Rights Act, which is discussed in greater detail in a subsequent section.

The Sixteenth Amendment's authorization for Congress to levy a graduated income tax has given Congress the means to raise sufficient funds to finance more than 500 categorical grant-in-aid programs for states and their political subdivisions.[6] Conditions attached to the program allow the Congress and federal administrative agencies to exercise considerable influence over matters reserved to states by the Tenth Amendment to the U.S. Constitution; responsibility for many of these matters typically are delegated by states to local governments.

Statutory Elaboration

The delegation of specific powers to the Congress by the U.S. Constitution upon its ratification in 1788 did not lead to the immediate exercise of all of these powers. The power to regulate interstate commerce was not employed in a comprehensive manner until enactment of the Interstate Commerce Act of 1887, and the power to regulate bankruptcies was not exercised until 1933.

Commencing with the Atomic Energy Act of 1946, Congress increasingly used its powers of total and partial preemption to supersede state laws and local ordinances. Congressional acts totally or partially preempting responsibility for abating environmental pollution have had the greatest impact upon the discretionary authority of states and their political subdivisions.

The Water Quality Act of 1965 required each state to adopt "water quality standards applicable to interstate waters or portions thereof within such State" as well as an implementation and enforcement plan.[7] The administrator of the Environmental Protection Agency (EPA) is authorized to promulgate water quality standards, which become effective at the end of six months in the event a state fails to establish and enforce adequate standards. The federal role was strengthened by the Federal Water

Pollution Control Act Amendments of 1972, which established July 1, 1977 as the deadline for the secondary treatment of sewage, and July 1, 1983 as the date for achieving "water quality which provides for protection and propagation of fish, shellfish, and wildlife" and requires the elimination of the "discharge of pollutants into navigable waters in 1985."[8] A similar procedure concerning state responsibility for air pollution abatement, with the exception of emissions from new motor vehicles, was established by the Air Quality Act of 1967.[9] The implications for states and local governments of federal partial preemption of responsibility for air pollution abatement are examined in a subsequent section.

Judicial Interpretation

Since the development of the doctrine of implied powers in *McCulloch v. Maryland* and the doctrine of the continuous journey in *Gibbons v. Ogden*, the U.S. Supreme Court generally has interpreted the delegated powers of Congress broadly.[10] In 1885 Woodrow Wilson wrote:

> Congress must wantonly go very far outside of the plain and unquestionable meaning of the Constitution, must bump its head directly against all right and precedent, must kick against the very pricks of all well-established rulings and interpretations, before the Supreme Court will offer its distinct rebuke.[11]

The decisions of the U.S. Supreme Court limiting the police power of the states and their political subdivisions concerning economic matters are well known and need no elaboration. Two 1980 decisions of the Court strike at the sovereign immunity of subnational governments and illustrate the tendency of the Court to issue expansive interpretations of acts of Congress.

In *Maine v. Thiboutot* and *Owen v. City of Independence*, the Court stripped states and their political subdivisions of immunity for the actions of their public servants by an expansive interpretation of a section of the Civil Rights Act of 1871.[12] Section 1983 of the act provides:

> Every person who, under color of any statute, ordinance, regulation, custom, or usage, of any State or territory, subjects, or causes to be subjected to, any citizen of the United States or other person within the jurisdiction thereof to the deprivation of any rights, privileges, or immunities secured by the Constitution and laws, shall be liable to the party injured in an action at law, suit in equity, or other proper proceeding for redress.

In the 1980 cases, the phrase "and laws" in section 1983 was interpreted to provide a cause for action for deprivation of rights secured by any law of the United States because Congress had not provided for state and municipal immunity. Section 1983 cases previously had been limited to infringements of rights protected by the equal protection of laws clause of the Fourteenth Amendment to the U.S. Constitution. State and local officials can be held entirely responsible under these decisions even though officials of federal administrative agencies have equal administrative responsibility for the affected programs. These decisions grant the judiciary unlimited authority to review actions of state and local officials totally unrelated to civil rights.

In his dissent in the *Thiboutot* case, Justice Lewis Powell, Jr. pointed out that "no one can predict the extent to which litigation from today's decision will harass State and local officials; nor can one foresee the number of new filings in our already overburdened courts. But no one can doubt that these consequences will be substantial."[13] Justice Powell included as an appendix to his dissent a long list of programs affected by the majority decision.[14]

Concerning local governments, Powell in his dissent in the *Owen* case lamented that:

> After today's decision, municipalities will have gone in two short years from absolute immunity under § 1983 to strict liability. As a policy matter, I believe that strict municipal liability unreasonably subjects local governments to damages judgments for actions that were reasonable when performed. It converts municipal governance into a hazardous slalom through constitutional obstacles that often are unknown and unknowable.[15]

In bringing the discussion of judicial interpretation to a close, attention must be focused upon federal court decisions resulting in the court monitoring the operation of a school system and issuing orders affecting its operation. The outstanding example of court assumption of many of the responsibilities of a school committee involves U.S. District Court Judge W. Arthur Garrity, Jr., who has issued approximately 240 court orders affecting the public schools in Boston and determined such miniscule issues as whether a ceiling in the Rogers School should be repaired.[16] We conclude this section by noting that U.S. Supreme Court decisions occasionally have favored the states and their political subdivisions and cite *San Antonio Independent School District v. Rodriguez*, discussed in Chapter 3, and *National League of Cities v. Usery*, which is examined in a subsequent section.

THE IMPACT OF FEDERAL PREEMPTION

Prior to 1965, formal powers of preemption were rarely exercised by Congress, as in 1933 when the Bankruptcy Act nullified the bankruptcy laws of the 48 states and in 1946 when complete responsibility for regulating ionizing radiation was assigned to the U.S. Atomic Energy Commission.[17] The exercise of formal preemptory powers by Congress had a minimal impact on local governments less than two decades ago. Support for this conclusion is based in part upon the January 1940 issue of *The Annals*, which was devoted to intergovernmental relations in the United States and contains no reference to formal federal preemption.[18] A similar volume of *The Annals*, published in 1974, contains several references to formal federal preemption.[19]

The national government, however, acquired significant influence over many state-local activities prior to 1960 by means of informal partial preemption, which was voluntarily initiated by state and local governments accepting conditional federal grants-in-aid and the use of tax credits by Congress.

Informal Preemption

The Hatch Act of 1887, designed to promote agricultural research, was the first federal law authorizing grants-in-aid to the states on a continuing basis. In 1894 Congress enacted the Carey Act, which contained the first condition, a type of de facto partial preemption, for the receipt of federal funds by states, that is, preparation of a comprehensive plan for the irrigation of arid land. Federal inspection of state forestry operations and matching requirements date from 1911.[20]

Federal grants to state and local governments increased from $7 million in 1902 to $12 million in 1913 to $232 million in 1932 to $1,031 million in 1939.[21] The impact of the sharp increase in federal grants upon state governments did not elude the scrutiny of perceptive observers. In 1940 G. Homer Durham pointed out that "some of the largest and politically most powerful state agencies such as highway administration with an almost total absence of merit personnel, are no longer dependent on their operating jurisdictions for funds."[22]

The dollar amounts of federal grants-in-aid to state and local governments exploded after World War II. In 1978 the U.S. Advisory Commission on Intergovernmental Relations pointed out that "at least through the 1950s, federal assistance activities were confined by an effort to restrict aid to fields clearly involving the national interest or an important national purpose."[23] Commencing with 1965, "the concept of the national interest lost most of its substantive content" with "any action passed by both legislative chambers and signed by the President being accepted as appropriate."[24]

Extensive informal preemption by the federal government by means of conditional grants-in-aid in recent years had led to fears that state and local governments are becoming stipendiaries and ministerial arms of the federal government. Some authorities feel that state and local governments are becoming too heavily dependent on federal funding and no longer possess discretion to modify federally aided programs, such as welfare, because the rule-making power resides in federal administrative agencies or to reduce the amount of funds for federally aided programs because of maintenance-of-effort provisions. Charles Schultze questions whether major national purposes are served by conditional grants-in-aid and maintains that the grants "simply reflect the substitution of the judgment of federal legislators and agency officials for that of state and local officials."[25]

It must also be recognized that federal administrators are granted a veto power over state and local government plans, policies, and implementation of programs. In other words, there has been a significant expansion of the decision-making powers of federal administrators, and the expansion has evoked fears of administrative imperialism. Former U.S. Senator James Buckley in 1978 expressed this viewpoint in strong terms:

> The federal bureaucracy has grown into what is essentially a fourth branch of government that has become virtually immune to political direction or control. It is peopled by men and women who are now possessed by broad discretionary power over many areas of American life—so many, in fact, that one begins to wonder to what extent ours can still be described as a government of laws rather than of men.[26]

Buckley is convinced the federal machinery has been overloaded and that only by reducing the federal involvement in the governance process by shifting responsibilities to the states and local governments will it be possible to "expand the amount of time that the President and the members of Congress can devote to each of the matters for which they remain responsible."[27]

Although the rhetoric of some state and local government officials suggests that states and their political subdivisions are becoming vassals of the federal government, this description is an inaccurate portrayal of the powers of states, which continue to be important units of government possessing relatively broad discretionary powers. Furthermore, states and local governments retain a considerable amount of discretionary authority in administering federally aided programs and also are able to influence federal policies in statutes enacted by Congress and in rules and regulations promulgated by federal agencies administering the grant programs.

Formal Preemption

Many federal laws contain an express provision for total federal preemption. The Flammable Fabrics Act stipulates that it "is intended to supersede any law of any State or political subdivision thereof inconsistent with its provisions."[28] A similar provision is found in the U.S. Grain Standards Act and the Radiation Control for Health and Safety Act of 1968.[29] And in 1967, Congress enacted the Air Quality Act, which totally preempted responsibility for establishing and enforcing automobile exhaust emission standards for 1968 and for subsequent model vehicles.[30]

The type of problem that can be caused by total federal preemption is illustrated by the experience of officials in Keene, New Hampshire, who in 1980 were planning to develop a city-owned industrial park and discovered that a small section of the lot had been deemed a "wetland" area by the U.S. Army Corps of Engineers and thereby was protected from development by federal environmental protection laws.[31]

Problems for local governments are also caused by partial federal preemption statutes, which establish minimum national standards and authorize states to continue to be responsible for regulatory activities provided the state standards are at least as high as the national standards. The Safe Drinking Water Act, for example, stipulates that "a State has primary enforcement responsibility for public water systems" provided the administrator of the Environmental Protection Agency determines that the State "has adopted drinking water regulations which . . . are no less stringent than" national standards.[32] Should a state fail to adopt or enforce such standards, the agency would apply national standards within that state.

A relatively large number of state mandates that are strenuously objected to by local government officials are "indirect" federal mandates under federal partial preemption statutes. In other words, if the state had failed to mandate certain actions by its political subdivisions, the federal government would have initiated the actions.

Many acts of Congress do not contain an explicit partial or total preemption section yet have been held by courts to be preemptive. In 1941 the U.S. Supreme Court stressed that each challenge of a state law on the ground of inconsistency with federal law must be determined on the basis of the particular facts of the case.

> There is not—and from the very nature of the problem—there can not be any rigid formula or rule which can be used to determine the meaning and purpose of every act of Congress. This Court, in considering the validity of State laws in the light of treaties or federal laws touching on the same subject has made use of the following expressions: Conflicting; contrary to; occupying the field; repugnance; difference; irrecon-

cilability; inconsistency; violation; curtailment; and interference. But none of these expressions provides an infallible constitutional test or an exclusive constitutional yardstick. In the final analysis, there can be no one crystal clear distinctly marked formula. Our primary function is to determine whether, under the circumstances of this particular case, Pennsylvania's law stands as an obstacle to the accomplishment and execution of the full purposes and objectives of Congress.[33]

In 1947 the U.S. Supreme Court explicated two tests of federal preemption: (1) "the question in each case is what the purpose of Congress was," and (2) does the act of Congress involve "a field in which the federal interest is so dominant that the federal system will be assumed to preclude enforcement of State laws on the same subject?"[34] Concerning the Noise Control Act of 1972, the Court wrote:

Our prior cases on preemption are not precise guidelines in the present controversy, for each case turns on the peculiarities and special features of the federal regulatory scheme in question. . . . Control of noise is of course deep-seated in the police power of the States. Yet the pervasive control vested in EPA [Environmental Protection Agency] and FAA [Federal Aviation Administration] under the 1972 Act seems to us to leave no room for local curfews or other local controls.[35]

The U.S. Supreme Court also occasionally voids only the portion of a state or local law held to be preempted. A three-section Washington state law pertaining to Puget Sound required that oil tankers be guided by state-licensed pilots, specified design standards for oil tankers, and banned all tankers over 125,000 deadweight tons.[36] The Court let stand the first section but ruled that the other two sections had been preempted by Congress.[37]

The U.S. Supreme Court has placed some limits on federal preemptory powers. In 1970 Congress lowered the voting age in all elections to 18, but the Court ruled that Congress lacked the power to lower the voting age for state and local elections.[38] Justice Hugo Black, in delivering the judgment of the Court, wrote that "the Equal Protection Clause of the Fourteenth Amendment was never intended to destroy the States' power to govern themselves, making the Nineteenth and Twenty-fourth Amendments superfluous."[39] Justice Black added that the power of Congress to enforce the guarantees of the Fourteenth and Fifteenth Amendments was subject to at least three limitations:

First, Congress may not by legislation repeal other provisions of the Constitution. Second, the power granted to Congress was not intended to strip the States of their power to govern themselves or to convert our

national government of enumerated powers into a central government
of unrestrained authority over every inch of the whole Nation. Third,
Congress may only "enforce" the provisions of the amendments and
may do so only by "appropriate legislation."[40]

In 1976 the Court invalidated the 1974 Fair Labor Standards Act
amendments extending minimum wage and overtime pay provisions to
nonsupervisory employees of state and local governments on the ground
that the extension violated the Tenth Amendment to the U.S. Constitution
and threatened the separate and independent existence of the units.[41] In
May 1979 the Court ruled that the statute giving federal courts jurisdiction
over allegations of violations of constitutional rights does not cover a suit
based simply on the fact that a state law conflicts with the federal Social
Security Act.[42] Conceding that the conflict between the laws violates the
supremacy clause of the U.S. Constitution, the Court held that such a
violation is not the type of constitutional allegation that confers jurisdiction
upon federal courts.

Commencing in 1971, questions began to be raised concerning formal
federal preemption, and fears began to be expressed about the potential
danger of the evolution of a monocentric system of government. In 1788
who would have believed that a bill approved by the state legislature and
signed by the governor, other than a bill falling within the purview of Section
10 of Article I of the U.S. Constitution, would require the approval of the
U.S. attorney general or the U.S. District Court for the District of Columbia
before the law could be implemented? Yet the federal Voting Rights Act
contains such a requirement for states and their political subdivisions,
which meet the two criteria for triggering the act, desiring to make even
minor changes in their electoral systems.[43]

Dissenting in *Perkins v. Matthews*, a voting rights case, Justice Hugo
Black wrote:

> In my view, the Constitution prohibits the Federal Government from
> requiring federal approval of State laws before they can become
> effective. Proposals for such congressional veto power over State laws
> were made at the Constitutional Convention and overwhelmingly
> rejected. The Fourteenth Amendment did not alter the basic structure
> of our federal system of government. The Fourteenth Amendment did
> bar discrimination on account of race and did give the Federal
> Government power to enforce the ban on racial discrimination. In this
> case the Congress has attempted to enforce the ban on racial
> discrimination by requiring States to submit their laws or practices to
> federal approval even before they are initiated. In my view that
> requirement attempts to accomplish the constitutional end of banning
> racial discrimination by a means—requiring submission of proposed

State laws to the Attorney General—that violates the letter and spirit of the Constitution.[44]

Preemptive decisions of the U.S. Supreme Court since 1954 have led to the filing in Congress of numerous bills limiting the Court's jurisdiction as authorized by the U.S. Constitution.[45] To cite one recent example, on February 21, 1979 Senator Jesse Helms of North Carolina introduced a bill, S. 438, stipulating that "the Supreme Court shall not have jurisdiction to review, by appeal, writ of certiorari, or otherwise, any case arising out of any State statute, ordinance, rule, regulation, or any part thereof, or arising out of any Act interpreting, applying, or enforcing a State statute, ordinance, rule, or regulation, which relates to voluntary prayers in public schools and public buildings."[46] The bill, which also denies jurisdiction over such cases to U.S. district courts, was approved by the Senate on April 5, 1979 by a vote of 47 to 37.[47]

Pressures to limit the jurisdiction of federal courts continued in 1980 and 1981. Congress in 1980 attached eight riders to appropriation bills that would effectively block enforcement of the major civil rights acts of the 1960s and 1970s.[48] In late 1981, U.S. Attorney General William French Smith criticized federal courts for judicial policy making and announced that the Department of Justice will "contest any expansion of the list of suspect classifications, which, once established by a court, almost inevitably result in the overturning of legislative judgments."[49]

A Case Study

Even in the functional areas partially preempted by Congress, local governments are not necessarily powerless to influence federal policies, as illustrated by New York City's experience with a federally mandated transportation control plan.

The federal Clean Air Amendments of 1970 represent a sharp break with the earlier federal approach to air pollution abatement, which relied upon state and local governments to provide the necessary leadership and took into consideration the economic and technical feasibility of abatement controls.[50] Direct federal action to protect public health was made national policy, and explicit dates for adoption of standards and abatement plans by states were specified. In contrast to earlier ones, the new standards were mandated without considering the economic or technical feasibility of pollution abatement systems.

The administrator of the Environmental Protection Agency was directed to publish within 90 days in the *Federal Register* a list of categories of stationary sources of air pollution subject to performance standards established under the amendments. He was given an additional 120 days following publication of the list to include in the *Federal Register* proposed regulations establishing federal standards for new sources of air pollution. Each state was authorized to submit to the administrator a proposed procedure for implementing and enforcing standards of performance for new sources located in the state, and the administrator was empowered to delegate authority to each state to implement and enforce the standards for other than new United States-owned sources. The administrator on February 24, 1974 published final regulations for reviewing the air quality impact prior to construction of new facilities, labeled indirect sources, which may generate significant amounts of automobile traffic.[51]

If stationary source controls combined with motor vehicle emission controls cannot guarantee the attainment of statutory ambient air quality standards within an air quality control region, transportation controls must be adopted and such controls will force significant changes on the life styles of many residents of the region.

In April 1973, Governor Rockefeller transmitted a plan, developed in cooperation with Mayor John Lindsay of New York City, to the administrator of the Environmental Protection Agency. The air quality implementation plan [52] for the New York City metropolitan area was approved by the agency in June 1973 and provided for the imposition of transportation controls, including mandatory vehicle emission inspection, tolling of East River and Harlem River bridges in New York City, staggering of work hours, a sharp reduction in the number of midtown Manhattan parking spaces, improved traffic management, designation of exclusive bus lanes, and a selective ban on taxicab cruising in midtown Manhattan. The U.S. Circuit Court of Appeals for the Second Circuit in 1974 upheld the validity of the plan.[53]

Newly elected Mayor Abraham Beame in 1975 sought to have the transportation control plan amended to eliminate the requirements for tolling of the bridges and vehicle emission inspection. Unsuccessful in his attempt to have the plan amended, Mayor Beame and other officials mobilized the New York State congressional delegation to work for the inclusion of a provision—the Moynihan-Holtzman Amendment—in the Clean Air Act Amendments of 1977, which would direct the administrator of the Environmental Protection Agency to delete from a transportation control plan a requirement for the tolling of bridges upon application of the governor of the concerned state. The provision was incorporated into the act, and Governor Hugh Carey on October 19, 1977 notified the administrator, and the requirement was deleted from the plan on November 28, 1977.[54]

The dispute over the transportation control plan was not ended since the Moynihan-Holtzman Amendment required the state to make a new submission to the Environmental Protection Agency outlining other actions that will be taken to reduce air pollution by an amount equal to the reduction that would have resulted from the tolling of the bridges. On June 30, 1980, the agency published a rule-making notice in the *Federal Register* proposing disapproval of the transit element of the New York State Implementation Plan (SIP) and the New York Moynihan-Holtzman Amendment submission.[55] The New York State Departments of Environmental Conservation and Transportation reacted to the proposed disapproval with a sharply worded statement maintaining that the agency's proposed action "is an ad hoc, subjective evaluation of New York State's submission" and the "proposed disapproval is not based upon any promulgated policy statement, definitions or measurable criteria."[56]

The election of Ronald Reagan as president led the Environmental Protection Agency in 1981 to reconsider and reverse its position on the ground that new evidence had been provided by the state that the public transit system would be improved by a $5.8 billion plan to purchase new equipment and make capital improvements.

FEDERAL FINANCIAL ASSISTANCE

The federal government financially assists local governments by categorical grants-in-aid, block grants-in-aid, services-in-aid, in-lieu tax payments, loans, technical assistance, special revenue sharing, general revenue sharing, and exemption of interest paid on municipal bonds from the federal income tax. The last item enables local governments to borrow funds at a lower rate of interest. The revenues of several local governments have increased because of a 1958 U.S. Supreme Court ruling that a local government could tax federally owned real property leased by a private corporation.[57]

The bulk of the federal financial assistance is provided to local governments by categorical grants-in-aid, block grants, special revenue sharing, and general revenue sharing.

Grants-in-Aid

Federal grants-in-aid to state and local governments increased by approximately 15 percent annually between fiscal 1960 and fiscal 1980, from $7 billion to more than $91 billion.[58] In fiscal 1977, local governments received $16,554,395,000 in direct aid from the federal government and many additional billions in the form of federal "pass through" aid from state governments.[59] Implementation of all President Reagan's budget proposals will reduce the annual rate of increase in federal financial assistance to state and local governments to under 7 percent. Furthermore, inflation has resulted in an actual decrease in federal financial assistance when measured in terms of purchasing power. The purchasing power of the $91.8 billion in federal assistance in 1981 was 8.3 percent less than the purchasing power of the $89.8 billion received in fiscal 1980.[60]

Categorical Grants-in-Aid

Considerable criticism has been directed at the categorical grant-in-aid programs since the early 1950s, including complaints of programmatic duplication and lack of coordination. Dr Carl Stenberg, assistant director of the U.S. Advisory Commission on Intergovernmental Relations, attributed "the presence of so many separate or functionally related programs administered by various agencies" to "differences in individual missions and clienteles."[61] Dr. Stenberg highlighted the accountability problem in the following terms: " . . . the highly fragmented intergovernmental assistance program provides many buck-passing opportunities. Local officials can always blame the 'feds' for unpopular actions or policy decisions such as fair share housing programs or community based corrections projects. Both can criticize the insensitivity, unwillingness, or inability of some States to provide needed assistance or authority to their local governments."[62]

One argument advanced in favor of federal categorical grants-in-aid is that the federal government can exert leverage on local governments to target their programs to meet national needs. While such grants may be stimulative and result in the launching of new programs by local governments, Dr. David Walker, assistant director of the U.S. Advisory Commission on Intergovernmental Relations, concluded that grant programs do not produce equity in terms of service delivery.

> Equally fanciful is any notion that the federal aid system as a whole protects the interests of the needy or equalizes levels of public service. The log-rolling style—whether explicit or, more often, implicit— through which most grant programs are adopted simply precludes any careful "targeting" of fiscal resources. "What's in it for me?" is the watchword for Congressmen (and their folks back home), for special interest lobbies, and for bureaucrats as well. Questions of equity are largely ignored in the scramble for benefits. If there were a genuine concern, direct federal performances of the function at least would be raised as a serious issue, but the last time this occurred was in the middle thirties.[63]

Most categorical grant-in-aid programs require substate units to match the federal grants, typically on a one-third local, two-thirds federal basis. A 1980 study by the U.S. General Accounting Office revealed that the matching requirement is not stimulating the recipient units, but is having an adverse impact on the federal, state, and local governments by:

— Screening out those State and local governments most in need of the federal program, but unable to fund the required match. As a result, federal grant funds may be diverted from those grantees that the program was intended to help.
— Distorting the priorities of States and localities, particularly those experiencing budget reductions, by forcing these jurisdictions to reduce resources in nonmatched programs to provide the match to continue or increase federal funding. This distortion process has intensified in recent years with the growth of federal grant program initiatives, reflected by the fact that the minimum non-federal match has increased from 8 to 12 percent of State and local own source spending over the past 10 years.[64]

One condition attached to the typical federal grant-in-aid program is a maintenance-of-effort requirement designed to ensure that the grant funds are employed to finance additional local programs and not to replace local financial support for these programs. A 1980 U.S. General Accounting Office report concluded that local governments experiencing a fiscal crisis or taxpayer revolt are unable to reduce spending for federally supported activities without losing the federal aid and may have to eliminate programs not supported by federal grants or not institute needed reductions in any program.[65]

A total of 31 requirements—affirmative action, citizen participation, environmental protection, equal access to public facilities for the handicapped, payment of prevailing wages, etc.—are attached to federal grant-in-aid programs to promote the achievement of social goals. A 1980 national survey by the author revealed that federal court decisions have not significantly reduced the discretion of local governments, but federal conditional grants-in-aid have reduced significantly the discretionary authority of substate units.[66] Sixty-four percent of the southern respondents and 57 percent of the western respondents reported such a reduction, compared to 44 percent of the northeastern respondents and 41 percent of the north central respondents.[67] Concerning state conditional grants-in-aid, 35 percent of the southern respondents and only 14 percent of the north central respondents reported a reduction in local discretionary authority.[68]

As mentioned in Chapter 3, Thomas Dye and Thomas Hurley found state grants-in-aid to be "more closely associated with size, growth rate, density, age of city, and segregation than federal grants-in-aid."[69] They concluded:

. . . State grants-in-aid appeared more closely associated with urban needs than federal grants-in-aid. . . . This generalization is subject to some exceptions: federal grants-in-aid are more closely associated with public assistance rates, death rates, and aged populations than state grants-in-aid. But even with regard to these indicators of dependent and aged populations, differences between state and federal responsiveness were slight.[70]

Block Grants and Special Revenue Sharing

Responding to criticisms of the categorical grant-in-aid system, Congress in 1966 commenced to fold a number of categorical grant programs into a single broader program labelled a block grant program or special revenue sharing, thereby increasing the discretionary authority of local governments relative to the expenditure of the federal funds.

Although often referred to as the community development block grant program (CDBG), the special revenue-sharing program for community development [71] differs from a conventional block grant program in that a local government is required to submit only a simple application, the U.S. Department of Housing and Community Development may not reject the application of an eligible unit, the recipient unit is not subject to federal administrative audits, and matching and maintenance of effort are not required.

A total of 32 categorical grant-in-aid programs were consolidated into block grant or special revenue-sharing programs for health, employment and training, and community development from 1966 to 1974, and "two other programs—law enforcement and social services—were block grants from the outset."[72] In 1977 and 1978, Congress consolidated grant programs in three additional fields—insular areas, forestry, and the elderly. In 1980 the law enforcement block grant program was terminated, and in 1981, the Reagan administration was successful in persuading Congress to consolidate 57 categorical grant programs into 9 "block" grant programs.[73]

With respect to the special revenue-sharing program for community development, the U.S. General Accounting Office in 1978 concluded that officials in the U.S. Department of Housing and Urban Development did an inadequate job of evaluating applications and discretionary grants made to a number of local governments in nonmetropolitan areas that did not have the most promising programs.[74] A 1980 study by the Congressional Budget Office contained the following findings:

> Local spending under the CDBG program appears to reflect some measures of need but not others. The majority of funds is targeted at poor households, but it is difficult to determine the nature of the benefits these households may derive from the program. In addition,

tracts with a majority of poor households do not account for all, or even most, of the poor households in grantee cities. . . . For at least one limited sample of grantees, . . . there were few clear relationships between measures of city need levels and the proportion of funds spent on different types of projects. This lack of correspondence does not mean that grantees are spending funds inappropriately. It does suggest that the needs to which local officials are responding in setting program priorities may differ from the needs—as represented by the CDBG formula items—to which federal policy responds in distributing CDBG funds.[75]

Concerning the 1977 changes in the program's funding formula, Patricia Dusenbury of the Southern Growth Policies Board and Professor Thad Beyle of the University of North Carolina in 1980 reported that "benefit . . . is associated with a large proportion of pre-40 housing, high population density, and population loss" and "is not significantly related to indicators of urban economic or social conditions or to a city's inadequate housing (units that are crowded or have incomplete plumbing)."[76]

Richard Nathan and Paul Dommel concluded in 1978 that the program represents a decentralization of decision making when compared to categorical grant-in-aid programs, but local officials believe after two years' experience that their discretionary authority is being reduced.[77]

In a major 1978 study, the U.S. Advisory Commission on Intergovernmental Relations reaffirmed its 1967 recommendation that the number of categorical grant programs be reduced and suggested that each program selected for merger should be:

a) closely related in terms of the functional area covered;
b) similar or identical with regard to their program objectives; and
c) linked to the same type(s) of recipient governmental jurisdictions.[78]

Recognizing that initiative for program changes is more apt to come from the President than from Congress, the commission recommended that:

... Congress enact legislation authorizing the President to submit plans for consolidating categorical grant programs to the Congress, that Congress be required to approve or disapprove such plans by resolution within 90 days of submission, and that if approved, such plans [would] go into effect upon approval by the President of the joint resolution.[79]

This proposal for a legislative veto of a presidentially initiated grant consolidation proposal is similar to a legislative veto authorized in 1932 and employed concerning plans for reorganizing the executive branch of the federal government.[80]

General Revenue Sharing

In contrast to federal grant-in-aid programs that promote intergovernmental functional contacts and strengthen the position of bureaucrats on all levels of government administering the programs, the general revenue-sharing program strengthens the ability of local elected officials to control bureaucrats since general revenue-sharing funds cannot be spent by bureaucrats until the local governing body has appropriated the funds.

The State and Local Fiscal Assistance Act of 1972 appropriated $30.2 billion over a five-year period for a program of general revenue sharing with the states and local governments.[81] As an entitlement program, the states and eligible local governments are not required to submit an application to the federal government, provide matching funds, comply with maintenance of efforts requirements, or contend with federal administrative audits. A major argument advanced against the program was the contention that the political accountability maxim would be violated since the units spending the funds are not responsible for raising the funds. Nevertheless, the program was renewed in 1976 for another five years and was renewed for the second time in 1980 for a three-year period with a provision that states would not receive funds in fiscal 1981.[82]

Since the House of Representatives and the Senate were unable to agree upon a common formula for the distribution of funds, both formulas were included in the law, and each state receives the higher amount resulting from the calculations utilizing the two formulas. The House formula is based upon population, urban population, per capita income, state income tax collections, and tax effort. The Senate formula is based upon population, relative income, and tax effort. Until 1980 states received one-third of the general revenue-sharing funds and local governments received two-thirds.

A 1980 report by the U.S. Bureau of the Census revealed that the general revenue-sharing program provides a significant proportion of the funds expended by several cities—Baton Rouge, Louisiana (10.8 percent), Miami, Florida (9.7 percent), New Orleans, Louisiana (7.8 percent), Pittsburgh, Pennsylvania (6.4 percent), and El Paso, Texas (6.2 percent).[83] In fiscal year 1978 more than 75 percent of the general revenue-sharing funds received by local governments were utilized for current expenses; approximately 23 percent were used for capital expenses, and less than 2 percent were used for debt redemption.[84]

A second major argument directed against the program is that funds are not distributed according to need. A 1980 U.S. General Accounting

Office report on the distribution of general revenue-sharing funds among 57 counties in New York based its conclusions upon three measures of need—fiscal effort, fiscal pressure, and per capita income. "Our analysis indicates that there was a tendency to distribute more revenue sharing aid to high 'effort' governments and to low income governments, and there was no observed tendency to target more aid to governments with high fiscal pressures." [85]

A third major argument advanced against the program is that too many local governments with relatively few functional responsibilities receive general revenue-sharing funds. The criticism is directed in particular at midwest townships, many of which are little more than bridge and highway districts, and New England counties that have limited court-related, law enforcement, and welfare functions. Approximately one-third of the eligible local governments are "limited purpose" rather than "general purpose" units.

A Tax Credit Program?

National experience with a tax credit program—as opposed to a tax "deduction" program—dates to the Federal Revenue Act of 1926, which provides eligible taxpayers with an 80 percent credit against the federal inheritance and estate tax for estate and inheritance taxes paid to a state.[86] In 1935 Congress provided for a 90 percent tax credit for employers who paid unemployment taxes to a state.[87] And the Economic Recovery Tax Act of 1981 authorizes urban public transit authorities to utilize sale-lease-backs as a device for selling their investment tax credits and depreciation.[88] For example, a private corporation could purchase buses from a public transportation authority for $10 million by using $2 million of its own funds and $8 million of the authority's funds. Since the corporation holds title to the buses, it may depreciate the total cost of the buses and lease them for a fee to the authority that is responsible for maintenance and operating costs. The authority has gained $2 million, and the corporation can take advantage of tax deductible interest payments and accelerated depreciation over a five-year period under the federal corporate income tax.

A tax credit program can be structured to achieve national objectives without having taxpayer funds flowing to Washington, D.C. to be redistributed to substate units by the federal bureaucracy, which administers grant programs with conditions attached and conducts audits of recipient units to determine compliance with the conditions. To a large extent, a tax credit program could replace conditional grants-in-aid.

Provision can be made in national law for either a full or partial tax credit, and provision also can be made for the type of local tax eligible for a tax credit. Since a 100 percent tax credit in effect would tranfer responsibility for raising funds to Congress, a partial tax credit would be preferable since local elected officials would share some of the responsibility for raising revenue. We suggest a 50 percent federal tax credit for new local taxes as desirable in terms of providing equitable responsibility for raising revenue.

While a case can be made for a national tax credit program that would exclude regressive local taxes, the lack of state authority to levy a tax other than the general property tax, and perhaps sales or excise taxes, suggests that any type of tax should be eligible for tax credits. Congress, of course, could pressure states to allow political subdivisions to levy more progressive taxes by restricting tax credits to these taxes.

Advantages

A national tax credit program would have nine major advantages, when contrasted with federal, conditional grant-in-aid programs.

First, substate units would be afforded the opportunity to raise additional tax revenue without overburdening their taxpayers. The additional revenue also could be raised quickly as needed and used for any legal purpose in contrast to the delays encountered in obtaining federal grants-in-aid and the required compliance with federal conditions.

Second, local elected officials know local conditions better than federal bureaucrats and will ensure that the lack of coordination and duplication associated with grant-in-aid programs do not occur.

Third, political subdivisions would be relieved of the expense of preparing detailed applications for federal conditional grants-in-aid.

Fourth, local governments would be relieved of complying with detailed conditions contained in federal rules and regulations and federal administrative audits.

Fifth, substate units would have a steady source of revenue in contrast to federal grants-in-aid that typically are not funded at authorization levels. In addition, tax credits cannot be denied by federal bureaucrats, whereas applications for federal grants-in-aid may be rejected.

Sixth, local governments would not be subject to distribution of federal funds by formulas that may not be equitable for all units or to the decisions of federal bureaucrats administering discretionary grant programs.

Seventh, a tax credit program can result in a significant drop in the size of the federal bureaucracy as conditional grant-in-aid programs are terminated.

Eighth, total federal spending would be reduced by a tax credit program.

Ninth, a tax credit system has the potential for reducing total government spending since there are no matching requirements as under grant-in-aid programs.

Possible Disadvantages

Whether a tax credit program would have significant disadvantages depends upon the structuring of the program. Federal bureaucrats losing their positions would oppose the program as would special interest groups benefiting from eliminated grant-in-aid programs. Of course, a tax credit program could be established that would supplement rather than replace the grant-in-aid programs and the general revenue-sharing program.

To some, a tax credit program would not be a desirable replacement for conditional grants-in-aid since the benefits of the former would accrue to the local governments that vote for tax increases, regardless of their need for additional revenue, in contrast to many grant-in-aid programs that tend to redistribute fiscal resources geographically on the basis of need. To others, the loss in federal revenue due to a tax credit program would be a disadvantage during an inflationary period.

SUMMARY AND CONCLUSIONS

The delivery of most governmental services has become intergovernmental in nature since most functional responsibilities no longer can be described as exclusively federal or state or local. A major development has been the increasing role played by the federal government in functional areas outside of those delegated to the Congress by Section 8 of Article I of the U.S. Constitution.

Although this chapter has emphasized the growing exercise of preempted powers by Congress, an examination of federal partial preemption statutes reveals that they generally are confined to health and environmental protection, and with the exceptions of these two functional areas local governments generally are not significantly affected by partial federal preemption.

Federal categorical grants-in-aid have had a major impact upon local governments and frequently distort their budgets. The principal criticism directed at federal grant programs involves conditions limiting the discretionary authority of recipient units. In functional areas where local government criticism was the strongest, Congress responded by replacing categorical grant-in-aid programs with block grant and special revenue-sharing programs. If local governments desire additional relief from conditions, they must mobilize their political resources more effectively and persuade Congress to make changes in the programs.

The rhetoric of some local officials notwithstanding, there is no evidence that the substantial expansion of federal power through informal and formal preemption has resulted in the atrophy of local governments. These political subdivisions retain substantial discretionary powers, can influence in a positive manner congressional and federal administrative policies, and will continue to be the chief providers of public services to the citizenry.

We are convinced that a federal tax credit program can prove to be beneficial for the intergovernmental system in the United States. A tax credit program has major advantages, ranging from providing relatively "string free" revenue to local governments to a reduction in total government spending, and merits serious consideration by the national administration and Congress.

To recapitulate, tensions will continue to characterize federal-local relations in the foreseeable future because federal and local officials do not hold a common perception of the nature of most domestic problems or agree on the best solutions. Nevertheless, cooperation between these levels of government will be more common than conflict.

NOTES

1. Formal preemption refers to the authority granted to the Congress by the U.S. Constitution to assume partial or total responsibility for a governmental function. See Joseph F. Zimmerman, "Frustrating National Policy: Partial Federal Preemption" in *The Nationalization of State Government*, ed. Jerome J. Hanus (Lexington, Mass.: Lexington Books, 1981), pp. 75–104.

2. *Atkins v. Kansas*, 191 U.S. 207 at 220–21 (1903). See also *City of Trenton v. New Jersey*, 262 U.S. 182 (1923).

3. Roscoe C. Martin, *The Cities and the Federal System* (New York: Atherton Press, 1965), p. 111.

4. Ibid., p. 191.

5. Ibid., p. 192.

6. *A Catalog of Federal Grant-in-Aid Programs to State and Local Governments: Grants Funded FY 1978* (Washington, D.C.: U.S. Advisory Commission on Intergovernmental Relations, February 1979), p. 1.

7. *Water Quality Act of 1965*, 79 STAT. 903, 33 U.S.C. 1151 (1965 supp.).

8. *Federal Water Pollution Control Amendments of 1972*, 70 STAT. 498, 33 U.S.C. 1151 (1972 supp.).

9. *Air Quality Act of 1967*, 81 STAT. 485, 42 U.S.C. 1857 (1969).

10. *McCulloch v. Maryland*, 4 Wheaton 316 (1819); *Gibbons v. Ogden*, 9 Wheaton 1 (1824).

11. Woodrow Wilson, *Congressional Government: A Study in American Politics* (Boston: Houghton Mifflin, 1925), pp. 36–37.

12. *Maine v. Thiboutot*, 100 S.Ct. 2502 (1980); *Owen v. City of Independence*, 100 S.Ct. 1398 (1980); *Civil Rights Act of 1871*, 42 U.S.C. 1983.

13. *Maine v. Thiboutot*, 100 S.Ct. 2502 at 2514 (1980).

14. Ibid., at 2519–521.

15. *Owen v. City of Independence*, 100 S.Ct. 1398 at 1423 (1980). See also *City of Newport v. Fact Concerts, Incorporated*, 100 S.Ct. 2748 (1981).

16. Gene I. Maeroff, "Integration in Boston Bringing Broad Educational Changes," *New York Times*, October 25, 1980, p. 7.

17. *Bankruptcy Act of 1933*, 47 STAT. 1467, 11 U.S.C. 101 (1933): *Atomic Energy Act of 1946*, 60 STAT. 755, 42 U.S.C. 2011 (1947 supp.).

18. W. Brooke Graves, ed. "Intergovernmental Relations in the United States," *The Annals* 207 (January 1940): 1–218.

19. Richard H. Leach, ed. "Intergovernmental Relations in America Today," *The Annals* 416 (November 1974): 1–169. In particular, see Deil S. Wright, "Intergovernmental Relations: An Analytical Overview," pp. 1–16; Brevard Crihfield and H. Clyde Reeves, "Intergovernmental Relations: A View from the States," pp. 99–107; Joseph F. Zimmerman, "The Metropolitan Area Problem," pp. 133–47.

20. 36 STAT. 961, 16 U.S.C. 552 (1911).

21. *Categorical Grants: Their Role and Design* (Washington, D.C.: U.S. Advisory Commission on Intergovernmental Relations, 1978), pp. 16, 22.

22. G. Homer Durham, Politics and Administration in Intergovernmental Relations," *The Annals* 207 (January 1940): 5.

23. *Categorical Grants*, p. 42.

24. Ibid., pp. 52–53.

25. Charles L. Schultze, "Federal Spending: Past, Present, and Future," in *Setting National Priorities: The Next Ten Years*, eds. Henry Owen and Charles L. Schultze, (Washington, D.C.: Brookings Institution, 1976), p. 367.

26. James L. Buckley, "The Trouble with Federalism: It Isn't Being Tried," *Commonsense* (Summer 1978), p. 13.

27. Ibid., p. 14.

28. *Flammable Fabrics Act*, 81 STAT. 574, 15 U.S.C. 1191 (1967).

29. *United States Grain Standards Act*, 82 STAT. 769, 7 U.S.C. 71 (1968 supp.); *Radiation Control for Health and Safety Act of 1968*, 82 STAT. 1186, 42 U.S.C. 262 (1968 supp.).

30. *Air Quality Act*, 81 STAT. 485, 42 U.S.C. 1857 et seq. (1969).

31. George Manlove, "Industrial Park Wetland Area Jeopardizes Development Plans," *Keene Sentinel* (Keene, N.H.), September 17, 1980, pp. 1, 11.

32. *Safe Drinking Water Act*, 88 STAT. 1665, 42 U.S.C. 200g-2 (1974 supp.).

33. *Hines v. Davidowitz*, 321 U.S. 52 at 67 (1941).

34. *Rice v. Santa Fe Elevator Corporation*, 331 U.S. 218 (1947).

35. *City of Burbank v. Lockheed Air Terminal Incorporated*, 411 U.S. 624 at 632 (1973).

36. *Washington Revised Code*, § § 88.16.170, 88.16.190 (1975 supp.).

37. *Ray v. Atlantic Richfield Company*, 435 U.S. 151 (1978).

38. *Oregon v. Mitchell*, 400 U.S. 112 (1970).

39. Ibid., at 126.

40. Ibid., at 128.

41. *National League of Cities v. Usery*, 426 U.S. 833 (1976).

42. *Chapman v. Houston Welfare Rights Organization*, 441 U.S. 600 (1979).

43. *Voting Rights Act of 1965*, 79 STAT. 437, 42 U.S.C. 1973 (1965 supp.); *Voting Rights Act Amendments of 1970*, 84 STAT. 314, 42 U.S.C. 1973 (1970 supp.); *Voting Rights Act Amendments of 1975*, 89 STAT. 400, 42 U.S.C. 1973 (1975 supp.). For an analysis of the act, see Joseph F. Zimmerman, "The Federal Voting Rights Act and Alternative Election Systems," *William & Mary Law Review* (Summer 1978), pp. 621–60.

44. *Perkins v. Matthews*, 400 U.S. 379 at 404 (1971).

45. *U.S. Constitution*, art. III, § 2.

46. *Congressional Record*, February 21, 1979, p. S1583.

47. Marjorie Hunter, "Senate, in a Surprise Move, Votes to Permit Prayer in Public Schools," *New York Times*, April 6, 1979, p. A14. The Senate subsequently rescinded its

approval of the Helm's amendment to the administration's Department of Education bill, but the U.S. House of Representatives on June 11, 1979 adopted an amendment to the Department of Education bill allowing voluntary prayers in public schools. See Marjorie Hunter, "Prayers in Schools Approved by House," *New York Times*, June 12, 1979, p. B20.

48. Spencer Rich, "8 Bills 'Riders' Seen Curtailing Civil Rights Laws," *Washington Post*, October 16, 1980, pp. A1, A13.

49. William French Smith, "Remarks before the Federal Legal Council," paper presented in Reston, Va., October 29, 1981, pp. 4, 6–7 (mimeographed).

50. *Clean Air Amendments of 1970*, 84 STAT. 1676, 42 U.S.C. 1857 et seq., 49 U.S.C. 1421, 1430 (1970 supp.).

51. 39 *Federal Register* 7271 et seq. (February 24, 1974).

52. 40 CFR 52.1670 (1973). For the latest version of this plan, see *New York State Air Quality Implementation Plan: Transportation Element, New York City Metropolitan Area* (Albany: New York State Department of Environmental Conservation, December 1978).

53. *Friends of the Earth v. EPA*, 499 F2d 1118 (2d Cir. 1974).

54. *Clean Air Act Amendments of 1977*, 91 STAT. 695, 42 U.S.C. 7510 (1977 supp.); 42 *Federal Register* 61453 (December 5, 1977).

55. 45 *Federal Register* 43794-3810 (June 30, 1980).

56. *New York State Comments to the June 30, 1980 Proposed Rulemaking by the U.S. Environmental Protection Agency* (Albany: New York State Department of Environmental Conservation and Department of Transportation, August 29, 1980), p. 2.

57. *Board of Assessors of Riverhead, New York et al. v. Grumman Aircraft Engineering Corporation*, 355 U.S. 814 (1958).

58. *Federal Aid to States: Fiscal Year 1980* (Washington, D.C.: U.S. Department of the Treasury, 1981), p. 1. See also *Perspectives on Intergovernmental Policy and Fiscal Relations* (Washington, D.C.: U.S. General Accounting Office, 1979), p. i.

59. Seymour Sacks, *Recent Trends in Federal and State Aid to Local Governments* (Washington, D.C.: U.S. Advisory Commission on Intergovernmental Relations, 1980), pp. 36–37, 62–75.

60. Al Davis and Frank Tippett, "A Fiscal Note," *Intergovernmental Perspective* (Summer 1980), p. 19.

61. Carl W. Stenberg, "Federal-Local Relations in a Cutback Environment: Issues and Future Directions," paper presented at the Annual Conference of the American Politics Group of the United Kingdom Political Studies Association, Manchester, England, January 4, 1980, p. 5.

62. Ibid., p. 13.

63. David B. Walker, "The Federal Role in Today's Intergovernmental Relations and the Emergence of Dysfunctional Federalism," paper presented at the 86th Annual National Conference on Government, Houston, Texas, November 15, 1980, p. 11.

64. *Proposed Changes in Federal Matching and Maintenance of Effort Requirements for State and Local Governments* (Washington, D.C.: U.S. General Accounting Office, 1980), p. 25.

65. Ibid., p. 61.

66. Joseph F. Zimmerman, *Measuring Local Discretionary Authority* (Washington, D.C.: U.S. Advisory Commission on Intergovernmental Relations, 1981), pp. 29–30.

67. Ibid.

68. Ibid.

69. Thomas R. Dye and Thomas L. Hurley, "The Responsiveness of Federal and State Governments to Urban Problems," *Journal of Politics* 40 (February 1978): 204.

70. Ibid.

71. *Housing and Community Development Act of 1974*, 88 STAT. 633, 42 U.S.C. 5301 (1974 supp.).

72. Stenberg, "Federal-Local Relations," p. 19.

73. *The Community Development Block Grant Program: Discretionary Grant Funds Not Always Given to the Most Promising Small City Programs.* (Washington, D.C.: U.S. General Accounting Office, 1978), p. 15.

74. *Omnibus Budget Reconciliation Act of 1981*, 95 STAT. 357, 31 U.S.C. 1331 (1981).

75. *Community Development Block Grants: Reauthorization Issues* (Washington, D.C.: Congressional Budget Office, U.S. Congress, 1980), p. 39.

76. Patricia J. Dusenbury and Thad L. Beyle, "The Community Development Block Grant Program: Policy by Formula," *State and Local Government Review* 12 (September 1980): 87–88.

77. Richard P. Nathan and Paul R. Dommel, "Federal-Local Relations under Block Grants," *Political Science Quarterly* 93 (Fall 1978): 442. See also Philip Rosenberg, "The Community Development Block Grant Program," *Urban Data Service Report* 9 (November 1977): 1–14.

78. *Summary and Concluding Observations* (Washington, D.C.: U.S. Advisory Commission on Intergovernmental Relations, 1978), p. 16.

79. *Categorical Grants: Their Role and Design* (Washington, D.C.: U.S. Advisory Commission on Intergovernmental Relations, 1978), p. 303.

80. *Legislative Appropriations Act of 1932*, 47 STAT. 382 at 413–14, 5 U.S.C. 133 (y) (1) (1932 supp.).

81. *State and Local Fiscal Assistance Act of 1972*, 86 STAT. 919, 33 U.S.C. 1221 (1972 supp.).

82. John Herbers, "Should Washington Share Revenue with the States?" *New York Times* January 22, 1981, p. B8.

83. U.S. Bureau of the Census, *Expenditures of General Revenue Sharing and Antirecession Fiscal Assistance Funds: 1977–78* (Washington, D.C.: U.S. Government Printing Office, 1980), pp. 97, 99, 102–3, 105.

84. Ibid., p. 2.

85. *How Revenue Sharing Formulas Distribute Aid: Urban-Rural Implications* (Washington, D.C.: U.S. General Accounting Office, 1980), p. 38.

86. *Revenue Act of 1926*, 44 STAT. 9, 48 U.S.C. 845 (1926).

87. *Social Security Act of 1935*, 49 STAT. 620, 42 U.S.C. 301 (1935).

88. *Economic Recovery Tax Act of 1981*, 95 STAT. 399, 26 U.S.C. 103 (1981 supp.).

CHAPTER 6

State-Local Relations:
A Partnership Approach

The governance system on the substate level, particularly within metropolitan areas, is a maze since responsibility is shared by the federal government and three to six tiers of subnational governments: state government; one or more regional special districts; county government(s); cities, towns, villages, and boroughs; special districts within a general purpose political subdivision; school districts; and community school districts within New York City.

Although rationally thinking governmental reformers are convinced the assignment of functional responsibilities is maladroit and advance proposals to eliminate the maze by sorting out and assigning responsibility for functions to specific types of governments, elimination of the maze is an impossibility since no function is entirely local in its impacts and a complex of political forces committed to the status quo is exceptionally strong.

The great governance problem on the subnational level involves an imbalance of state and local interests. States must initiate action to ensure that the interests of the statewide public are advanced yet must frame the action to prevent a significant erosion of local self-government. Developing a proper balance between state authority and local authority has been the goal of reformers since major industrialization and urbanization occurred in the post–Civil War period. The task always has been difficult because of competing perceptions of the proper respective roles of the state and its local governments. Rapidly changing economic, social, and technological conditions in the latter part of the twentieth century make the task increasingly difficult, and some observers may argue the task is impossible in view of the systemic ferment.

EXPANSION OF LOCAL DISCRETIONARY AUTHORITY

The grass roots tradition is revered in the United States, yet local governments historically occupied a highly subordinate role in the governance system, and there is general agreement that granting local units unlimited power by constitutional provision would be unwise. A key characteristic of state-local relations in the typical state during the past three decades has been the legal broadening of the discretionary authority of local governments. In several states, the most profound changes have involved county governments that originally were quasi-municipal corporations lacking legislative powers and serving as administrative arms of the state.

While states generally have broadened the powers of their political subdivisions, the grass roots movement in the 1970s acquired a more important role as voters employed the initiative and the referendum with greater frequency and produced important statewide results in California and Massachusetts. In many other states, the initiative and referendum have been employed only on the local level. In most instances, the initiative and referendum have been employed to restrict the ability of local governments to exercise their discretionary authority by placing limits on property tax revenue, and the popularity of these "direct democracy" devices portends a reduction in the ability of many local elected officials to exercise their discretionary powers fully.

Citizens' and local officials' unhappiness with stringent state control of political subdivisions was responsible for the movement, commencing in the nineteenth century, to prevent state legislative interference with local governments and to provide them with additional discretionary authority. The case for local self-government is supported by the diversity of local conditions, which makes statewide uniformity in all functional areas undesirable if local problems are to be solved and services delivered to the citizenry in the most economic and efficient manner. More recently, the public choice theory was developed, which innately advocates broad local discretionary authority.[1] Public choice theorists favor a large number of small units of local government on the grounds that such units maximise citizen participation, governmental responsiveness to citizens, and choice of residential location on the basis of services offered and taxes levied. This theory, of course, is largely predicated on the existence of a broad grant of discretionary authority by the state to its general purpose political subdivisions.

An examination of state-local relations leads to the conclusion that the relations are not based upon a systematic theory but rather are the product of historical evolution on a piecemeal basis with adjustments being made periodically to meet emerging problems and changing conditions. A great need exists for a model whose implementation would ensure a proper balance of state and local interests and relieve the state legislature of the inordinate burden of considering numerous local bills and relying upon the legislative delegation from the concerned units for advice on the action to be taken on the bills.

A STATE-LOCAL RELATIONS MODEL

The analysis contained in the preceding chapters serves as the basis for a positive approach to the reform of state-local relations involving:

Constitutional prohibition or provision for a local veto of special legislation unless requested by the governing body of the concerned local units;

Constitutional devolution of all powers capable of devolution upon general purpose political subdivisions subject to preemption by general law;

Constitutional authorization for classified legislation provided there are no more than three classes of local governments and at least three political subdivisions in each class;

Constitutional requirement for the enactment by the state legislature of a code of restrictions upon local government powers;

Recodification of state laws clearly identifying powers totally or partially preempted by the state legislature;

Partial or total state reimbursement of added costs associated with state mandates;

Removal of constitutional debt, levy, and tax limits on local governments;

Creation of a state boundary commission;

Reservation to the state legislature of authority to establish areawide governments; and

State-established minimum levels of service provisions in the most important functional areas.

Constitutional safeguards to prevent inappropriate action by the state legislature that would erode local discretionary authority are absolutely essential. Particularly helpful in the typical state would be a shortening and simplification—removal of ephemeral and statutorylike provisions and restrictions upon local governments—of the state constitution since such action would do much to revitalize state and local governments.

Special Legislation

Long experience with special legislation demonstrated conclusively that the state legislature cannot be entrusted with this power because the power will be abused. A need exists for special laws, yet the need does not have to be satisfied by granting the legislature unrestricted authority to enact special laws.

To supply the flexibility inherent in special legislation, the legislature should be authorized by the state constitution to enact a special law upon the petition of the governing body of the concerned general purpose political subdivision, or the special law enacted by the legislature should be subject to an absolute veto by the governing body of the local unit. The latter provision makes the special act an acceptance statute differing from the generally employed acceptance statute, described in Chapter 2, that may be adopted by any local government or a specific class of local governments.

To reduce the burden placed upon the state legislature by requests for special legislation, local elected officials must be disciplined by the local government committees of the state legislature not to seek special legislation in an area falling under their discretionary authority. In part, the problems could be reduced by recodification of state laws to define more clearly powers devolved upon local governments and powers preempted by the state legislature.

Two less desirable alternatives exist for handling the special legislation problem. First, the state legislature by an extramajority vote of each house could be authorized by the state constitution to enact a special law upon the receipt of a message from the governor certifying the existence of a genuine emergency necessitating the enactment of the special law. Second, local governments could be granted a suspensory veto over special laws; that is, if the local governing body disapproved a special law, it would be returned to the state legislature, which could reenact the law and send it to the governor for his action.

Devolution of Powers

Of the various methods of ensuring that local political subdivisions will be granted broad discretionary powers, the devolution of powers approach is the most satisfactory as demonstrated by experience. While this approach is a legislative supremacy approach, it can incorporate a decentralization model at one extreme should the state legislature fail to exercise its powers of preemption or a centralized model if the powers of preemption are exercised fully. The approach in practice tends to be more decentralized than centralized and generally takes the judiciary out of its role as the arbiter of state-local disputes provided the legislature periodically reexamines the powers of general purpose local governments and exercises its powers of preemption where necessary.

To guarantee that there will not be undue judicial interference with the powers devolved upon local political units, the constitutional provision specifically can reverse the Ultra Vires Rule and stipulate that an *Imperium in Imperio* is not to be created by judicial action.

The narrow judicial interpretation of local discretionary authority in several states is the principal reason accounting for the large number of local or special bills enacted into law each year by the state legislature. In the extreme case of Rhode Island's legislature, the end product of the practice of enacting special acts is a separate set of laws for each general purpose local government superseding many sections of the general laws.

A particularly difficult problem is the issuance by the highest court in a state of conflicting decisions interpreting the scope of local discretionary authority. When faced by court decisions broadly and narrowly interpreting the scope of local discretionary authority, the corporation counsel or local government attorney will be cautious and suggest the securing of a special state law, thereby contributing to the overload of the state legislature. This problem is most acute in states with a constitutional limit on the length of the legislative session.

In devolving powers upon general purpose local governments by constitutional provision, care must be exercised in framing the provision to permit eligible local units to exercise the devolved powers without the necessity of adopting a new charter since the units may be satisfied with the existing charters yet desire to exercise all devolved powers and to supersede certain state laws. The Ultra Vires Rule (Dillon's Rule) should be replaced except in areas reserved to the state legislature by the state constitution and the areas preempted by the state legislature by means of general laws.

With respect to charters, the state legislature should provide for the adoption of a broad variety of optional charters by local governments since the adoption of a charter under the optional charter law can be accomplished more rapidly and at less expense than the drafting and adopting of a charter by a local government. Short optional charters, confined to fundamentals, are preferable.

Combined with the prohibition of special legislation outlined above and other elements of the model for state-local relations, the devolution of powers approach can produce in a satisfactory manner a balance of state and local political power.

To assist local government attorneys and officials to understand the limits placed by the state legislature upon local discretionary authority, the state constitution should direct the legislature to enact and update periodically a code of restrictions clearly defining the restrictions placed upon the exercise of local discretionary authority.

Classified Legislation

To reduce the need for special legislation and provide a degree of uniformity among similar groups of political subdivisions, the constitutional local government article in the typical state should authorize the state legislature to group local governments into a maximum of three classes based upon population provided there are at least three political subdivisions in each class.

Classified legislation is not inherently bad. If groups of cities with a population over 500,000 have problems not experienced by other cities while cities under 25,000 have common problems, classified legislation can serve a legitimate purpose by making legal distinctions between groups of substate units.

The maximum number of classes of general purpose local governments in the typical state should be three in order to prevent the legislature from establishing a separate class for each unit of government. To prevent abuses associated with special legislation in the past, each class should have a minimum of three units. Under no circumstance should the local government article of the state constitution be framed to allow judicial interpretation to place a single local government in a class.

Code of Restrictions

Surveys of local elected officials by the author reveal that one reason they seek special legislation is that they are uncertain about the extent of their powers. Advised by the corporation counsel or local government attorney, both of whom tend to be conservative and cautious in interpreting grants of powers, local officials decide to "play it safe" by securing the enactment of a special law authorizing the unit to undertake an activity or provide a service.

Bond counsels also are conservative in interpreting the grant of local discretionary authority, as we saw with reference to Vermont in Chapter 2, and advise the concerned officials to seek the enactment of authorizing state legislation should the bond counsels have the slightest doubt as to the authority of the local unit and/or its officials.

To clarify the extent of local discretionary authority, the local government article of the state constitution should mandate the state legislature to enact a code of restrictions upon local government powers and periodically—perhaps every five years—review and amend the code. A code of restrictions would be most helpful in reassuring local officials of the extent of their powers and also should reduce the number of occasions on which bond counsels advise the local government to seek the enactment of a special law. With a code, power exercised by local officials can become the equivalent of power potential.

Recodification of State Laws

The municipal laws of several states are in need of recodification, and surveys of officials in the 50 states, conducted by the author, reveal that these laws are not recodified often and typically are in need of major revision to remove obsolete and conflicting provisions.

The various municipal laws in New York State—County Law (1972), General City Law (1968), General Municipal Law (1977), Local Finance Law (1968), Municipal Home Rule Law (1969), Statute of Local Governments (1969), Optional County Law (1956), Second Class Cities Law (1952), Town Law (1965), and Village Law (1973)—are lengthy and contain complex and conflicting provisions. As a result, local government officials often are confused with respect to the extent of their legal powers. Some local officials with long experience take advantage of the divergent provisions in the various general laws and operate under one set of laws for one purpose and under a second set of laws for another purpose. One undesirable consequence is the citizens' lack of understanding of the local governance system.

A careful recodification of a state's local government laws undertaken in conjunction with the enactment of a code of restrictions upon local governments would greatly facilitate citizens' and local government officials' understanding of the extent of local discretionary authority.

State Mandate Reimbursement

As described in Chapters 2 and 3, the greatest irritant in state-local relations is the state mandate. Although not all mandates increase the cost of operating local governments or result only in a minor cost increase, certain mandates significantly raise local government expenditures.

State mandates are justifiable in functional areas where the importance of the functions demands the provision of services on a uniform basis statewide and reliance upon local discretion to provide the services would result in the services not being provided by some political subdivisions and provision on a nonuniform basis by other subdivisions.

In view of the limited ability of numerous local governments to raise revenue directly on an equitable basis, state mandates imposing significant additional costs on local governments should provide for full reimbursement by the state since the local governments in effect are acting as agents of the state in performing the mandated activities and the state would directly have to provide the functions in the absence of local governments. An alternative approach would be the adoption by states of the provision in the Alaska Constitution stipulating that "local acts necessitating appropriations by a political subdivision may not become effective unless approved by a majority of the qualified voters voting thereon in the sub-division affected." [2]

Removal of Constitutional Restrictions

Reckless financing, as well as corruption, in the nineteenth century is responsible for the various fiscal limits—debt, levy, and tax—placed upon local governments by state constitutions. While these restrictions may have been justifiable at the time of their adoption, evidence that there is a general need for constitutional restrictions today is lacking. On the contrary, current evidence demonstrates that these restrictions create hardships for financially distressed units, particularly the older central cities with large numbers of high-cost citizens, and in many instances have been evaded totally or partially by pragmatic substate officials and legislative ingenuity. Tax limits alone are undesirable because they encourage reckless borrowing.

Removal of constitutional restrictions upon the state government and its political subdivisions in most instances will eliminate the need for public authorities which, as described in Chapter 4, tend to be accountable to no one, fractionalize responsibility, and result in higher costs because of frequent reliance upon moral obligation bonds described in Chapter 3.

State Boundary Commissions

Chapter 4 described boundary commissions and their activities. While there has been strong local government opposition to such commissions in a few states, the commissions offer the best prospects for flexibly adjusting local government boundaries in accordance with changing conditions.

In most states, local boundaries are the result of historical accidents, natural features, or a deliberate decision to limit the size of local governments in terms of available means of transportation such as the location of county boundaries at the end of a one-day horse ride from the county seat. Whereas current local boundaries at one time may have made sense, urbanization and modern communications and transportation systems have removed the rationale for many current boundaries.

Two major questions regarding local government boundaries are raised. First, are some units of local government too small in terms of population to be viable units offering a range of services considered essential by most citizens? Second, does competition between cities for annexation of the same land and defensive incorporations suggest that local government boundary problems are not being solved in the most rational and efficient manner?

One of the most serious governmental problems on the local level, in terms of accountability and responsibility, is the product of a proliferation of special districts other than school districts; over 27,000 such districts are in existence. These districts reduce the discretionary authority of local governments, may fragment responsibility to the extent that services are not provided in the most economical manner, are less visible to the citizenry, and produce coordination problems. The state boundary commission should be granted the authority to dissolve existing special districts, subject to bondholders' approval if bonds are outstanding, if accountability and responsibility are to be improved and services provided at a lower cost by other governmental units. Where a special district exists within the confines of a county, abolition of the district and its replacement by a county service and tax district would be highly desirable. In addition, the commission should be granted jurisdiction over the creation of special districts.

Areawide Governments

The growing together of urbanized areas to form metropolitan areas makes constitutional authorization for the state legislature essential to establish areawide governments where needed. With problems overspilling local political boundaries and interlocal cooperation unable to resolve all such problems, the alternatives are state assumption of responsibility for solving the problems or the establishment of an areawide government with sufficient areal jurisdiction to cope with the problems. To keep functions as close to the citizenry as possible, it is preferable to create substate units with sufficient areal jurisdiction and adequate powers than to transfer functional or regulatory responsibility to the heights of the state government. In several states, state-controlled regional public authorities could be converted into popularly controlled multifunctional areawide governments.

State Minimum Service Levels

For many years, states have had minimum standards in the fields of education, finance, and personnel to ensure an acceptable quality of education, prevention of financial irregularities, and selection of the most competent personnel by local governments. While any state mandate imposing costs upon local governments evokes controversy, the state legislature should not shy away from the establishment of minimum service levels in important areas—such as health and environmental protection— since local officials desiring reelection may be hesitant to authorize the expenditure of funds required to provide services meeting what are perceived to be generally minimum levels of service. In each functional field where the state legislature establishes a minimum level of service, political subdivisions should be permitted to provide a higher level of service and issue regulations with standards exceeding the mandated state standards.

A DEFENDER OF LOCAL DISCRETIONARY AUTHORITY

Implementation of the foregoing model will provide substate elected officials with sufficient discretionary authority to cope with problems caused by rapidly changing conditions and relieve the state legislature of the burden of dealing with most bills previously filed to solve local problems. Nevertheless, the model is not entirely self-executing, and the judiciary will continue to play a major referee role in many states in the foreseeable future since the demands upon the time of the state legislature probably will prevent it from reassessing the distribution of political power between the state and its political subdivisions on a systematic and continuing basis. As a consequence, the courts will be called upon to determine the dividing line between state and local powers where there is a joint state-local concern and conflict. Although the Alaska Constitution totally incorporated the devolution of powers approach, the Alaska Supreme Court in 1974 converted the devolution of powers into a type of *Imperium in Imperio*.[3]

Courts must weigh the intramural and extramural aspects of the exercise of a power by a local government as well as the intent of the framers of the enabling constitutional or statutory provision(s) in question. It would be preferable to have state-local disputes handled on a political basis by the state legislature rather than on a legal basis by the courts.

Substate general purpose units are in palpable need of a discretionary authority paraclete. Experience in New York State since 1979 clearly demonstrates that the attorney general is the state official best qualified to serve as a defender and promoter of local discretionary authority since the attorney general issues opinions that should influence courts in the event they are called upon to resolve a conflict over the respective powers of the state and its general purpose political subdivisions.

The attorney general can provide the courts with guidance concerning the intent of the framers of the local government constitutional and/or statutory provisions and ensure that judges educated in Dillon's Rule understand that the devolution of powers approach to local discretionary authority is designed to reverse the Ultra Vires Rule except in the instances where the state constitution reserved authority to the legislature or the legislature affirmatively exercised its powers of preemption by general law.

A PARTNERSHIP APPROACH

In conclusion, the typical state in the foreseeable future will be neither a silent partner nor a paternalistic partner in its relationships with political subdivisions since the seriousness of local problems in general will necessitate a genuine partnership approach for their effective resolution. Such an approach, however, will result in an erosion of the locally controlling sphere of power since conditions in the last two decades of the twentieth century will make the complete insulation of general purpose local governments from state interference impossible. A few states—Utah is a prime example—historically did not "meddle in local affairs," but rapidly occurring developments, including partial federal preemption, are forcing states to play a larger role in the substate governance system.

While states continue to hold paramount power on the subnational level, the epoch of state centralization has ended in spite of attempts by pertinacious state officials to centralize control. General purpose local governments, however, will not be entirely free of state control since political power neither can be completely centralized nor totally decentralized. The two competing theories—centralization and decentralization—will continue to influence the assignment of functional responsibility, and tensions will characterize state-local relations, particularly with respect to the transfer of fiscal resources through state categorical grants-in-aid and state revenue sharing. State intervention in the local governance system is inevitable on occasion because of the state's special responsibility to ensure that actions taken by one local government do not cause problems for other local governments or abridge the rights of minorities.

The state's role in the local governance system should be primarily that of a facilitator and, only where essential, that of an initiator as local government should continue to be the principal deliverers of services to citizens. In practice, a type of federation exists in each state because of necessity. It is impossible for the state to control all local governments tightly, and an attempt to do so would be unwise.

The Ultra Vires Rule will become anachronistic by the year 2000 if states adopt the model of state-local relations outlined in this chapter; local governments will then become a coordinate element in the governance system. The greatest degree of local discretionary authority will involve structure of government and functions inherently intramural. Experience with a broad grant of discretionary authority demonstrates that local officials generally have been conservative in the exercise of the powers granted. It is unrealistic to anticipate that local officials in a state with an Ultra Vires Rule tradition will immediately take full advantage of the new powers flowing from adoption by the state of the model outlined in this chapter. Even if the tradition is overcome, financial restraints will continue to limit the ability of numerous local governments to take full advantage of the discretionary authority devolved upon them by the state constitution and statutes.

Fluidity will characterize federal-state-local relations in the foreseeable future since the delivery of most services to citizens will have intergovernmental elements. A movement toward converting federal categorical grants into block grants, if successful, will reduce the controls typically associated with a growing centralization of fiscal resources.

In sum, the local governance system in the United States has proved to be a resilient and kaleidoscopic one allowing multiple units and levels of government to play roles in solving problems and providing services, but the system will continue to be viewed as a labyrinth by reformers urging the state to "rationalize" the system.

NOTES

1. See Charles M. Tiebout, "A Pure Theory of Local Expenditures," *Journal of Political Economy* 64 (October 1956): 416–24; Robert L. Bish and Vincent Ostrom, *Understanding Urban Government: Metropolitan Reform Reconsidered* (Washington, D.C.: American Enterprise Institute for Public Policy Research, 1973).

2. *Constitution of Alaska*, art. II § 19.

3. *Jefferson v. State*, 527 P.2d 37 (1974).

Appendix

TABLE A.1 States Classified by Region, Restriction on Length of Legislative Session, Degree of State Dominance of Fiscal Partnership, and State-Local Legal Relationship, 1980

States	Region[a]	Restriction on Legislative Session[b]	Degree of State Dominance of Fiscal Partnership[c]	State-Local Legal Relationship[d]
Alabama	3	1	1	3
Alaska	4	2	1	1
Arizona	4	2	2	1
Arkansas	3	1	1	3
California	4	2	3	1
Colorado	4	2	2	1
Connecticut	1	1	2	1
Delaware	3	1	1	2
Florida	3	1	2	1
Georgia	3	1	2	1
Hawaii	4	1	1	1
Idaho	4	2	2	1
Illinois	2	2	2	1
Indiana	2	1	2	3
Iowa	2	2	2	1
Kansas	2	2	2	1
Kentucky	3	1	1	3
Louisiana	3	1	1	1
Maine	1	2	2	1
Maryland	3	1	2	1
Massachusetts	1	2	3	1
Michigan	2	2	2	1
Minnesota	2	1	2	1
Mississippi	3	1	1	3
Missouri	2	1	2	1
Montana	4	1	3	1
Nebraska	2	1	3	1
Nevada	4	1	2	3[e]
New Hampshire	1	1	3	1
New Jersey	1	2	3	2

(continued)

[a]1 = Northeast, 2 = North Central, 3 = South, 4 = West.
[b]1 = yes, 2 = no.
[c]1 = state dominant fiscal partner, 2 = state strong fiscal partner, 3 = state junior partner.
[d]1 = constitutional grant of power, 2 = statutory grant of power, 3 = Dillion's Rule state.
[e]The constitutional provision has not been implemented by the legislature.

States	Region[a]	Restriction on Legislative Session[b]	Degree of State Dominance of Fiscal Partnership[c]	State-Local Legal Relationship[d]
New Mexico	4	1	1	1
New York	1	2	3	1
North Carolina	3	2	1	2
North Dakota	2	1	2	1
Ohio	2	2	3	1
Oklahoma	3	1	1	1
Oregon	4	2	2	1
Pennsylvania	1	2	2	1
Rhode Island	1	1	2	1
South Carolina	3	2	1	1
South Dakota	2	1	3	3[f]
Tennessee	3	1	2	1
Texas	3	1	2	1
Utah	4	1	2	1
Vermont	1	2	2	3[g]
Virginia	3	1	2	2
Washington	4	1	2	1
West Virginia	3	1	1	1
Wisconsin	2	2	2	1
Wyoming	4	1	2	1

[f]The constitutional provision has not been utilized.

[g]The statutory provision is a dead letter because of rulings by bond counsels.

Source: Joseph F. Zimmerman, *Measuring Local Discretionary Authority* (Washington, D.C.: U.S. Advisory Commission on Intergovernmental Relations, 1981), p. 33.

TABLE A.2 Index of Town Discretionary Authority by States, 1980

States	Structure	Functional Areas	Finance	Personnel
U.S. (Unweighted average)	2.65	2.43	3.41	2.40
Alabama	4.50	3.00	2.00	1.75
Alaska	—	—	—	—
Arizona	4.25	2.00	1.75	1.75
Arkansas	5.00	4.00	3.00	2.00
California	—	—	—	—
Colorado	2.50	3.00	3.50	2.00
Connecticut	1.00	1.00	3.50	2.00
Delaware	1.00	2.00	3.00	4.00
Florida	—	—	—	—
Georgia	—	—	—	—
Hawaii	—	—	—	—
Idaho	—	—	—	—
Illinois	1.00	2.00	1.50	2.50
Indiana	4.50	2.50	4.00	2.00
Iowa	—	—	—	—
Kansas	—	—	—	—
Kentucky	—	—	—	—
Louisiana	1.00	1.50	3.00	2.00
Maine	1.50	1.50	2.00	2.00
Maryland	—	—	—	—
Massachusetts	1.00	2.00	5.00	3.00
Michigan	—	—	—	—
Minnesota	—	—	—	—
Mississippi	2.00	2.00	4.00	2.00
Missouri	—	—	—	—
Montana	1.00	2.00	5.00	2.00
Nebraska	—	—	—	—
Nevada	3.00	4.00	4.00	4.00
New Hampshire	2.00	1.75	4.00	1.00
New Jersey	3.00	2.00	4.00	2.00

(continued)

Note: Scale is 1 to 5 with 1 indicating the greatest degree of freedom from state control and 5 indicating the smallest degree of freedom.

Source: Joseph F. Zimmerman, *Measuring Local Discretionary Authority* (Washington, D.C.: U.S. Advisory Commission on Intergovernmental Relations, 1981), p. 56.

TABLE A.2 *(continued)*

States	Structure	Functional Areas	Finance	Personnel
New Mexico	—	—	—	—
New York	1.50	3.00	3.75	4.00
North Carolina	1.00	1.00	2.50	1.00
North Dakota	—	—	—	—
Ohio	—	—	—	—
Oklahoma	4.00	2.50	3.50	2.50
Oregon	—	—	—	—
Pennsylvania	—	—	—	—
Rhode Island	1.00	2.00	5.00	3.00
South Carolina	4.00	2.00	2.00	2.00
South Dakota	5.00	3.00	5.00	3.00
Tennessee	3.00	3.00	3.00	2.00
Texas	3.50	2.50	4.00	2.50
Utah	2.50	2.00	3.50	2.00
Vermont	5.00	3.00	3.00	3.00
Virginia	3.50	2.50	3.00	2.25
Washington	—	—	—	—
West Virginia	5.00	3.00	5.00	3.00
Wisconsin	3.00	5.00	4.00	5.00
Wyoming	1.00	3.00	3.00	2.00

TABLE A.3 Index of Village Discretionary Authority by States, 1980

States	Structure	Functional Areas	Finance	Personnel
U.S. (Unweighted average)	2.84	2.55	3.46	2.50
Alabama	—	—	—	—
Alaska	—	—	—	—
Arizona	—	—	—	—
Arkansas	—	—	—	—
California	—	—	—	—
Colorado	—	—	—	—
Connecticut	—	—	—	—
Delaware	—	—	—	—
Florida	—	—	—	—
Georgia	—	—	—	—
Hawaii	—	—	—	—
Idaho	—	—	—	—
Illinois	1.80	2.30	2.30	2.50
Indiana	—	—	—	—
Iowa	—	—	—	—
Kansas	—	—	—	—
Kentucky	—	—	—	—
Louisiana	1.00	1.50	3.00	2.00
Maine	4.50	4.50	2.00	4.50
Maryland	—	—	—	—
Massachusetts	—	—	—	—
Michigan	2.00	1.50	2.00	1.50
Minnesota*	1.00	2.00	3.00	2.00
Mississippi	2.00	2.00	4.00	2.00
Missouri	5.00	4.00	3.00	3.00
Montana	—	—	—	—
Nebraska	5.00	5.00	5.00	5.00
Nevada	—	—	—	—
New Hampshire	5.00	3.50	4.50	1.00
New Jersey	3.00	2.00	4.00	2.00

(continued)

*Officially entitled statutory cities.

Note: Scale is 1 to 5 with 1 indicating the greatest degree of freedom from state control and 5 indicating the smallest degree of freedom.

Source: Joseph F. Zimmerman, *Measuring Local Discretionary Authority* (Washington, D.C.: U.S. Advisory Commission on Intergovernmental Relations, 1981), p. 57.

TABLE A.3 *(continued)*

States	Structure	Functional Areas	Finance	Personnel
New Mexico	—	—	—	—
New York	1.50	3.00	4.00	4.00
North Carolina	1.00	1.00	2.50	1.00
North Dakota	—	—	—	—
Ohio	1.00	1.50	2.50	1.50
Oklahoma	—	—	—	—
Oregon	—	—	—	—
Pennsylvania	—	—	—	—
Rhode Island	—	—	—	—
South Carolina	—	—	—	—
South Dakota	—	—	—	—
Tennessee	—	—	—	—
Texas	3.50	2.50	4.00	2.50
Utah	—	—	—	—
Vermont	5.00	2.00	5.00	3.00
Virginia	—	—	—	—
Washington	—	—	—	—
West Virginia	5.00	3.00	5.00	3.00
Wisconsin	1.00	2.00	3.00	2.00
Wyoming	—	—	—	—

TABLE A.4 Index of Township Discretionary Authority by States, 1980

States	Structure	Functional Areas	Finance	Personnel
U.S. (Unweighted average)	4.35	3.92	4.29	3.65
Alabama	—	—	—	—
Alaska	—	—	—	—
Arisona	—	—	—	—
Arkansas	—	—	—	—
California	—	—	—	—
Colorado	—	—	—	—
Connecticut	—	—	—	—
Delaware	—	—	—	—
Florida	—	—	—	—
Georgia	—	—	—	—
Hawaii	—	—	—	—
Idaho	—	—	—	—
Illinois	4.30	4.00	4.00	4.00
Indiana	4.50	3.50	4.00	2.00
Iowa	5.00	3.50	4.30	4.50
Kansas	5.00	5.00	5.00	5.00
Kentucky	—	—	—	—
Louisana	—	—	—	—
Maine	—	—	—	—
Maryland	—	—	—	—
Massachusetts	—	—	—	—
Michigan	3.50	3.00	4.00	3.00
Minnesota	4.50	4.50	5.00	4.00
Mississippi	—	—	—	—
Missouri	5.00	5.00	5.00	5.00
Montana	—	—	—	—
Nebraska	5.00	5.00	5.00	5.00
Nevada	—	—	—	—
New Hampshire	—	—	—	—
New Jersey	3.00	2.00	4.00	2.00

(continued)

Note: Scale is 1 to 5 with 1 indicating the greatest degree of freedom from state control and 5 indicating the smallest degree of freedom.

Source: Joseph F. Zimmerman, *Measuring Local Discretionary Authority* (Washington, D.C.: U.S. Advisory Commission on Intergovernmental Relations, 1981), p. 58.

TABLE A.4 *(continued)*

States	Structure	Functional Areas	Finance	Personnel
New Mexico	—	—	—	—
New York	—	—	—	—
North Carolina	—	—	—	—
North Dakota	3.70	3.00	3.50	2.00
Ohio	5.00	4.50	4.50	3.50
Oklahoma	—	—	—	—
Oregon	—	—	—	—
Pennsylvania	3.00	3.00	2.50	2.50
Rhode Island	—	—	—	—
South Carolina	—	—	—	—
South Dakota	5.00	5.00	5.00	5.00
Tennessee	—	—	—	—
Texas	—	—	—	—
Utah	—	—	—	—
Vermont	—	—	—	—
Virginia	—	—	—	—
Washington	—	—	—	—
West Virginia	—	—	—	—
Wisconsin	—	—	—	—
Wyoming	—	—	—	—

TABLE A.5   Index of Borough Discretionary Authority by States, 1980

States	Structure	Functional Areas	Finance	Personnel
U.S. (Unweighted average)	2.50	2.50	2.83	2.17
Alabama	—	—	—	—
Alaska*	—	—	—	—
Arizona	—	—	—	—
Arkansas	—	—	—	—
California	—	—	—	—
Colorado	—	—	—	—
Connecticut	2.00	2.00	2.00	2.00
Delaware	—	—	—	—
Florida	—	—	—	—
Georgia	—	—	—	—
Hawaii	—	—	—	—
Idaho	—	—	—	—
Illinois	—	—	—	—
Indiana	—	—	—	—
Iowa	—	—	—	—
Kansas	—	—	—	—
Kentucky	—	—	—	—
Louisiana	—	—	—	—
Maine	—	—	—	—
Maryland	—	—	—	—
Massachusetts	—	—	—	—
Michigan	—	—	—	—
Minnesota	—	—	—	—
Mississippi	—	—	—	—
Missouri	—	—	—	—
Montana	—	—	—	—
Nebraska	—	—	—	—
Nevada	—	—	—	—
New Hampshire	—	—	—	—
New Jersey	3.00	2.00	4.00	2.00

(continued)

*Alaska boroughs are the equivalent of counties in other states.

Note: Scale is 1 to 5 with 1 indicating the greatest degree of freedom from state control and 5 indicating the smallest degree of freedom.

Source: Joseph F. Zimmerman, *Measuring Local Discretionary Authority* (Washington, D.C.: U.S. Advisory Commission on Intergovernmental Relations, 1981), p. 58.

181

TABLE A.5 *(continued)*

States	Structure	Functional Areas	Finance	Personnel
New Mexico	—	—	—	—
New York	—	—	—	—
North Carolina	—	—	—	—
North Dakota	—	—	—	—
Ohio	—	—	—	—
Oklahoma	—	—	—	—
Oregon	—	—	—	—
Pennsylvania	2.50	3.50	2.50	2.50
Rhode Island	—	—	—	—
South Carolina	—	—	—	—
South Dakota	—	—	—	—
Tennessee	—	—	—	—
Texas	—	—	—	—
Utah	—	—	—	—
Vermont	—	—	—	—
Virginia	—	—	—	—
Washington	—	—	—	—
West Virginia	—	—	—	—
Wisconsin	—	—	—	—
Wyoming	—	—	—	—

BIBLIOGRAPHY

BOOKS AND MONOGRAPHS

Altshuler, Alan A. *Community Control: The Black Demand for Participation in Large American Cities*. New York: Pegasus, 1970.

American County Action for Home Rule. Washington, D.C.: National Association of Counties, 1962.

Archer, Jules, *Washington vs. Main Street: The Power Struggle between Federal and Local Power*. New York: Thomas Y. Crowell, 1975.

Baldinger, Stanley. *Planning and Governing the Metropolis: The Twin Cities Experience*. New York: Praeger, 1971.

Banfield, Edward C. *The Unheavenly City: The Nature and Future of Our Urban Crisis*. Boston: Little Brown, 1968.

Banfield, Edward C. *The Unheavenly City Revisited*. Boston: Little Brown, 1974.

Beasley, Kenneth E. *State Supervision of Municipal Debt in Kansas: A Case Study*. Lawrence: Governmental Research Center, University of Kansas, 1961.

Benson, George C. S. *The Politics of Urbanism: The New Federalism*. Woodbury, N.Y.: Baron's Educational Series, 1972.

Bingham, David A. *Constitutional Municipal Home Rule in Arizona*. Tucson: Bureau of Business and Public Research, University of Arizona, 1960.

Birkhead, Guthrie S., Campbell, Alan K., and Weissman, Marsha. *Massachusetts Substate Government: A Report to the Secretary of Environmental Affairs*. Syracuse, N.Y.: Maxwell Graduate School, Syracuse University, 1972.

Bish, Robert L., and Ostrom, Vincent. *Understanding Urban Government: Metropolitan Reform Reconsidered*. Washington, D.C.: American Enterprise Institute for Public Policy Research, 1973.

Bollens, John C. *American County Government*. Beverly Hills: Sage Publications, 1969.

Bollens, John C. *States and the Metropolitan Problem: A Report to the Governors' Conference*. Chicago: Council of State Government, 1956.

The Book of the States: 1980–1981. Lexington, Council of State Governments, 1980.

Braden, George D., and Cohn, Rubin G. *The Illinois Constitution: An Annotated and Comparative Analysis.* Urbana: Institute of Government and Public Affairs, University of Illinois, 1969.

Brown, Peter G. *Personal Liability of Public Officials, Sovereign Immunity, and Compensation for Loss.* Columbus, Ohio: Academy for Contemporary Problems, 1977.

Campbell, Alan K., and Bahl, Roy W., eds. *State and Local Government: The Political Economy of Reform.* New York: The Free Press, 1976.

Campbell, Alan K., ed. *The States and the Urban Crisis.* Englewood Cliffs, N.J.: Prentice-Hall, 1970.

Carroll, James D., and Campbell, Richard W., eds. *Intergovernmental Administration: 1976.* Syracuse, N.Y.: Maxwell Graduate School of Citizenship and Public Affairs, Syracuse University, 1976.

Cease, Ronald C. *A Report on State and Provincial Boundary Review Boards.* Portland, Oreg.: Portland State College, 1968.

Center for Policy Research and Analysis. *States' Responsibilities to Local Governments: An Action Agenda.* Washington, D.C.: National Governors' Conference, 1975.

Childs, Richard S. *The Charter Problem of Metropolitan Cities.* New York: Citizens Union Research Foundation, 1960.

City-State Relations. Philadelphia: Institute of Local and State Relations, 1937.

Cleaveland, Frederick N. et al. *Congress and Urban Problems: A Casebook on the Legislative Process.* Washington, D.C.: Brookings Institution, 1969.

Coduri, Joseph E. *Home Rule Charters in Rhode Island.* Kingston: Bureau of Government Research, University of Rhode Island, 1973.

Cole, Stephanie, ed. *Partnership within the States: Local Self-Government in the Federal System.* Philadelphia and Urbana: Center for the Study of Federalism, Temple University, and Institute of Government and Public Affairs, University of Illinois, 1976.

Colman, William G. *Cities, Suburbs, and States: Governing and Financing Urban America.* New York: The Free Press, 1975.

Connery, Robert H., and Caraley, Demetrios, eds. *Governing the City: Challenges and Options for New York.* New York: Academy of Political Science, 1969.

Cooley, Thomas M. *A Treatise on the Constitutional Limitations Which Rest Upon the Legislative Power of the States of the American Union.* 7th ed. Boston: Little Brown, 1903.

CPES Membership Questionnaire on Issues: Summary of Results. Albany: Citizens Public Expenditure Survey, 1980.

Derthick, Martha. *Between State and Nation: Regional Organizations of the United States.* Washington, D.C.: Brookings Institution, 1974.

————— . *The Influence of Federal Grants.* Cambridge, Mass.: Harvard University Press, 1970.

Dillon, J. F. *Commentaries on the Law of Municipal Corporations.* Boston: Little Brown, 1911.

Dommel, Paul R. *The Politics of Revenue Sharing.* Bloomington: Indiana University Press, 1974.

Drury, James W. *Home Rule in Kansas.* Lawrence: Governmental Research Center, University of Kansas, 1965.

Due, John F., and Mikesell, John L. *State and Local Sales Taxation.* Chicago: Public Administration Service, 1971.

Ecker-Racz, L. L. *The Politics and Economics of State-Local Finance.* Englewood Cliffs, N.J.: Prentice-Hall, 1970.

Eels, John M. *LAFCO Spheres of Influence: Effective Planning for the Urban Fringe?* Berkeley: Institute of Governmental Studies, University of California, 1977.

Elazar, Daniel J. *American Federalism: A View from the States.* 2nd ed. New York: Harper & Row, 1972.

Eppes, M. Henry. *Home Rule in Maryland Counties.* College Park: Bureau of Governmental Research, University of Maryland, 1975.

Farkas, Suzanne. *Urban Lobbying: Mayors in the Federal Arena.* New York: New York University Press, 1971.

The Federalist Papers. New York: New American Library, 1961.

Fesler, James W., ed. *The 50 States and Their Local Governments.* New York: Alfred A. Knopf, 1967.

First National Bank of Boston and Touche Ross. *Urban Fiscal Stress: A Comparative Analysis of 66 U.S. Cities*. New York: Touche Ross, 1979.

The Fleischmann Report on the Quality, Cost and Financing of Elementary and Secondary Education in New York State. New York: Viking Press, 1973.

Fordham, Jefferson B. *Local Government Law: Legal and Related Materials*. Rev. ed. Mineola, N.Y.: Foundation Press, 1975.

———. *Model Constitutional Provisions for Municipal Home Rule*. Chicago: American Municipal Association, 1953.

Frieden, Bernard J., and Kaplan, Marshall. *The Politics of Neglect: Urban Aid from Model Cities to Revenue Sharing*. Cambridge: MIT Press, 1975.

Friedman, Milton. *Capitalism and Freedom*. Chicago: University of Chicago Press, 1962.

The Future of Property Tax Limits in California. Sacramento: California Taxpayers Association, 1976.

Gelfand, Mark I. *A Nation of Cities: The Federal Government and Urban America, 1933–1965*. New York: Oxford University Press, 1975.

Goodnow, Frank J. *Municipal Home Rule: A Study in Administration*. New York: Columbia University Press, 1895.

———. *Municipal Problems*. New York: Macmillan, 1904.

Graves, W. Brooke. *American Intergovernmental Relations: Their Origins, Historical Development, and Current Status*. New York: Charles Scribner's Sons, 1964.

Greene, Lee S., Grant, Daniel R., and Jewell, Malcolm E. *The States and the Metropolis*. University: University of Alabama Press, 1968.

Grodzins, Morton. *The American System*. Chicago: Rand McNally, 1967.

Gulick, Luther H. *The Metropolitan Problem and American Ideas*. New York: Alfred A. Knopf, 1962.

Haider, Donald. *When Governments Come to Washington: Governors, Mayors, and Intergovernmental Lobbying*. Riverside, N.J.: The Free Press, 1974.

Handbook for Mayors and Council Members in Home Rule Cities. Austin: Texas Municipal League, 1980.

Gere, Edwin A., and Curran, Michael P., eds. *Home Rule*. Amherst and Boston:

Bureau of Government Research, University of Massachusetts, and Bureau of Public Affairs, Boston College, n.d.

Hill, Melvin B., Jr. *State Laws Governing Local Government Structure and Administration*. Athens: Institute of Government, University of Georgia, 1978.

Hirsch, Werner A. *The Economics of State and Local Government*. New York: McGraw-Hill, 1970.

Home Rule in Action. Boston: Bureau of Public Affairs, Boston College, 1970.

Jarrett, James E., and Hicks, Jimmy E. *The Bond Bank Innovation: Maine's Experience*. Lexington, Ky: Council of State Governments, 1977.

Keith, John P. *City and County Home Rule in Texas*. Austin: Institute of Public Affairs, University of Texas, 1951.

Kilpatrick, Wylie. *State Supervision of Local Budgeting*. New York: National Municipal League, 1939.

Kochan, Thomas A., et al. *An Evaluation of Impasse Procedures for Police and Firefighters in New York State: A Summary of Findings, Conclusions, and Recommendations*. Ithaca: New York State School of Industrial and Labor Relations, Cornell University, 1976.

Kotler, Milton. *Neighborhood Government*. Indianapolis: Bobbs-Merrill, 1969.

Krefetz, Sharon P. *Welfare Policy Making and City Politics*. New York: Praeger, 1976.

Larkey, Patrick D. *Evaluating Public Programs: The Impact of General Revenue Sharing on Municipal Government*. Princeton: Princeton University Press, 1979.

Legates, Richard T. *California Local Agency Formation Commissions*. Berkeley: Institute of Governmental Studies, University of California, 1970.

Lepawsky, Albert. *Home Rule for Metropolitan Chicago*. Chicago: University of Chicago Press, 1935.

Lewis, Carol W. *State Mandates: Responsibility and Accountability in Massachusetts*. Boston: Massachusetts League of Cities and Towns, 1978.

Littlefield, Neil. *Metropolitan Area Problems and Municipal Home Rule*. Ann Arbor: Legislative Research Center, University of Michigan Law School, 1962.

Local Government Study. Denver: Governor's Local Affairs Study Commission, 1966.

Lockard, Duane. *New England State Politics*. Princeton: Princeton University Press, 1959.

Lovell, Catherine, et al. *Federal and State Mandating on Local Governments: An Exploration of Issues and Impacts*. Riverside: University of California, 1979.

Maine Municipal Bond Banks: 1975 Series A, B, C and D. Bonds. New York: Goldman Sachs, 1975.

Martin, David L., and Ward, Keith J. *Home Rule for Local Governments*. Auburn: Office of Public Service and Research, Auburn University, 1978.

Martin, Roscoe C. *The Cities and the Federal System*. New York: Atherton Press, 1965.

————. *Grass Roots*. University: University of Alabama Press, 1957.

Maxwell, James A. *Financing State and Local Governments*. Rev. ed. Washington, D.C.: Brookings Institution, 1969.

————. *Tax Credits and Intergovernmental Fiscal Relations*. Washington, D.C.: Brookings Institution, 1962.

McBain, Howard L. *American City Progress and the Law*. New York: Columbia University Press, 1918.

————. *The Law and Practice of Municipal Home Rule*. New York: Columbia University Press, 1916.

McCarthy, David J., Jr. *Local Government Law in a Nutshell*. St. Paul, Minn.: West Publishing Company, 1975.

McFarland, M. Carter. *Federal Government and Urban Problems. HUD: Successes, Failure, and the Fate of Our Cities*. Boulder, Colo.: Westview Press, 1978.

McGoldrick, Joseph D. *Law and Practice of Municipal Home Rule: 1916–1930*. New York: Columbia University Press, 1933.

McMillan, T. E., Jr. *State Supervision of Municipal Finance*. Austin: Institute of Public Affairs, University of Texas, 1953.

McQuillin, Eugene. *The Law of Municipal Corporations*. Chicago: Callaghan, 1949.

Metropolitan Surveys: A Digest. Chicago: Public Administration Service, 1958.

Minge, David. *Effect of Law on County and Municipal Expenditures as Illustrated by the Wyoming Experience*. Laramie: Wyoming Law Institute, University of Wyoming, 1975.

Model City Charter. 6th ed. New York: National Municipal League, 1964.

Model County Charter. New York: National Municipal League, 1956.

Model State Constitution. 6th ed. New York: National Municipal League, 1963.

Modernizing Local Government. New York: Committee for Economic Development, 1966.

Morris, David. *The Nature and Purpose of A Home Rule Charter*. Detroit: Citizens Research Council of Michigan, 1971.

Mott, Rodney L. *Home Rule for America's Cities*. Chicago: American Municipal Association, 1949.

The Municipal Year Book: 1980. Washington, D.C.: International City Management Association, 1980.

Nathan, Richard P., Navel, Allen D., and Calkins, Susannah E. *Monitoring Revenue Sharing*. Washington, D.C.: Brookings Institution, 1975.

Nathan, Richard P., Adams, Charles F., Jr., et al. *Revenue Sharing: The Second Round*. Washington, D.C.: Brookings Institution, 1977.

Netzer, Dick. *State-Local Finance and Intergovernmental Fiscal Relations*. Washington, D.C.: Brookings Institution, 1969.

New Hampshire Municipal Bond Bank: 1980 Series A. Bonds. New York: Goldman Sachs, 1980.

A New Look at Home Rule: A Symposium. New York: National Municipal League, 1955.

New York City's Fiscal Crisis: A Redefinition. New York: Citizens Budget Commission, 1980.

Oates, Wallace E. *Fiscal Federalism*. New York: Harcourt, Brace, Jovanovich, 1972.

Oberholtzer, Ellis P. *The Referendum in America*. Charles Scribner's Sons, 1912.

Omdahl, Lloyd B. *Implementing Home Rule in North Dakota*. Grand Forks: Bureau of Governmental Affairs, University of North Dakota, 1971.

Owen, Henry, and Schultze, Charles L. *Setting National Priorities: The Next Ten Years*. Washington, D.C.: Brookings Institution, 1976.

Petersen, John E., Stallings, Wayne, and Spain, Catherine L. *State Roles in Local Government Financial Management: Nine Case Studies.* Washington, D.C.: Municipal Finance Officers Association, 1980.

Pontius, Dale. *State Supervision of Local Governments.* Washington: American Council on Public Affairs, 1942.

Prescott, Frank W., and Zimmerman, Joseph F. *The Politics of the Veto of Legislation in New York State.* 2 vols. Washington, D.C.: University Press of America, 1980.

Pressman, Jeffrey L. *Federal Programs and City Politics.* Berkeley: University of California Press, 1975.

The Problems with Philadelphia Real Property Assessment Practices and Solutions. Philadelphia: Eastern Division, Pennsylvania Economy League, 1980.

Property Tax Limits. Chicago: International Association of Assessing Officers, 1978.

Public Authorities in the States. Chicago: Council of State Governments, 1953.

Ravitch, Diane. *The Great School Wars: New York City, 1805–1973.* New York: Basic Books, 1974.

Reagan Michael D., and Sanzone, John G. *The New Federalism.* 2nd ed. New York: Oxford University Press, 1981.

Report of the Committee on State-Urban Relations. Chicago: Council of State Governments, 1968.

Reshaping Government in Metropolitan Areas. New York: Committee for Economic Development, 1970.

Rhyne, Charles S. *The Law of Local Government Operations.* Washington, D.C.: Law of Local Government Operations Project, 1980.

Rhyne, Charles S., Rhyne, William S., and Elmendorf, Stephen P. *Tort Liability and Immunity of Municipal Officials.* Washington, D.C.: National Institute of Municipal Law Officers, 1976.

Rockefeller, Nelson A. *The Future of Federalism.* New York: Atheneum Press, 1964.

Rossi, Peter H., Berk, Richard A., and Edison, Betty A. *The Roots of Urban Discontent: Public Policy, Municipal Institutions, and the Ghetto.* New York: John Wiley and Sons, 1974.

Ruben, Elisabeth A., and Williams, Constance. *Comprehensive Permits for Housing*

Lower Income Households in Massachusetts. Boston: Citizens Housing and Planning Association, 1979.

A Sane Fiscal Policy for Louisiana. Baton Rouge: Louisiana Association of Business and Industry, 1977.

Sato, Sho, and Van Alstyne, Arvo. *State and Local Government Law.* Boston: Little Brown, 1970.

Savitch, H. V. *Urban Policy and the Exterior City: Federal, State, and Corporate Impacts Upon Major Cities.* New York: Pergamon Press, 1979.

Schmandt, Henry J., and Standing, William H. *The Milwaukee Metropolitan Study Commission.* Bloomington: Indiana University Press, 1965.

Selected Provisions of Philadelphia's Home Rule Charter Compared with Charters of 11 Other Cities with Population over 700,000. Philadelphia: Eastern Division, Pennsylvania Economy League, 1973.

Shalala, Donna E. *The City and the Constitution: The 1967 New York Convention's Response to the Urban Crisis.* New York: National Municipal League, 1972.

Shurtleff, Nathaniel B., ed. *Records of the Governor and Company of the Massachusetts Bay in New England.* Boston: From the Press of William White, Printer to the Commonwealth, 1853.

Smith, Robert G. *Ad Hoc Governments.* Beverly Hills, Calif.: Sage Publications, 1975.

Staff Reports. Albany, N.Y.: Temporary State Commission on State and Local Finances, 1975.

State Constitutional Restrictions on Local Borrowing and Property Tax Powers. Albany, N.Y.: Government Affairs Foundation, 1964.

State and Local Government Finance and Financial Management: A Compendium of Current Research. Washington, D.C.: Government Finance Research Center, Municipal Finance Officers Association, 1978.

State-Local Relations. Chicago: Council of State Governments, 1946.

State Offices of Community Affairs: Their Functions, Organization and Enabling Legislation. Lexington, Ky.: Council of State Governments, 1969.

State Public Authorities. Lexington, Ky.: Council of State Governments, 1970.

The States and the Metropolitan Problem. Chicago: Council of State Governments, 1957.

The States and Urban Problems. Washington, D.C.: National Governors' Conference, 1967.

Stein, Jane L., et al., eds. *The Effects of Public Safety Employee Bargaining.* Lexington, Mass.: D. C. Heath, 1975.

Stephens, G. Ross, and Olson, Gerald W. *Pass-Through Federal Aid and Interlevel Finance in the American Federal System, 1957 to 1977.* Kansas City: University of Missouri-Kansas City, 1979.

Sundquist, James L., and Davis, David W. *Making Federalism Work.* Washington, D.C.: Brookings Institution, 1970.

Sutton, Robert W., ed. *Rhode Island Local Government: Past, Present, Future.* Kingston: Bureau of Government Research, University of Rhode Island, 1974.

Syed, Anwar. *The Political Theory of American Local Government.* New York: Random House, 1966.

Teaford, Jon C. *The Municipal Revolution in America: Origins of Modern Urban Government.* Chicago: University of Chicago Press, 1975.

Tollenaar, Kenneth C., et al. *Local Government Boundary Commissions: The Oregon Experience.* Eugene: Bureau of Governmental Research and Service, University of Oregon, 1978.

Vermont Municipal Bond Bank: 1972 Series A Bonds. New York: Goldman Sachs, 1972.

Walker, David B. *Toward a Functioning Federalism.* Cambridge, Mass.: Winthrop Publishers, 1981.

Wallace, S. C. *State Administrative Supervision over Cities in the United States.* New York: Columbia University Press, 1928.

Warner, Sam Bass, Jr. *The Private City: Philadelphia in Three Periods of Its Growth.* Philadelphia: University of Pennsylvania Press, 1968.

Westbrook, James E. *A Model Charter for Missouri Cities: A Guide for City Charter Commissions in Missouri.* Jefferson City: Missouri Municipal League, 1973.

Wichwar, W. Hardy. *The Political Theory of Local Government.* Columbia: University of South Carolina Press, 1970.

Wilson, Woodrow. *Congressional Government: A Study of American Politics.* Boston: Houghton Mifflin, 1925.

Wood, Robert C. *1400 Governments*. Cambridge, Mass.: Harvard University Press, 1961.

Wright, Deil. *Understanding Intergovernmental Relations*. North Scituate, Mass.: Duxbury Press, 1978.

Zimmerman, Joseph F. *The Federated City: Community Control in Large Cities*. New York: St. Martin's Press, 1972.

——— . *The Government and Politics of New York State*. New York: New York University Press, 1981.

——— . *Home Rule in Massachusetts: Some Historical Perspectives*. Albany: Graduate School of Public Affairs, State University of New York at Albany, 1970.

——— . *The Massachusetts Town Meeting: A Tenacious Institution*. Albany: Graduate School of Public Affairs, State University of New York at Albany, 1967.

——— . *Metropolitan Surveys*. Albany: Graduate School of Public Affairs, State University of New York at Albany, 1966–68.

——— . *State and Local Government*. 3rd ed. New York: Barnes and Noble, 1978.

——— . *Subnational Politics*. New York: Holt, Rinehart, and Winston, 1970.

GOVERNMENT REPORTS AND DOCUMENTS

Abt Associates. *Property Tax Relief Programs for the Elderly: Final Report*. Washington, D.C.: U.S. Department of Housing and Urban Development, 1975.

ACIR State Legislative Program: Local Government Modernization. Washington, D.C.: U.S. Advisory Commission on Intergovernmental Relations, 1975.

ACIR State Legislative Program: State and Local Revenues. Washington, D.C.: U.S. Advisory Commission on Intergovernmental Relations, 1975.

The Adequacy of Federal Compensation to Local Governments for Tax Exempt Federal Lands. Washington, D.C.: U.S. Advisory Commission on Intergovernmental Relations, 1978.

An Advisory Committee Report on Local Government Submitted to the Commission on

Intergovernmental Relations. Washington, D.C.: U.S. Government Printing Office, 1955.

An Analysis of the Effect of Proposition 13 on Local Governments. Sacramento: California Legislative Analyst, 1979.

An Analysis of Proposition 4: The Gann 'Spirit of 13' Initiative. Sacramento: California Legislative Analyst, 1979.

Aronson, J. Richard. *Municipal Fiscal Indicators*. Washington, D.C.: U.S. Department of Housing and Urban Development, 1980.

An Assessment of 1980 Census Results in 10 Urban Areas. Washington, D.C.: U.S. General Accounting Office, 1980.

Awakening the Slumbering Giant: Intergovernmental Relations and Federal Grant Law. Washington D.C.: U.S. Advisory Commission on Intergovernmental Relations, 1980.

BLS File of State, County, and Municipal Collective Bargaining Agreements, Fall 1979. Washington, D.C.: U.S. Bureau of Labor Statistics, 1980.

Boynton, Robert P., ed. *Occasional Papers in Housing and Community Affairs*. Vol. IV. Washington, D.C.: U.S. Department of Housing and Urban Development, 1979.

Carey, Hugh L. *Message to the Legislature*. Albany: Executive Chamber, January 8, 1975.

————. *Message to the Legislature*. Albany: Executive Chamber, January 7, 1981.

————. *State of New York Annual Budget Message, 1980–1981*. Albany: Executive Chamber, 1980.

A Catalog of Federal Grant-in-Aid Programs to State and Local Governments: Grants Funded FY 1978. Washington, D.C.: U.S. Advisory Commission on Intergovernmental Relations, 1979.

Categorical Grants: Their Role and Design. The Intergovernmental Grant System: An Assessment and Proposed Policies. Washington, D.C.: U.S. Advisory Commission on Intergovernmental Relations, 1978.

Changing Public Attitudes on Governments and Taxes. Washington, D.C.: U.S. Advisory Commission on Intergovernmental Relations, 1980.

Chicago's Government: Its Structural Modernization and Home Rule Problems. Chicago: Chicago Home Rule Commission, 1954.

Cities—Message from the President. Washington, D.C.: House of Representatives, 89th Cong., 1st sess. Document no. 99, 1965.

Citizen Participation in the American Federal System. Washington, D.C.: U.S. Advisory Commission on Intergovernmental Relations, 1979.

City Financial Emergencies : The Intergovernmental Dimension. Washington, D.C.: U.S. Advisory Commission on Intergovernmental Relations, 1973.

City Government Finances in 1978–79. Washington, D.C.: U.S. Bureau of the Census, 1980.

City and Town Centers: A Program for Growth. Boston: Massachusetts Office of State Planning, 1977.

The Commission on Intergovernmental Relations: A Report to the President for Transmittal to the Congress. Washington, D.C.: U.S. Government Printing Office, 1955.

Committee on Education and Labor, U.S. House of Representatives. *Task Force Report on Public Employee Retirement Systems.* Washington, D.C.: U.S. Government Printing Office, 1978.

Committee on Government Operations, U.S. House of Representatives. *Unshackling Local Government: A Survey of Proposals by the Advisory Commission on Intergovernmental Relations.* Rev. ed. Washington, D.C.: U.S. Government Printing Office, 1968.

The Community Development Block Grant Program: Discretionary Grant Funds Not Always Given to the Most Promising Small City Programs. Washington, D.C.: U.S. General Accounting Office, 1978.

Community Development Block Grants: Reauthorization Issues. Washington, D.C.: Congressional Budget Office, 1980.

Cook, Frederick W. *Historical Data Relating to Counties, Cities, and Towns in Massachusetts.* Boston: Commonwealth of Massachusetts, 1948.

Comparative Analysis of New York City's Financial and Economic Indicators. New York: Office of the New York City Comptroller, 1981.

County Government Finances in 1978–79. Washington, D.C.: U.S. Bureau of the Census, 1980.

Cuciti, Peggy L. *Federal Constraints on State and Local Governments.* Washington, D.C.: Congressional Budget Office, 1979.

Curran, Michael P. *Model Charter for Cities in Massachusetts.* Boston: Massachusetts Department of Community Affairs, 1970.

A Decent Home: The Report of the President's Committee on Urban Housing. Washington, D.C.: U.S. Government Printing Office, 1968.

Distribution of the Property Tax: What It Is and Where It Goes. Sacramento: California Senate Committee on Local Government, 1981.

Dorchester Town Records: Fourth Report of the Records Commissioners of the City of Boston. 2nd ed. Boston, 1883.

Effects of Local Option Tax and Implementation of Property Tax Control on Local Finance in Indiana. Indianapolis: Indiana Legislative Council, 1974.

Federal Aid Simplification: White House Status Report. Washington, D.C.: The White House, 1978.

Federal Aid to States: Fiscal Year 1980. Washington, D.C.: Fiscal Service Bureau, U.S. Department of the Treasury, 1981.

Federal Grants: Their Effects on State-Local Expenditures, Employment Levels, Wage Rates. Washington, D.C.: U.S. Advisory Commission on Intergovernmental Relations, 1977.

Federal Legislation and Education in New York State. Albany: State Education Department, 1981.

The Federal Role in the Federal System: The Dynamics of Growth, A Crisis of Confidence and Competence. Washington, D.C.: U.S. Advisory Commission on Intergovernmental Relations, 1980.

Final Report. Albany: Temporary State Commission on Constitutional Tax Limitations, 1975.

Final Report of the Assembly Select Committee on Local Implementation of Tax and Spending Initiatives. Sacramento: California Assembly Select Committee on Implementation of Tax and Spending Limitations, 1980.

The Final Report of the Commission on State-Local Relations and Financing Policy. Madison: State of Wisconsin, 1977.

Final Report of the Decentralization Study Committee. Detroit Public Schools, January 1, 1978.

Final Report of the Home Rule Commission. Boston: City of Boston, 1971.

Final Report of the Subcommittee on Education to the Task Force to Study State-Local Fiscal Relationships. Annapolis: Maryland General Assembly, 1981.

Finances of Employee-Retirement Systems of State and Local Governments in 1978–79. Washington, D.C.: U.S. Bureau of the Census, 1980.

Finances of Selected Public Employee Retirement Systems. Washington, D.C.: U.S. Bureau of the Census, March 1981.

Finances of Public School Systems in 1977–78. Washington, D.C.: U.S. Bureau of the Census, 1980.

Financing the Public Pension Systems. Part I: Actuarial Assumptions and Funding Policies. New York: Permanent Commission on Public Employee Pension and Retirement Systems, 1975.

Fiscal Overview of Minnesota Local Governments. St. Paul: State Planning Agency, 1980.

First Steps toward a Modern Constitution. Albany: New York State Temporary Commission on the Revision and Simplification of the Constitution, 1959.

Fiscal Balance in the American Federal System. Vol. 2: *Metropolitan Fiscal Disparities.* Washington, D.C.: U.S. Advisory Commission on Intergovernmental Relations, 1967.

Fiscal Effect of State School Mandates. Albany: New York State Legislative Commission on Expenditure Review, 1978.

Fox, William F. *Size Economies in Local Government Services: A Review.* Washington, D.C.: U.S. Department of Agriculture, 1980.

Funding of State and Local Government Pension Plans: A National Problem. Washington, D.C.: U.S. General Accounting Office, 1979.

The Gann Initiative. Sacramento: California Department of Finance, 1979.

General Revenue Sharing: An ACIR Re-evaluation. Washington, D.C.: U.S. Advisory Commission on Intergovernmental Relations, 1974.

Governing Urban Areas: Realism and Reform. Albany: New York State Joint Legislative Committee on Metropolitan and Regional Areas Study, 1967.

Governmental Finances in 1978–79. Washington, D.C.: U.S. Bureau of the Census, 1980.

Governmental Structure, Organization, and Planning in Metropolitan Areas. Washington, D.C.: U.S. Advisory Commission on Intergovernmental Relations, 1961.

Harris, Dale A. *Home Rule in Montana*. Helena: Montana Commission on Local Government, 1975.

Hein, C. J., Keys, Joyce M., and Robbins, G. M. *Regional Governmental Arrangements in Metropolitan Areas: Nine Case Studies*. Washington, D.C.: U.S. Government Printing Office, 1974.

Hendler, Charles I., and Reid, J. Norman. *Federal Outlays in Fiscal 1978: A Comparison of Metropolitan and Nonmetropolitan Areas*. Washington, D.C.: U.S. Department of Agriculture, 1980.

Hinckley, Russell J. *State Grants-in-Aid*. Albany: New York State Tax Commission, 1935.

How Are the States Helping Distressed Communities? Washington, D.C.: U.S. Advisory Commission on Intergovernmental Relations, 1979.

How Revenue Sharing Formulas Distribute Aid: Urban-Rural Implications. Washington, D.C.: U.S. General Accounting Office, 1980.

Impact of School Decentralization in New York City on Municipal Decentralization. New York: State Charter Commission for New York City, 1974.

The Interaction of Federal and State Aid in New York State: Trends and Patterns, 1969–75. Washington, D.C.: U.S. General Accounting Office, 1980.

Intergovernmental Cooperation and Intergovernmental Consolidation in New York State. Albany: New York State Commission on Management and Productivity in the Public Sector, 1978.

The Intergovernmental Grant System: An Assessment & Proposed Policies. Washington, D.C.: U.S. Advisory Commission on Intergovernmental Relations, 1976–78.

Interim Report of the Task Force to Study State-Local Fiscal Relationships. Annapolis: Maryland General Assembly, 1980.

Jarrett, J., and Hicks, J. E. *Retirement System Consolidation: The South Dakota Experience*. Lexington, Ky.: Council of State Governments, 1976.

Joint Economic Committee. *Trends in the Fiscal Condition of Cities: 1978–1980*. Washington, D.C.: U.S. Government Printing Office, 1980.

Labor-Management Policies for State and Local Government. Washington, D.C.: U.S. Advisory Commission on Intergovernmental Relations, 1969.

Legislator's Guide to State and Local Fiscal Relationships. Annapolis: Maryland General Assembly, 1978.

Lehman, Maxwell, et al. *Home Rule vs. Super-Government.* New York: Metropolitan Regional Council, 1961.

Local Government Reform. Sacramento: California Task Force on Local Government Reform, 1974.

Local Revenue Diversification: Income, Sales Tax & User Charges. Washington, D.C.: U.S. Advisory Commission on Intergovernmental Relations, 1974.

Logue, Edward J. *Goals, Guidelines, Concerns of the New York State Urban Development Corporation.* New York: New York State Urban Development Corporation, 1971.

Long-Term Local Government and School Financing. Sacramento: California Senate Local Government Committee, 1979.

Management and Evaluation of the Community Block Grant Program Need to be Strengthened. Washington, D.C.: U.S. General Accounting Office, 1978.

Mann, Bettie. *State Constitutional Restrictions on Local Borrowing and Property Taxing Powers.* Albany: Government Affairs Foundation, 1964.

Marshlow, Robert W. *Home Rule in New York: A Brief Survey.* Albany: New York State Office for Local Government, 1965.

Matz, Deborah, and Petersen, John. *Trends in the Fiscal Condition of Cities: 1978–1980.* Washington, D.C.: Joint Economic Committee, U.S. Congress, 1980.

Meeting Metropolitan Problems. Sacramento: Governor's Commission on Metropolitan Area Problems, 1960.

Message from the President of the United States Transmitting Recommendations for City Demonstration Programs. Washington, D.C.: House of Representatives, 89th Cong., 2d sess., Document no. 368, 1966.

Municipal Government—Home Rule: State Assistance. Frankfort, Ky.: Legislative Research Commission, 1957.

Municipal Insurance Pools: An Appropriate Alternative for Local Governments? Albany: New York State Assembly Ways and Means Committee, 1980.

Naftalin, Arthur, and Brandl, John. *The Twin Cities Regional Strategy*. St. Paul, Minn.: Metropolitan Council, 1980.

National Commission on Urban Problems. *Building the American City*. Washington, D.C.: U.S. Government Printing Office, 1968.

New York's Role in the Fiscal Affairs of its Local Governments: New Directions for an Old Partnership. Albany: New York State Assembly Ways and Means Committee, 1979.

New York State Air Quality Implementation Plan: Transportation Element, New York City Metropolitan Area. Albany: New York State Department of Environmental Conservation, 1978.

New York State Comments to the June 30, 1980 Proposed Rulemaking by the U.S. Environmental Protection Agency. Albany: New York State Department of Environmental Conservation and Department of Transportation, 1980.

New York State Public Assistance Cost-Sharing Policies: Implications for Federal Policy. Washington, D.C.: U.S. General Accounting Office, 1980.

1980: Changing Public Attitudes on Governments and Taxes. Washington, D.C.: U.S. Government Printing Office, 1980.

Non-Property Taxes in a Fair and Equitable Tax System. Trenton: New Jersey Tax Policy Committee, 1972.

O'Hare, Robert J. M. *Local Structure: Home Rule*. Boston: Massachusetts Department of Community Affairs, 1969.

Office of Management and Budget Circular No. A-95: An Assessment. Washington, D.C.: U.S. Office of Management and Budget, 1978.

OMB Circular No. A-95: What It Is, How It Works. Washington, D.C.: U.S. Office of Management and Budget, n.d.

Ostrom Elinor, Parks, Roger B., and Whitaker, Gordon P. *Policing Metropolitan America*. Washington, D.C.: U.S. Government Printing Office, 1977.

Perspectives on Intergovernmental Policy and Fiscal Relations. Washington, D.C.: U.S. Government Printing Office, 1979.

President's Urban and Regional Policy Group. *A New Partnership to Conserve America's Communities: A National Urban Policy*. Washington, D.C.: U.S. Department of Housing and Urban Development, 1978.

Problems Relating to Taxation and Finance. Albany: New York State Constitutional Convention, 1938.

The Property Tax. Trenton: New Jersey Tax Policy Committee, 1972.

Property Tax Assessment. Sacramento: California Assembly Revenue and Taxation Committee, 1979.

Property Tax Circuit-Breakers: Current Status and Policy Issues. Washington, D.C.: U.S. Advisory Commission on Intergovernmental Relations, 1975.

Property Tax Relief Programs for the Elderly. Washington, D.C.: U.S. Department of Housing and Urban Development, 1975.

Property Values Subject to Local General Property Taxation in the United States: 1979. Washington, D.C.: U.S. Bureau of the Census, 1980.

Proposed Changes in Federal Matching and Maintenance of Effort Requirements for State and Local Governments. Washington, D.C.: U.S. General Accounting Office, 1980.

Proposition 2½: Estimated Impacts. Boston: Massachusetts Executive Office of Communities and Development, 1980.

Proposition 13—How California Governments Coped with a $6 Billion Revenue Loss. Washington, D.C.: U.S. General Accounting Office, 1979.

Public Authorities in New York State. Albany: Office of the State Comptroller, 1975.

Public Employment in 1979. Washington, D.C.: U.S. Bureau of the Census, 1980.

Recent Trends in Federal and State Aid to Local Governments. Washington, D.C.: U.S. Advisory Commission on Intergovernmental Relations, 1980.

Recommended Roles for California State Government in Federal Urban Programs. Sacramento: California Intergovernmental Council on Urban Growth, 1967.

Reid, J. Norman, et al. *Federal Programs Supporting Substate Regional Activities: An Analysis.* Washington, D.C.: Economics, Statistics, and Cooperative Service, U.S. Department of Agriculture, 1980.

The Role of the State in Urban Affairs. Columbus: Ohio Legislative Service Commission, 1969.

Report on Home Rule to the Governor. Atlanta: Georgia Commission on Intergovernmental Relations, 1968.

Report of the Lane County Local Government Boundary Commission: 1969–1973. Eugene, Oreg.: Lane County Local Government Boundary Commission, 1974.

Report Relative to Establishing a Metropolitan Services Financing District in the Boston Metropolitan Area. Boston: Massachusetts Legislative Research Council, 1976.

Report Relative to Municipal Home Rule. Boston: Massachusetts Legislative Research Council, 1961.

Report of the Subcommittee on Education to the Task Force to Study State-Local Fiscal Relationships. Annapolis: Maryland General Assembly, 1980.

Reports of the Subcommittee on Spending Patterns and Intergovernmental Assistance to the Task Force to Study State-Local Fiscal Relationships. Annapolis: Maryland General Assembly, 1979.

Report Submitted by the Special Commission on Municipal Home Rule. Boston: Commonwealth of Massachusetts, 1962.

Report of the Temporary State Commission on the Powers of Local Governments. New York, 1973.

Report of the Temporary State Commission on State and Local Finances. Vol. 3: *State Mandates.* Albany, 1975.

Restricting the Application of State Laws Adding to Local Government Costs. Boston: Massachusetts Legislative Research Council, 1975.

The Revenue Gap and Tax Burden. Trenton: New Jersey Tax Policy Committee, 1972.

Revising the Municipal Home Rule Amendment. Boston: Massachusetts Legislative Research Council, 1972.

The Role of the States in Strengthening the Property Tax. Washington, D.C.: U.S. Advisory Commission on Intergovernmental Relations, 1963.

Sacks, Seymour, Ross, Robert, and Palumbo, George. *Central City-Suburban Fiscal Disparity & City Distress: 1977.* Washington, D.C.: U.S. Advisory Commission on Intergovernmental Relations, 1980.

Second Interim Report. Albany: New York State Special Task Force on Equity and Excellence in Education, 1980.

Self-Government Powers in Montana: A Citizen's Guide. Bozeman: Cooperative Extension Service, Montana State University, 1978.

Significant Features of Fiscal Federalism: 1979–80 Edition. Washington, D.C.: U.S. Advisory Commission on Intergovernmental Relations, 1980.

Staff Reports. Albany: Temporary State Commission on State and Local Finances, 1975.

Stam, Jerome M., and Reid, J. Norman. *Federal Programs Supporting Multicounty Substate Regional Activities: An Overview.* Washington, D.C.: U.S. Department of Agriculture, 1980.

State Aids and Service Levels. Trenton: New Jersey Tax Policy Committee, 1972.

The State's Biggest Business—Local and Regional Problems. Hartford: Connecticut Commission to Study the Necessity and Feasibility of Metroplitan Government, 1967.

State Community Assistance Initiatives: Innovations of the Late 70s. Washington, D.C.: U.S. Advisory Commission on Intergovernmental Relations, 1979.

State Constitutional and Statutory Restrictions on Local Government Debt. Washington, D.C.: U.S. Government Printing Office, 1961.

State Constitutional and Statutory Restrictions on Local Taxing Powers. Washington, D.C.: U.S. Advisory Commission on Intergovernmental Relations, 1962.

State Constitutional and Statutory Restrictions upon the Structural, Functional, and Personnel Powers of Local Governments. Washington, D.C.: U.S. Advisory Commission on Intergovernmental Relations, 1962.

The States and Distressed Communities: Indicators of Significant Actions. Washington, D.C.: National Academy of Public Administration and U.S. Advisory Commission on Intergovernmental Relations, 1979.

State Government Finances in 1979. Washington, D.C.: U.S. Bureau of the Census, 1980.

State Limitations on Local Taxes and Expenditures. Washington, D.C.: U.S. Advisory Commission on Intergovernmental Relations, 1977.

State-Local Relations Bodies: State ACIRs and Other Approaches. Washington, D.C.: U.S. Advisory Commission on Intergovernmental Relations, 1981.

State and Local Governments' Views on Technical Assistance. Washington, D.C.: U.S. General Accounting Office, 1978.

State and Local Government Pension Reforms. Washington, D.C.: U.S. Advisory Commission on Intergovernmental Relations, 1979.

State and Local Pension Systems: Federal Regulatory Issues. Washington, D.C.: U.S. Advisory Commission on Intergovernmental Relations, 1980.

State and Local Ratio Studies, Property Tax Assessment, and Transfer Taxes. Washington, D.C.: U.S. Bureau of the Census, 1980.

State and Local Roles in the Federal System. Washington, D.C.: U.S. Advisory Commission on Intergovernmental Relations, 1982.

State Mandates to Counties. Albany: New York Legislative Commission on Expenditure Review, 1981.

State Mandating of Local Expenditures. Washington, D.C.: U.S. Advisory Commission on Intergovernmental Relations, 1978.

State of New York Annual Budget Message, 1980–1981. Albany: Executive Chamber, 1980.

State of New York Executive Budget, Submitted by Hugh L. Carey, Governor, to the New York State Legislature. Albany: Executive Chamber, 1979.

State Regulation of Local Accounting, Auditing, and Financial Reporting. Washington, D.C.: U.S. Advisory Commission on Intergovernmental Relations, 1979.

State Reimbursement of Mandated Local Costs. Sacramento: California Legislative Analyst, 1980.

State Revenue Sharing. Albany: Temporary State Commission on State and Local Finances, 1975.

State Sponsored Local Government Investment Pools. Washington, D.C.: U.S. Advisory Commission on Intergovernmental Relations, 1978.

The State of State-Local Revenue Sharing. Washington, D.C.: U.S. Advisory Commission on Intergovernmental Relations, 1980.

State Technical Assistance to Local Debt Management. Washington, D.C.: U.S. Government Printing Office, 1965.

State of Wisconsin Local Government Pooled Investment Funds: An Analysis of Local Government Reactions and their Implications. Madison: State Budget Office, 1977.

Statewide Public Authorities: A Fourth Branch of Government? Albany: Office of the State Comptroller, 1972.

Stenberg, Carl W. *State Involvement in Federal-Local Grant Programs: A Case Study of the "Buying In" Approach.* Washington, D.C.: U.S. Advisory Commission on Intergovernmental Relations, 1970.

Stoner, John E. *Interlocal Governmental Cooperation: A Study of Five States.* Washington, D.C.: U.S. Department of Agriculture, 1967.

Streamlining Federal Assistance Administration: The Final Report to the President by the Federal Assistance Monitoring Project. Washington, D.C.: U.S. Advisory Commission on Intergovernmental Relations, 1978.

Strengthening Local Government in New York. Part I: The Capacity for Change. New York: Temporary State Commission on the Powers of Local Government, 1973.

Strengthening Local Government in New York. Part 2: Services, Structure & Finance. New York: Temporary State Commission on the Powers of Local Governments, 1973.

A Study of the Local Government Impacts of Proposition 13. 4 vols. Sacramento: California Department of Finance, 1979.

Summary. Albany: Temporary State Commission on State and Local Finances, 1975.

Summary and Concluding Observations: The Intergovernmental Grant System: An Assessment and Proposed Policies. Washington, D.C.: U.S. Advisory Commission on Intergovernmental Relations, 1978.

Understanding State and Local Cash Management. Washington, D.C.: U.S. Advisory Commission on Intergovernmental Relations, 1977.

U.S. Advisory Commission on Intergovernmental Relations. *Substate Regionalism and the Federal System. Volume I: Regional Decision Making: New Strategies for Substate Districts.* Washington, D.C.: U.S. Government Printing Office, 1973.

U.S. Bureau of the Census. *Expenditure of General Revenue Sharing and Antirecession Fiscal Assistance Funds: 1977–78.* Washington, D.C.: U.S. Government Printing Office, 1980.

————. *1977 Census of Governments.* Vol. 1, no. 2: *Popularly Elected Officials.* Washington, D.C.: U.S. Government Printing Office, 1979.

————. *Property Values Subject to Local General Property Taxation in the United States: 1979.* Washington, D.C.: U.S. Government Printing Office, 1980.

U.S. Bureau of the Census and U.S. Labor Management Services Administration. *Labor-Management Relations in State and Local Governments: 1979.* Washington, D.C.: U.S. Government Printing Office, 1980.

U.S. Department of the Treasury. *Public Participation in Revenue Sharing.* Washington, D.C.: U.S. Government Printing Office, 1979.

U.S. Office of Management and Budget. *1980 Catalog of Federal Domestic Assistance.* Washington, D.C.: U.S. Government Printing Office, 1980.

The Urban Fiscal Crisis: Fact or Fantasy? Washington, D.C.: Office of Policy Development and Research, U.S. Department of Housing and Urban Development, 1979.

The Use and Costs of Public Credit. Trenton: New Jersey Tax Policy Committee, 1972.

Watertown Records. Watertown, Mass., 1894.

What is Revenue Sharing? Washington, D.C.: Office of Revenue Sharing, U.S. Department of the Treasury, 1978.

Zimmerman, Joseph F. *Measuring Local Discretionary Authority.* Washington, D.C.: U.S. Advisory Commission on Intergovernmental Relations, 1981.

——— . *Pragmatic Federalism: The Reassignment of Functional Responsibility.* Washington, D.C.: U.S. Advisory Commission on Intergovernmental Relations, 1976.

ARTICLES

Allman, Bruce M. "Impact of the 1974 Ohio Code on a Municipality's Constitutionally Delegated Power to Impose Sentences for Misdemeanors: A New Boundary." *University of Cincinnati Law Review* 43 (1974): 410–15.

Amdursky, Robert S. "A Public-Private Partnership for Urban Progress." *Journal of Urban Law* 46 (1969): 199–215.

Andersen, William R. "The Current Meaning of Home Rule in Washington." *Washington Public Policy Notes* 8 (Spring 1980): 1–5.

——— . "Resolving State/Local Government Conflict—A Tale of Three Cities." In *Urban Law Annual,* pp. 129–52. St. Louis: Washington University, 1980.

Aron, Joan. "New York Public Authorities: Changing Form and Function." *National Civic Review* 64 (June 1974): 295–300.

Austermann, Winnifred M., and Pilcher, Dan. "The Tax Revolt Transformed." *State Legislatures* (July/August 1980): 25–33.

Bahl, Roy. "Fiscal Retrenchment in a Declining State: The New York Case." *National Tax Journal* 32 (June 1979 supp.): 277–87.

Baer, Jon A. "Cooperation and Conflict: Overlapping Police Jurisdictions." *National Civic Review* 68 (September 1979): 417–22.

————. "Municipal Debt and Tax Limits: Constraints on Home Rule." *National Civic Review* 70 (April 1981): 204–10.

Bailey, Stephen K. "Improving Federal Governance." *Public Administration Review* 40 (November/December 1980): 548–52.

Bates, F. G. "State Control of Local Finance in Indiana." *The American Political Science Review* 20 (May 1926): 325–60.

Baum, David C., ed. "The Scope of Home Rule: The Views of the Con-Con Local Government Committee." *Illinois Bar Journal* 59 (June 1971): 814–30.

————. "A Tentative Survey of Illinois Home Rule (Part I): Powers and Limitations." *The University of Illinois Law Forum* (1972): 137–57.

————. "A Tentative Survey of Illinois Home Rule (Part II): Legislative Control, Transition Problems, and Intergovernmental Conflict." *The University of Illinois Law Forum* (1972): 559–88.

Benedetto, Richard. "State Education Funding: Cash and Carey." *Empire State Report* 7 (January 26, 1981): 48–50.

Benson, George C. S. "Sources of Municipal Powers." In *The Municipal Year Book: 1938*, pp. 149–65. Chicago: International City Managers Association, 1938.

Biebel, Paul P., Jr., "Home Rule in Illinois After Two Years: An Uncertain Beginning." *John Marshall Journal of Practice and Procedure* 6 (December 1973): 253–330.

Billingsley, Alan G., and Moore, Paul D. "Defining New York State's Role in Monitoring Local Fiscal Affairs." *Governmental Finance* 8 (December 1979): 12–16.

Bingham, David A. "No Home Rule in West Virginia." *National Civic Review* 69 (April 1980): 213–14.

Bowman, John H. "Urban Revenue Structures: An Overview of Patterns, Trends and Issues." *Public Administrative Review* 41 (January 1981): 131–43.

Brammer, Dana B. "State-Sponsored Investment Pools for Local Governments." *Public Administration Survey* 28 (Autumn 1980): 1–4.

Brennan, Geoffrey, and Buchanan, James. "The Logic of Tax Limits: Alternative Constitutional Constraints on the Power to Tax." *National Tax Journal* 32 (June 1979 supp.): 11–22.

Bromage, Arthur W. "Advantages of County Home Rule." *National Municipal Review* 23 (October 1934): 514–17.

———. "Home Rule-NML Model." *National Municipal Review* 44 (March 1955): 132–36.

———. "Reflections on County Home Rule." *Michigan Municipal Review* 64 (January 1971): 11, 16, 23.

Brown, George D. "Home Rule in Massachusetts: Municipal Freedom and Legislative Control." *Massachusetts Law Quarterly* 58 (March 1973): 29–57.

Brugger, Sam. "Municipal Corporations: Home Rule in Wisconsin." *Wisconsin Law Review* (1955): 145–53.

Buchholz, Duane C. " Home Rule: A Solution for Municipal Problems." *Wyoming Law Journal* 16 (Fall 1961): 47–73.

Buckley, James L. "The Trouble with Federalism: It Isn't Being Tried." *Commonsense* 1 (Summer 1978): 1–17.

Calhoun, Charles A. "Ohio's Property Tax System." *County News* (Ohio) 31 (July-August 1980): 11–15.

"California's 'Prop 13' Slows State-Local Tax Growth; Tax Increases in Rest of States Continue Unabated." *Monthly Tax Features* 24 (November-December 1980): 1, 4.

Caputo, David A., ed. "General Revenue Sharing and Federalism." *The Annals* 418 (May 1975): 1–142.

Carter, Jimmy. "Comprehensive National Urban Policy—Message from the President of the United States." *Congressional Record* (April 3, 1978): H 2364–368.

Clark, Barkley. "State Control of Local Government in Kansas: Special Legislation and Home Rule." *University of Kansas Law Review* 20 (Summer 1972): 631–83.

Clines, Francis X. "Wilson to Study Bond-Curb Plans." *New York Times*, March 15, 1974, p. 39.

Coduri, Joseph E. "State-Local Relations in Rhode Island." In *Rhode Island Local*

Government: Past, Present, Future, edited by Robert W Sutton, pp. 56–60. Kingston: Bureau of Government Research, University of Rhode Island, 1974.

Coe, Charles K. "State Supervision and Assistance in Local Government Financial Management." *State Government* 51 (Summer 1978): 187–91.

Cogen, Joel. "Gov. O'Neill's Wrong Plan to Hold Down Connecticut Spending." *New York Times*, January 14, 1981, p. A22.

Cole, Stephanie, and Dutton, Terence G. "Chicago Under Home Rule." In *Home Rule*, pp. 7–12. Urbana: Institute of Government and Public Affairs, University of Illinois, May 1974.

"Connecticut's New School Finance Plan is Much More Costly and Still Inequitable." *CPEC News and Views* 93 (August 1980): 1–2.

"Constitution Revision: How Will It Impact on Cities?" *Urban Georgia* 31 (July 1981): 10–13.

"Court Extends Assessment Criteria." *Georgia County Government* 32 (November 1980): 12–13.

Crihfield, Brevard, and Reeves, H. Clyde. "Intergovernmental Relations: A View from the States." *The Annals* 416 (November 1974): 88–107.

Crowley, Joseph H. "Home Rule for 'Whole City.' " *National Municipal Review* 39 (April 1950): 178–81.

"Dallas Rejects Bid for a 30% Tax Cut." *New York Times*, January 19, 1981, p. A18.

Davis, Al, and Tippett, Frank. "A Fiscal Note." *Intergovernmental Perspective* 6 (Summer 1980): 19.

Day, Adrian. "The Impact of Federal Grants on Local Governments: A Case Study." *Ripon Forum* 15 (May 1979): 4–10.

Desmond, Richard K., and Sefcovic, Paul F. "Municipal Debt and Tax Limitations." *Ohio State Law Journal* 37 (1972): 606–20.

Dewey, Addison E. "Municipal Income Taxes in Ohio: Limitations on the Tax Base by State Pre-Emptions." *The University of Toledo Law Review* 7 (Winter 1976): 501–16.

Dionne, E. J., Jr. "Financing Method for Schools Ruled Valid in New York." *New York Times*, June 24, 1982, pp. 1 and B7.

" 'District Power Equalization' in Present Plan Could Reduce Disparity in School

Finance." *Georgia County Government Magazine* 32 (March 1981): 10–11, 24, 26–27.

Dunn, Martha D. "Proposition 2½: It's Right—It's Wrong—It's Not the Real Issue." *New England Journal of Human Services* 1 (Fall 1981): 13–20.

Durham, G. Homer. "Politics and Administration in Intergovernmental Relations." *The Annals* 207 (January 1940): 1–6.

Dusenbury, Patricia J., and Beyle, Thad L. "The Community Development Block Grant Program: Policy by Formula." *State and Local Government Review* 12 (September 1980): 82–90.

Dye, Thomas R., and Hurley, Thomas L. "The Responsiveness of Federal and State Governments to Urban Problems." *Journal of Politics* 40 (February 1978): 196–207.

Eisel, John L. "Municipal Finance: Home Rule Taxation." *The University of Illinois Law Forum* (1973): 508–22.

Ellinghaus, William M. "Business Involvement Helps Cities Work." *National Civic Review* 70 (January 1981): 17–21.

Ennis, Eva M. "State Actions Affecting Local Affairs." In *The Book of the States: 1980–1981*, pp. 615–22. Lexington, Ky.: Council of State Governments, 1980.

Eribes, Richard A., and Hall, John S. "Revolt of the Affluent: Fiscal Controls in Three States." *Public Administration Review* 41 (January 1981): 107–21.

Farney, Dennis. "The Twin City Experiment." *Wall Street Journal*, March 21, 1974, p. 1.

Farrell, William E. "State 'Financing Schemes' Are Questioned by Levitt." *New York Times*, January 22, 1973, p. 59.

Finer, Herman. "The Case for Local Self-Government." *Public Administration Review* 3 (Winter 1943): 51–58.

Fischer, John "The Minnesota Experiment: How to Make a Big City Fit to Live In." *Harper's Magazine* 250 (April 1969): 12, 17–18, 20, 24, 26, 28, 30, 32.

Fitzgerald, Michael R., and Durant, Robert F. "Citizen Evaluations and Urban Management: Service Delivery in an Era of Protest." *Public Administration Review* 40 (November/December 1980): 585–94.

Florestano, Patricia S. "Revenue-Raising Limitations on Local Government: A

Focus on Alternative Responses." *Public Administration Review* 41 (January 1981): 122–31.

Florestano, Patricia S., and Marando, Vincent L. "State Commissions on Local Government: Implications for Municipal Officials." *National Civic Review* 67 (September 1978): 358–61, 384.

Fordham, Jefferson B. "Home Rule—AMA Model." *National Municipal Review* 44 (March 1955): 137–42.

————. "Local Government in the Larger Scheme of Things." *Vanderbilt Law Review* 13 (June 1955): 667–77.

————. "Ohio Constitutional Review—What of Local Government?" *Ohio State Law Journal* 33 (1972): 575–88.

Fox, William T. R., and Fox, Annette B. "Municipal Government and Special-Purpose Authorities." *The Annals* 207 (January 1940): 176–84.

Freedman, Eric. "The Politics of Public Employee Pensions." *Empire State Report* 6 (October 1–15, 1980): 358–61, 365–68.

————. "State: Free Goodies at Local Events OK." *Knickerbocker News* (Albany), March 14, 1980, p. 5A.

French, Gary E. "Home Rule in Pennsylvania." *Dickinson Law Review* 81 (Winter 1977): 265–95.

Froelich, Kurt P. "Illinois Home Rule in the Courts." *Illinois Bar Journal* 63 (February 1975): 320–29.

Gabler, L. Richard, and Zimmerman, Joseph F. "State Mandating of Local Expenditures." *Urban Data Service Report* (July 1978): 1–13.

Gelfand, M. David. "The Burger Court and the New Federalism: Preliminary Reflections of the Roles of Local Government Actors in the Political Dramas of the 1980's." *Boston College Law Review* 21 (May 1980): 763–850.

Glassberg, Andrew. "The Urban Fiscal Crisis Becomes Routine." *Public Administration Review* 41 (January 1981): 165–72.

Gordon, Stephen. "Most Towns Still Lack Septage Disposal Sites." *The Keene Sentinel* (Keene, N.H.), June 27, 1980, pp. 1, 6.

Gotherman, John E. "Municipal Home Rule in Ohio Since 1960." *Ohio State Law Journal* 33 (1972): 589–605.

Grad, Frank P. "Home Rule and the New York Constitution." *Columbia Law Review* 66 (June 1966): 1145–63.

Grant, Daniel R. "General Metropolitan Surveys: A Summary." *Metropolitan Surveys: A Digest.* Chicago: Public Administration Service, 1958.

Grant, William R. "Community Control vs. School Integration—The Case of Detroit." *The Public Interest* (Summer 1971): 62–79.

Graves, W. Brooke, ed. "Intergovernmental Relations in the United States." *The Annals* 207 (January 1940): 1–218.

————. "Readjusting Governmental Areas and Functions." *The Annals* 207 (January 1940): 203–9.

Green, S. William. "Report on the Administration's Urban Proposals." *Congressional Record* (October 14, 1978): E 5839.

Greene, Richard. "The Second Boston Tea Party." *Forbes* 126 (November 24, 1980): 34–35.

Greenhalgh, Leonard, and McKersie, Robert S. "Cost-Effectiveness of Alternative Strategies for Cut-Back Management." *Public Administration Review* 40 (November/December 1980): 575–84.

Greenhouse, Linda. "U.D.C. Head Seeks Banks' Guarantee." *New York Times*, February 4, 1975, p. 11.

Grumm, John G., and Murphy, Russell D. "Dillon's Rule Reconsidered." *The Annals* 416 (November 1974): 120–32.

Gutekunst-Roth, Gayle. "New York—A City in Crisis: Fiscal Emergency Legislation and the Constitutional Attacks." *The Fordham Urban Law Journal* 6 (Fall 1977): 65–100.

Harriss, C. Lowell. "Property Taxation: Classifying Types of Property to Differentiate Burdens." *Tax Foundation's Tax Review* 41 (May 1980): 19–22.

————. "Property Taxation: What's Good and What's Bad about It." *The American Journal of Economics and Sociology* 33 (January 1974): 89–102.

Healy, Howard. "Tax Shift to Homeowners a Worry." *Empire State Report* 7 (January 26, 1981): 50–53.

Henderson, Henry. "Risk Management—Municipal, County and Personal Tort Liability." *Public Sector* (Auburn University) 1 (October 1977): 1–9, 11.

Herbers, John. "Minneapolis Area Council Is Emerging as a Pioneer in Strong Regional Government." *New York Times*, February 2, 1971, p. 62.

————. "Should Washington Share Revenue with the States?" *New York Times*, January 22, 1981, p. B8.

Herman, Robin. "Carey Alters Medicaid Plan to Calm Mayors' Criticism." *New York Times*, February 20, 1981, p. B3.

————. "State School Aid Sought by Carey Called Too Small." *New York Times*, January 21, 1981, p. B10.

Hershman, Marc J., and Mistric, Marsha M. "Coastal Zone Management and State-Local Relations under the Louisiana Constitution of 1974." *Loyola Law Review* 22 (Winter 1975–76): 273–300.

Hill, Donald R. "Power of a Municipal Corporation to Enact a Civil Rights Ordinance." *Washburn Law Journal* 4 (1964–65): 128–44.

Hoffman, Charles. "Pennsylvania Legislation Implements Home Rule." *National Civic Review* 61 (September 1972): 390–93.

Hunter, Marjorie. "Prayers in Schools Approved by House." *New York Times*, June 12, 1979, p. B20.

————. "Senate, in Surprise Move, Votes to Permit Prayer in Public Schools." *New York Times*, April 6, 1979, p. A14.

Hyman, J. D. "Home Rule in New York, 1941–1965: Retrospect and Prospect." *Buffalo Law Review* 15 (1965): 335–69.

Jaffe, Jacob M. "The States' Stake in the Urban Fiscal Crisis." *State Government* 42 (Winter 1969): 23–30.

Karlen, Douglas M. "Municipal Finance: Tax Anticipation Notes." *The University of Illinois Law Forum* (1973): 523–39.

Katzman, Martin T. "Measuring the Savings from State Municipal Bank Banking." *Governmental Finance* 9 (March 1980): 19–25.

Kean, R. Gordon, Jr. "Local Government and Home Rule." *Loyola Law Review* 21 (1975): 63–79.

"Keeping Connecticut Solvent: Round Two." *New York Times*, February 12, 1981, p. A26.

Kemp, Roger L. "California's Taxpayers' Revolt: An Update." *The Bureaucrat* 10 (Spring 1981): 55–58.

Kittl, Donald F. "Managing Federal Grants in the City of Richmond." *The University of Virginia Newsletter* 57 (October 1980): 5–8.

Kiernan, William J., Jr. "The Power to Become Indebted and Its Limits." *Wisconsin Law Review* (1964): 173–251.

Knight, Michael. "Boston Prepared to Retrench as Tax Cut Drains Treasury." *New York Times*, February 16, 1981, p. A10.

Kolderie, Ted. "Minnesota Legislature Aids Metropolitan Setup." *National Civic Review* 58 (July 1969): 321, 326.

―――. "Regionalism in the Twin Cities of Minnesota." In *The Regionalist Papers*, edited by Kent Mathewson, pp. 26–47. Detroit: Metropolitan Fund, 1974.

Kopcke, Richard W., and Kimball, Ralph C. "Investment Incentives for State and Local Governments." *New England Economic Review* (January/February 1979): 20–40.

Kratovil, Robert, and Ziegweid, John T. "Illinois Municipal Home Rule and Urban Land: A Test Run of the New Constitution." *DePaul Law Review* 22 (Winter 1972): 359–87.

Kreskey, Edward M. "Local Government." In *Salient Issues of Constitutional Revision*, edited by John P. Wheeler, pp. 150–62. New York: National Municipal League, 1961.

Ladd, Helen F. "An Economic Evaluation of State Limitations on Local Taxing and Spending Powers." *National Tax Journal* 31 (March 1978): 1–18.

Lancaster, Lane W. "State Limitations on Local Indebtedness." In *The Municipal Year Book: 1936* pp. 313–27. Chicago: International City Managers' Association, 1936.

Leach, Richard H., ed. "Intergovernmental Relations in America Today." *The Annals* 416 (November 1974): 1–169.

Levine, Charles H., and Posner, Paul L. "The Centralizing Effects of Austerity on the Intergovernmental System." *Political Science Quarterly* 96 (Spring 1981): 67–85.

Levine, Gordon V. "The 'Clean Slate' Doctrine: A Liberal Construction of the Scope of the Illinois Home Rule Powers—Kanellos v. County of Cook." *DePaul Law Review* 23 (Spring 1974): 1298–313.

"Local and Metropolitan Government Organization." *The Urban Lawyer* 10 (Summer 1978): 452–69.

Lovell, Catherine H. "Evolving Local Government Dependency." *Public Administration Review* 41 (January 1981): 189–202.

Mabbutt, Richard. *Major Forces Shaping Idaho's Future: The Potential Impacts on Local Government.* Boise, Idaho: Governor's Task Force on Local Government, 1977.

Macchiarola, Frank J. "Constitutional, Statutory, and Judicial Restraints on Local Finance in New York State." *New York Law Forum* 15 (Winter 1969): 852–72.

———. "Local Government Home Rule and the Judiciary." *Journal of Urban Law* 48 (1971): 335–59.

Madden, Richard L. "Connecticut's Budget." *New York Times*, February 6, 1981, p. B2.

Maeroff, Gene I. "Integration in Boston Bringing Broad Educational Changes." *New York Times*, October 25, 1980, p. 7.

Magleby, David B. "The Movement to Limit Government Spending in American States and Localities, 1970–1979." *The University of Virginia Newsletter* 57 (November 1980): 9–12.

Manlove, George. "Industrial Park Wetland Area Jeopardizes Development Plans." *The Keene Sentinel* (Keene, N.H.), September 17, 1980, pp. 1, 11.

Marando, Vincent L., and Florestano, Patricia S. "State Commission on Local Government." *State & Local Government Review* 9 (May 1977): 49–53.

Martin, Albert B. "Home Rule for Kansas Cities." *Kansas Law Review* 10 (May 1962): 501–14.

Mattis, James M. "Home Rule— At the Crossroads?" *Current Municipal Problems* 20 (Summer 1978): 30–46.

Mauck, Elwyn A. "Home Rule for Counties Continues Its Progress." *National Municipal Review* 28 (February 1939): 89–95, 179.

May, Peter J., and Meltsner, Arnold J. "Limited Actions, Distressing Consequences: A Selected View of the California Experience." *Public Administration Review* 41 (January 1981): 172–79.

McBain, Howard L. "The Doctrine of an Inherent Right of Local Self-Government." *Columbia Law Review* 16 (1916): 190–216, 299–322.

McCaffery, Jerry, ed. "The Impact of Resource Scarcity on Urban Public Finance." *Public Administration Review* 41 (January 1981): 105–202.

McDowell, Bruce D. "Substate Regionalism Matures Gradually." *Intergovernmental Perspective* 6 (Fall 1980): 20–26.

"McGrath To Recommend 442 City Jobs Be Abolished." *The Evening Gazette* (Worcester, Mass.), January 10, 1981, pp. 1–2.

McKinney, Jerome B. "Process Accountability and the Creative Use of Intergovernmental Resources." *Public Administration Review* 41 (January 1981): 144–50.

Minetz, Robert S. "Recent Illinois Supreme Court Decisions Concerning the Authority of Home Rule Units to Control Local Environmental Problems." *DePaul Law Review* 26 (Winter 1977): 306–24.

Moore, Allen. "Development and Present Status of County Home Rule." *American County Government* 34 (April 1969): 16–21.

Moser, M. Peter. "County Home Rule—Sharing the State's Legislative Power with Maryland Counties." *Maryland Law Review* 28 (Fall 1968): 327–59.

Mosher, Frederick C. "The Changing Responsibilities and Tactics of the Federal Government." *Public Administration Review* 40 (November/December 1980): 541–48.

Mott, Rodney L. "Strengthening Home Rule." *National Municipal Review* 39 (April 1950): 172–77.

Muller, Thomas, and Fix, Michael. "Federal Solicitude, Local Costs: The Impact of Federal Regulations on Municipal Finances." *Regulation* 4 (July/August 1980): 29–36.

"Municipal Home Rule Power: Impact on Private Legal Relationships." *Iowa Law Review* 56 (February 1971): 631–45.

Mushkin, Selma J., and Biederman, Kenneth R. "Defining Tax and Revenue Relations." In *States' Responsibilities to Local Governments: An Action Agenda*, pp. 153–81. Washington, D.C.: National Governors' Conference, 1975.

Nathan, Richard P. "The Nationalization of Proposition 13." *P.S.* 14 (Fall 1981): 752–56.

―――. "The New Federalism Versus the Emerging New Structuralism." *Publius* 5 (Summer 1975): 111–29.

Nathan, Richard P., and Dommel, Paul R. "Federal-Local Relations under Block Grants." *Political Science Quarterly* 93 (Fall 1978): 421–42.

"The National Urban Policy: One Year Later." In *Information Bulletin*, pp. 1–11. Washington, D.C.: U.S. Advisory Commission on Intergovernmental Relations, May 1975.

"New York City: On the Comeback Trail." *The Morgan Guaranty Survey* (April 1981): 10–15.

Nichols, F. Glenn. "Debt Limitations and the Bona Fide Long-Term Lease with an Option to Purchase: Another Look at Lord Coke." *Urban Lawyer* 9 (Spring 1977): 403–20.

Petersen, John E. "City Finances 1978–1980: The JEC/MFOA Survey Results." *Governmental Finance* 9 (June 1980): 3–8.

Petersen, John E., Spain, Catherine L., and Stallings, C. Wayne. "From Monitoring to Mandating: State Roles in Local Government Finance." *Governmental Finance* 8 (December 1979): 3–11.

Porter, David O. "The Ripper Clause in State Constitutional Law: An Early Experiment—Part I." *Utah Law Review* (1969): 287–325.

————. "The Ripper Clause in State Constitutional Law: An Early Urban Experiment—Part II." *Utah Law Review* (1969): 450–91.

Porter, Kirk H. "County Home Rule a Mistake." *National Municipal Review* 23 (October 1934): 517–19, 535.

"Proposition 13 Update: State Cupboard Bare." *The Keene Sentinel* (Keene, N.H.), September 20, 1980, p. 16.

Proxmire, William. "The Limits of New York City Loan Guarantees." *New York Times*, September 23, 1980, p. A22.

Puryear, David L., and Ross, John P. "Tax and Expenditure Limitations: The Fiscal Context." *National Tax Journal* 32 (June 1979 supp.): 23–35.

Rampton, Calvin L. "An Address to the National Association of Counties, July 1974." In *States' Responsibilities to Local Governments: An Action Agenda*, p. iii. Washington, D.C.: National Governors' Conference, 1975.

Ravitch, Diane. "School Decentralization, and What It Has Come To." *New York Times*, June 30, 1974, sec. 4, p. E5.

Reed, Leonard. "The Budget Game and How to Win It." *Washington Monthly* 10 (January 1979): 23–33.

Rehmus, Charles M. "Constraints on Local Governments in Public Employee Bargaining." *Michigan Law Review* 67 (March 1969): 191–230.

Reschovsky, Andrew, and Knaff, Eugene. "Tax Base Sharing: An Assessment of the Minnesota Experience." *Journal of the American Institute of Planners* 43 (October 1977): 361–70.

"Revenue Sharing: Report from the Grass Roots." *Carnegie Quarterly* 24 (Winter 1976): 1–5.

Richter, Albert J. "Strengthening Local Government: A Call for Restructuring." *Intergovernmental Perspective* 6 (Fall 1980): 13–19.

Richetts, Jay. "Governor Signs Local Government Fiscal Note Act." *Georgia County Government Magazine* 33 (May 1981): 22–23.

Rosenberg, Philip. "The Community Development Block Grant Program." *Urban Data Service Report* 9 (November 1977): 1–14.

Ross, John P., and Calkins, Susannah E. "The State-Local Role in Federal Economic Stabilization." *Intergovernmental Perspective* 4 (Summer 1978): 16–20.

Rowell, David T. "Massachusetts Law Spurs Subsidized Housing." *National Civic Review* 65 (September 1976): 406–07, 432.

Rutledge, Philip J. "Federal-Local Relations and the Mission of the City." *The Annals* 417 (November 1974): 77–90.

Ruud, Millard H. "Legislative Jurisdiction of Texas Home Rule Cities." *Texas Law Review* 37 (June 1959): 682–720.

Ryan, Earl M. "The Wayne County Dilemma: Insolvency through Inaction." *National Civic Review* 69 (April 1980): 204–10.

Salsich, Peter W., Jr., and Tuchler, Dennis J. "Missouri Local Government: A Criticism of a Critique." *St. Louis University Law Journal* 14 (Winter 1969): 207–45.

Sayre, Wallace S. "New York City and State." In *Modern-State Government: The New York Constitutional Convention of 1967*, edited by Sigmund Diamond, pp. 106–13. New York: Academy of Political Science, 1967.

Sandalow, Terrance. "The Limits of Municipal Power under Home Rule: A Role for the Courts." *Minnesota Law Review* 48 (1963–64): 643–721.

Scheiber, Harry N. "Federalism and Legal Process: Historical and Contemporary

Analysis of the American System." *Law & Society Review* 14 (Spring 1980): 663–722.

Schmidt, Karl M. "Equal Justice under Law for Public Employees Too?" *Syracuse Guide* 19 (March 1977): 16–17, 26–28.

Schultze, Charles L. "Federal Spending: Past, Present, and Future." In *Setting National Priorities: The Next Ten Years*, edited by Henry Owen and Charles L. Schultze, pp. 323–69. Washington, D.C.: Brookings Institution, 1976.

Sentell, R. Perry, Jr. "When a Mother Hurts Her Young: Local Government Constitutional Protection Against the State." Pt. I. *Urban Georgia* 31 (May 1981): 31, 34–35.

———. "When a Mother Hurts Her Young: Local Government Constitutional Protection Against the State." Pt. II. *Urban Georgia* 31 (June 1981): 33, 35, 37–38, 40–41.

Shannon, John, Bell, Michael, and Fisher, Ronald. "Recent State Experience with Local Tax and Expenditure Controls." *National Tax Journal* 29 (September 1976): 276–85.

Shannon, John, and Cooper, Chris. "Tough Questions for Local Government Finances." *National Civic Review* 69 (May 1980): 267–71.

Shannon, John, and Gabler, L. Richard. "Tax Lids and Expenditure Mandates: The Case for Fiscal Fair Play." *Intergovernmental Perspective* 3 (Summer 1977): 7–12.

Shapiro, Perry, Puryear, David, and Ross, John. "Tax and Expenditure Limitation in Retrospect and in Prospect." *National Tax Journal* 32 (June 1979 supp.): 1–10.

Sharp, Gerald L. "Home Rule in Alaska: A Clash between the Constitution and the Court." *UCLA-Alaska Law Review* 3 (1973): 1–54.

Shestack, Jerome J. "The Public Authority." *The University of Pennsylvania Law Review* 105 (February 1957): 553–69.

Shick, J. Randle. "Illinois Home Rule in the Courts—Continued." *Illinois Bar Journal* 66 (December 1976): 214–18.

Shore, William B. "What's Next for American Cities?" *National Civic Review* 67 (April 1978): 168–72.

Shubnell, Lawrence D. "Home Rule or Home Ruin?" *American County Government* 34 (April 1969): 22–25.

Simmons, Peter. "Home Rule and Exclusionary Zoning: An Impediment to Low and Moderate Income Housing." *Ohio State Law Journal* 33 (1972): 621– 38.

Smith, Russell L., and Lyons, William. "The Impact of Fire Fighter Unionization on Wages and Working Hours in American Cities." *Public Administration Review* 40 (November/December 1980): 568–74.

Solheim, Thomas P. "Conflicts between State Statute and Local Ordinance in Wisconsin." *Wisconsin Law Review* (1975): 840–59.

Spicer, George W. "Fiscal Aspects of State-Local Relations." *The Annals* 207 (January 1940): 151–60.

"State Tax Action in 1980." *Tax Foundation's Tax Review* 41 (October 1980): 35– 38.

Stelzer, Leigh. "Electoral Participation, Competition and Budget Defeats in School Districts." *Journal of the New York State School Boards Association, Incorporated* 38 (March 1974): 24–29.

Stephens, G. Ross. "State Centralization and the Erosion of Local Autonomy." *Journal of Politics* 36 (February 1974): 44–76.

Still, Bayrd. "Patterns of Mid-Nineteenth Century Urbanization in the Middle West." *Mississippi Valley Historical Review* 28 (September 1941): 187–206.

Stine, Susan B. "Proposition 2½ Lessens Property Tax Reliance." *Public Administration Times* 4 (January 15, 1981): 1, 3.

Stitely, John O. "Home Rule in Rhode Island: Twenty Years Later." *Bureau of Government Research Newsletter* (University of Rhode Island) 14 (November 1972): 1–4.

Straussman, Jeffrey D. "More Bang for Fewer Bucks? Or How Local Governments Can Rediscover the Potentials (and Pitfalls) of the Market." *Public Administration Review* 41 (January 1981): 150–58.

Sullivan, Joseph F. "Byrne Budget: Thorny Adieu." *New York Times*, February 3, 1981, p. B3.

"Tax Reduction Proposals Lose." *National Civic Review* 70 (January 1981): 46–47.

Teaford, Jon. "City Versus State: The Struggle for Legal Ascendancy." *American Journal of Legal History* 17 (January 1973): 51–65.

"Text of Letter from Mayor Koch Accompanying Proposed Budget for Fiscal '82." *New York Times*, January 17, 1981, p. 28.

Thomas, Robert D., and Marando, Vincent L. "Local Governmental Reform and Territorial Democracy: The Case of Florida." *Publius* 11 (Winter 1981): 49–63.

Thornburgh, Dick. "States Have Responsibility in Partnerships for Progress." *National Civic Review* 70 (January 1981): 11–16.

Tiebout, Charles M. "A Pure Theory of Local Expenditures." *Journal of Political Economy* 64 (October 1956): 416–24.

Trautman, Philip A. "Legislative Control of Municipal Corporations in Washington." *Washington Law Review* 36 (1963): 743–83.

Turner, Wallace. "1978 Coast Tax Initiative Now Spurs Budget Crisis." *New York Times*, January 10, 1981, p. 8.

Tvedt, Sherry. "Enough is Enough: Proposition 2½ in Massachusetts." *National Civic Review* 70 (November 1981): 527–33.

"Twin Cities Metropolitan Council Anticipates and Supplies Orderly Growth." *Urban Action Clearinghouse*, Case Study No. 20. Washington, D.C.: Chamber of Commerce of the United States, 1971.

VanLandingham, Kenneth E. "Constitutional Municipal Home Rule since the AMA (NLC) Model." *William and Mary Law Review* 17 (Fall 1975): 1–34.

————. "Municipal Home Rule in the United States." *William and Mary Law Review* 10 (Winter 1968): 269–314.

Vaubel, George D. "Of Concern to Painesville—Or Only to the State: Home Rule in the Context of Utilities Regulation." *Ohio State Law Journal* 33 (Spring 1972): 257–348.

Vaughan, Donald S. "Mississippi's Optional Charter Plan." *Public Administration Survey* 21 (September 1973): 1–6.

Vitullo, Vincent F. "Local Government: Recent Developments in Local Government Law in Illinois." *DePaul Law Review* 22 (Fall 1972): 85–95.

Wager, Paul W. "State Centralization in the South." *The Annals* 207 (January 1940): 144–50.

Walker, David B. "Proposition 13 and California's System of Governance." *Intergovernmental Perspective* 4 (Summer 1978): 13–15.

————. "The States' Role in Meeting the Urban Crisis: Positive or Negative." *Metropolitan Viewpoints* 2 (May 1967): 1–4.

————. "The States and the System: Changes and Choices." *Intergovernmental Perspective* 6 (Fall 1980): 6–12.

Walsh, Roger E. "Constitutional Debt Limitations of Wisconsin Municipalities—A Survey." *Marquette Law Review* 45 (1962): 614–29.

Webster, Charles W., and FitzGerald, John L. "Municipal Corporations." *Southwestern Law Journal* 20 (1967): 221–36.

Westbrook, James E. "Municipal Home Rule: An Evaluation of the Missouri Experience." *Missouri Law Review* 33 (Winter 1968): 45–80.

Woolsey, Thomas R. "Local Government: Annexation." *The University of Illinois Law Forum* (1973): 582–603.

Wright, Deil S. "Intergovernmental Relations: An Analytical Overview." *The Annals* 416 (November 1974): 1–16.

Zimmerman, Joseph F. "Can Cities and Towns Meet the Challenges of the Space Age?" *New Hampshire Town and City* 15 (June 1972): 4/104–10/110.

————. "The Cooperative Approach to Environmental Enhancement." In *Managing the Environment*, U.S. Environmental Protection Agency, pp. 367–83. Washington, D.C.: U.S. Government Printing Office, 1974.

————. "Coping with Metropolitan Problems: The Boundary Review Commission." *State Government* 48 (Autumn 1975): 257–60.

————. "Developing a Balanced Transportation System." In *States' Responsibilities to Local Governments: An Action Agenda*, pp. 121–33. Washington, D.C.: National Governors' Conference, 1975.

————. "Direct State Action to Help Solve Metropolitan Problems." *State Government* 44 (Winter 1971): 37–41.

————. "The Discretionary Authority of Local Governments." *Urban Data Service Report* 13 (November 1981): 1–13.

————. "Ethics in Local Government." *Management Information Service Report* 8 (August 1976): 1–11.

————. "Evolving State-Local Relations in New England." In *Partnership within the States: Local Self-Government in the Federal System*, edited by Stephanie Cole, pp. 213–47. Philadelphia and Urbana: Center for the Study of Federalism, Temple University, and Institute of Government and Public Affairs, University of Illinois, 1976.

————. "The Federal Voting Rights Act and Alternative Election Systems." *William and Mary Law Review* 19 (Summer 1978): 621–60.

————. "The Federal Voting Rights Act: Its Impact on Annexation." *National Civic Review* 66 (June 1977): 278–83.

————. "Frustrating National Policy: Partial Federal Preemption." In *The Nationalization of State Government*, edited by Jerome J. Hanus, pp. 75–104. Lexington, Mass.: Lexington Books, 1981.

————. "Governing the Metropolitan Area: Why Some Systems Work and Others Don't." *Georgia County Government Magazine* 30 (February 1979): 58, 60–62, 64–68.

————. "Governing the Metropolitan Area: Why Some Systems Work and Others Don't, Part II." *Georgia County Government Magazine* 30 (March 1979): 10–11, 33–35.

————. "A Growing Trend." *National Civic Review* 58 (November 1969): 462–68.

————. "Intergovernmental Service Agreements for Smaller Cities." *Urban Data Service Report* 5 (January 1973): 1–12.

————. "Intergovernmental Service Agreements and Transfer of Functions." In *Substate Regionalism and the Federal System*. Vol. III: *Challenge of Local Government Reorganization*, U.S. Advisory Commission on Intergovernmental Relations, pp. 29–52, 176–84. Washington, D.C.: U.S. Government Printing Office, 1974.

————. "Lease-Purchase Fails." *National Civic Review* 48 (May 1959): 241–45.

————. "Local Discretionary Authority in New England." *Suffolk University Law Review* 15 (December 1981): 1125–156.

————. "Mandating in New York State." In *State Mandating of Local Expenditures*, pp. 69–85. Washington, D.C.: U.S. Advisory Commission on Intergovernmental Relations, 1978.

————. "Meeting Service Needs through Intergovernmental Agreements." In *The Municipal Year Book: 1973*, pp. 79–88. Washington, D.C.: International City Management Association, 1973.

————. "The Metropolitan Area Problem." *The Annals* 416 (November 1974): 133–47.

————. "Metropolitan Ecumenism: The Road to the Promised Land?" *Journal of Urban Law* 44 (Spring 1967): 433–57.

————. "Metropolitan Governance: The Intergovernmental Dimension." In *State and Local Government*, edited by Alan K. Campbell and Roy W. Bahl, pp. 54–64. New York: The Free Press, 1976.

————. "The Metropolitan Governance Maze in the United States." *Urban Law and Policy* 2 (1979): 265–84.

————. "The Municipal Stake in Environmental Protection." In *Municipal Year Book: 1972*, pp. 105–09. Washington, D.C.: International City Management Association, 1972.

————. "Neighborhood Control of Schools." In *Revitalizing Cities*, edited by Herrington J. Bryce, pp. 243–56. Lexington, Mass.: Lexington Books, 1979.

————. "Opposition to Unreimbursed State Mandates Gives Rise to Push for Constitutional Changes." *The Daily Bond Buyer—MFOA Supplement* (April 18, 1977): 19–21.

————. "The Patchwork Approach: Adaptive Responses to Increasing Urbanization." In *Metropolitan America in Contemporary Perspective*, edited by Amos H. Hawley and Vincent P. Rock, pp. 431–98. New York: Halsted Press, 1975.

————. "Pollution Abatement by Regional Action." In *An Anthology of Selected Readings for the National Conference on Managing the Environment*, edited by Steven Carter and Lyle Sumek, pp. III-44 to III-56. Washington, D.C.: International City Management Association, 1973.

————. "Reforming the Single Member District Electoral System." *Georgia County Government Magazine* 32 (March 1981): 12, 21–24.

————. "Regionalism." *The Massachusetts Selectman* 31 (April 1972): 7–10, 15–16.

————. "The Single-Member District System: Can It Be Reformed?" *National Civic Review* 70 (May 1981): 255–59.

————. "Solving Areawide Problems in Rhode Island." *Bureau of Government Research Newsletter* (University of Rhode Island) 14 (September 1972): 1–4.

————. "State-Local Relations: The State Mandate Irritant." *National Civic Review* 65 (December 1976): 548–52.

————. "The State Role in Metropolitan Governance in the U.S. Federal System." *Planning and Administration* 1 (Winter 1974): 75–87.

———— . "Substate Regional Governance: The Intergovernmental Dimension." *National Civic Review* 67 (June 1978): 272–74, 300.

UNPUBLISHED MATERIAL

Baer, Jon A. "Municipal Debt and Tax Limitations in New York State: A Constraint on Home Rule." Albany: Graduate School of Public Affairs, State University of New York at Albany, 1980.

Florestano, Patricia S. "Areawide Government and Multiple Jurisdictions: An Examination of Selected Counties in Maryland." College Park: Institute for Urban Studies, University of Maryland, 1978.

"Memorandum of the Association of Towns of The State of New York to the Assembly Ways and Means Committee and Assembly Standing Committee on Local Governments." Albany: Association of Towns, September 21, 1979. Mimeographed.

Lawther, Wendell C. "The Changing Role of the Federal Official in an Era of New Federalism: The Case of the Intergovernmental Personnel Act of 1970." Paper presented at the Annual Meeting of the Northeast Political Science Association, Mount Pocono, Pa., November 11, 1977.

Morgan, James R. "The Growing Tension in State-Local Relations." Paper presented at the Conference on Mining in Northern Wisconsin, Rhinelander, Wis., May 18, 1978.

O'Hare, Robert J. M. "Constitutional Home Rule—Yes or No?" Paper presented at the National Conference on Government, Atlanta, November 16, 1971.

Stenberg, Carl W. "Federal-Local Relations in a Cutback Environment: Issues and Future Directions." Paper presented at the Annual Conference of the American Politics Group of the United Kingdom Political Studies Association, Manchester, England, January 4, 1980.

Walker, David B. "The Changing Dynamics of Federal Aid to Cities." Paper presented at the Annual Meeting of the American Political Science Association, New York City, September 4, 1981.

———— . "The Federal Role in Today's Intergovernmental Relations and the Emergence of Dysfunctional Federalism." Paper presented at the 86th Annual National Conference on Government, Houston, November 15, 1980.

Zimmerman, Joseph F. "Alternative Means of Delivering Public Services." Paper presented at a Seminar on State Development Strategies sponsored by the

New York State Department of State and the State University of New York, Binghamton, N.Y., February 15, 1980.

———— . "Alternative Service Delivery Mechanism and Areawide Tax Savings." Paper presented at a meeting of "Industries for Amsterdam," Amsterdam, N.Y., November 10, 1981.

———— . "Federal Preemption and the Erosion of Local Discretionary Authority." Paper presented at the Congress of Cities, Atlanta, December 1, 1980.

———— . "Governing Metropolitan Areas through Intergovernmental Cooperation." Paper presented at Urban Studies Workshop, State University of New York College at Potsdam, November 6, 1980.

———— . "The Impact of Federal Preemption on the American Governance System." Paper presented at the Annual Conference of the American Politics Group of the United Kingdom Political Studies Association, Manchester, England, January 4, 1980.

———— . "Preemption, Federal Mandates, and Goal Achievement." Paper presented at the Annual Conference of the Council of University Institutes of Urban Affairs, Washington, D.C., March 20, 1980.

———— . "Reforming the Single Member District System." Paper presented at the 86th Annual National Conference on Government, Houston, November 17, 1980.

———— . "Regional Governance: The Greater Dublin and Greated London Models." Paper presented at the 87th National Conference on Government, Pittsburgh, November 16, 1981.

———— . "State-Local Relations: State Dominance or Local Autonomy?" Paper presented at the 1980 Annual Meeting of the American Political Science Association, Washington, D.C., August 28, 1980.

———— . "The State Response to Local Problems." Paper presented at the Maxwell School of Citizenship and Public Affairs, Syracuse University, March 24, 1981.

Index

Abrams, Robert, 34-35, 47-48 (n. 73)
Acceptance statute, 7, 23-24, 162
Acute fiscal distress, 75-79
Adirondack Park Reserve, 121
Adler v. Deegan, 46 (n. 38-40)
Administrative Code of New York City, 81 (n. 35)
Advisory Commission on Intergovernmental Relations, v, 37, 42, 47 (n. 48), 48 (n. 84-86), 51, 56, 64-65, 67-68, 70, 76-77, 80 (n. 3), 81 (n. 7, 12, 23-24, 32), 82 (n. 60, 62), 83 (n. 65, 68, 70, 80-82, 84-86, 93-95), 84 (n. 100, 115, 119-20), 86-87, 92, 104, 110-11, 119, 126 (n. 4-6, 11-18), 127 (n. 25, 27, 29), 129 (n. 95), 131 (n. 144), 138-39, 146, 149, 154 (n. 6)
Advisory opinions, 34-36
Air Quality Act of 1967, 136, 154 (n. 9), 155 (n. 30)
Alaska, 68, 83 (n. 74), 113, 130 (n. 108-09), 165-66, 168, 170 (n. 2)
  Constitution, 68, 83 (n. 74), 113, 130 (n. 108-09), 165-66, 168, 170 (n. 2)
  Local Boundary Commission, 113
  Supreme Court, 30, 168
Amdursky, Robert S., 127 (n. 43)
American Municipal Association, 25, 28, 46 (n. 23)
Angell v. Toledo, 82 (n. 56)
Annals, The, 138
Annexation, 85-86, 110-13, 125
  Commission on Municipal Annexation and Consolidation, 111
Areawide government, 88-89
Aron, Joan, 99, 127 (n. 42)

Assembly Ways and Means Committee, 101
Association of the Bar of the City of New York, 100, 128 (n. 50)
Atkins v. Kansas, 45 (n. 9), 154 (n. 2)
Atomic Energy Act of 1946, 135
Attorney general, 34-36, 42-43, 168

Back-door financing, 102
Baer, Jon A., 28, 46 (n. 43-44)
Balanced budgets, 56, 76
Baldinger, Stanley, 106-07, 129 (n. 77-78, 81)
Bankruptcy Act, 138, 155 (n. 17)
Beame, Abraham, 144
Bell, Michael, 81 (n. 17)
Benefit overspill, 79
Bethlehem Steel Corporation v. Board of Education, 81 (n. 22)
Beyle, Thad L., 149, 157 (n. 76)
Bill of attainder, 3
Bill of Rights, 3
Bingham, David A., 15 (n. 17)
Birkhead, Guthrie S., 127 (n. 34)
Bish, Robert L., 170 (n. 1)
Black, Hugo L., 141-42
Block grants, 148-50, 153, 170
Board of Appeals of Hanover v. Housing Appeals Committee, 131 (n. 156)
Board of Assessors of Riverhead v. Grumman Aircraft Engineering Corporation, 156 (n. 57)
Board of Education v. Nyquist, 84 (n. 107, 110)
Board of ethics, 57
Bond
  banks, 94
  counsels, 38, 164
  indenture, 128 (n. 67)

referenda, 50, 54-55, 59, 81 (n. 25), 82 (n. 46), 89-90, 100-02, 111-12, 115-16

Boundary, 110-20

changes, 110-20

review commissions, 111-20

Braden, George D., 34-36, 47 (n. 69-70, 72), 48 (n. 77)

Brandl, John, 108-09, 129 (n. 83, 85)

Brown, Edmund, Jr., 60

Buckley, James L., 139, 155 (n. 26)

Budgets, 7, 56

balanced, 56

state approval, 7, 56

Business Week, 101, 128 (n. 52)

Byrne, Brendan, 75

California, 69, 74, 84 (n. 103), 119-20, 131 (n. 145-46)

Constitution, 84 (n. 103)

Property Tax Reform Act of 1972, 69

Supreme Court, 74

Task Force on Local Government Reform, 119-20, 131 (n. 145-46)

Campbell, Alan K., 127 (n. 34)

Canons of a good tax, 61

Cardozo, Benjamin N., 27

Carey Act, 138

Carey, Hugh L., 71-73, 75, 83 (n. 88-89), 102, 128 (n. 53, 55), 144

Catalog of Federal Domestic Assistance, 38

Categorical grant-in-aid programs, 71-73, 135, 144-48, 170

Cease, Ronard C., 119, 131 (n. 143)

Certificate of necessity, 30

Chamber of Commerce of the United States, 129 (n. 77)

Chapman v. Houston Welfare Rights Organization, 155 (n. 42)

Charter, 22, 26, 29, 33

classified, 22

commission, 33

ordinance, 29

Chatters, Carl H., 25, 46 (n. 33)

Chief of Police of Dracut v. Town of Dracut, 46 (n. 30)

Chisholm v. City Council of Lynn, 46 (n. 32)

Christoph v. City of Chilton, 46 (n. 15)

Citizens Housing and Planning Association, 131 (n. 158-59)

Citizens Public Expenditure Survey, Incorporated, 1, 14 (n. 2)

City Annexation Commission, 117

City of Beloit v. Kallas, 47 (n. 55)

City of Burbank v. Lockheed Air Terminal Incorporated, 155 (n. 35)

City of Clinton v. Cedar Rapids and Missouri Railroad Company, 45 (n. 5)

City-county consolidation, 96

City index, 38-40

City of Newport v. Facts Concerts, Incorporated, 48 (n. 79), 154 (n. 15)

City of Trenton v. New Jersey, 45 (n. 10), 154 (n. 2)

City of West Allis v. County of Milwaukee, 47 (n. 51, 65)

Civil Rights Act of 1871, 37, 48 (n. 80), 136-37

Classes of local government, 22-23, 30, 164

Classified laws, 22-23, 30, 164

Clean Air Act Amendments of 1977, 156 (n. 50, 54)

Clean Air Amendments of 1970, 143-44

Clines, Francis X., 128 (n. 58)

Code of restrictions, 31, 163-64

Codes of ethics, 52, 57

Coduri, Joseph E., 32, 47 (n. 61)

Cogen, Joel, 84 (n. 97)

Collective bargaining, 121

Colorado Constitution, 130 (n. 126)

Commission on Metropolitan Area
    Problems, 114, 129 (n. 96)
Commission on Municipal Annexation
    and Consolidation, 111
Community development block grant,
    148-50
Compacts, 3
    interstate, 3
    political, 3
Compliance costs, 63
Compulsory binding arbitration, 11,
    121
Concurrent majority, 88-89
Concurrent powers, 3
Conflict of interest laws, 57
Congressional Budget Office, 148-49,
    157 (n. 75)
Connecticut
    Conference of Municipalities, 73
    Public Expenditure Council, 74, 84
        (n. 106)
    Supreme Court, 32, 52, 74
Constitutional amendments, 134-35
Cooley's Rule, 19-20
Cooley, Thomas M., 19-20, 45 (n. 8)
Council of State Governments, 82 (n.
    45), 83 (n. 71), 84 (n. 101),
    86, 126 (n. 3, 11), 131 (n.
    147)
Councils of governments, 91
County, 42-44, 56, 88-89
    convention, 56
    government, 88-89
    index, 42-44
Crihfield, Brevard, 155 (n. 19)
Cummings v. Godin, 47 (n. 59)

Davis, Al, 156 (n. 60)
Debt limits, 43, 52, 54-55, 80, 89-
    90, 166
Deficit limits, 51-54, 80
Delegated powers, 3
Democracy
    direct, 2
    pure, 2
Democratic theory, 2

Detroit, 123-24, 132 (n. 167)
    Board of Education, 123-24
    regional school boards, 123-24
Devolution of powers, 26-34, 43-44,
    47 (n. 47)
    charter, 30
Dillon, John F., 19
Dillon's Rule, 19-21, 29-30, 33, 43-
    44, 64, 87, 96, 163, 168
Dionne, E. J., Jr., 84 (n. 110)
Direct democracy, 2
Discretionary authority, v, 5-6, 25-
    34, 36-45, 70, 89, 147, 160-
    70
    determinants, 5-6
    expansion of, 160-68
    indexes of, 37-42, 175-82
District Reorganization Act, 114
Doctrine of the continuous journey,
    136
Doctrine of implied powers, 136
Dommel, Paul R., 149, 157 (n. 77)
Dual federalism, 3
Due process of law, 134-35
Durham, G. Homer, 138, 155 (n. 22)
Dusenbury, Patricia J., 149, 157 (n.
    76)
Dye, Thomas R., 72-73, 83 (n. 96),
    147-48, 156 (n. 69-70)

East Ohio Gas Company vs. Akron,
    82 (n. 58)
Economic Recovery Tax Act of
    1981, 151, 157 (n. 88)
Education, 84 (n. 103-04, 107, 110),
    122-24
    Board of Education v. Nyquist, 84
        (n. 107, 110)
    Detroit, 123-24
    Fleischmann Report, 84 (n. 102)
    New York City, 122-23
    political decentralization, 122-24
    San Antonio Independent School
        District v. Rodriguez, 84 (n.
        104)
    Serrano v. Priest, 84 (n. 103)

Eels, John M., 114–15, 130 (n. 120–22)
Elazar, Daniel N., 15 (n. 11, 15)
Elitist theory, 2
Emergency Finance Control Board, 76–77, 120
  New York City, 76, 120
  Yonkers, 77
Ennis, Eva M., 83 (n. 71)
Entitlement program, 150
Enumerated powers, 2, 3, 43
Environmental Facilities Corporation, 98–100, 127 (n. 37)
Environmental Protection Agency, 135, 140, 143–45
Equal protection of laws, 135, 137, 141
Ethics, codes of, 52, 57
Expenditure limits, 89
Ex post facto law, 3
Expressed powers, 3
Expressio unius est excusio alterius, 26
Extra majority requirements, 54–55, 162

Fair Labor Standards Act Amendments, 142
Farney, Dennis, 109, 129 (n. 86)
Farrell, William E., 128 (n. 59)
Farrington v. Pinckney, 46 (n. 17)
Federal preemption, 3, 7, 67, 80, 121, 125, 133, 135, 138–45, 169
  informal, 138–39
  partial, 3, 80, 121, 133, 135, 169
  total, 121, 133, 135
Federal Revenue Act of 1926, 151
Federal Voting Rights Act of 1965, 135, 142, 155 (n. 43)
Federal Water Pollution Control Act Amendments of 1972, 135–36, 154 (n. 8)
Federalism, 3
  dual, 3
  layer cake, 3

Federalist Papers, 3, 15 (n. 10)
Fifteenth Amendment, 135, 141
First Amendment, 135
First National Bank of Boston et al. v. Bellotti, 82 (n. 46)
Fiscal notes, 67–68, 80
Fiscal resource equalization, 78–79
Fiscal restraints, 88–90
Fiscal zoning, 129 (n. 90)
Fischer, John, 129 (n. 77)
Fisher, Ronald, 81 (n. 77)
Flammable Fabrics Act, 140, 155 (n. 28)
Fleischmann Report, 84 (n. 102)
Florida Environmental Land and Water Management Act of 1972, 121
Fordham, Jefferson B., 23, 28–30, 44, 46 (n. 23, 33), 47 (n. 45–47), 53, 68–69, 83 (n. 72–73)
Forwood v. City of Taylor, 47 (n. 46)
Fourteenth Amendment, 74, 134–35, 137, 141–42
Fox v. City of Racine, 47 (n. 59)
Freedman, Eric, 48 (n. 78)
Friends of the Earth v. EPA, 156 (n. 53)
Full faith and credit bonds, 55, 90, 100–01, 104–05
Functional transfers, 87, 91, 93, 167

Garrity, W. Arthur, Jr., 137
General city law, 35
General Court, 18, 24, 33, 56
General law cities, 7
General laws, 28, 35–36, 44
General Municipal Law, 35, 48 (n. 74)
General property tax, 49–51, 57–62
  assessment, 49–50, 58
  exemptions, 52–53, 58
  senior citizen circuit breaker laws, 58–59
General revenue sharing, 38, 145 150–51

Gibbons v. Ogden, 136
Goodnow, Frank J., 46 (n. 13-14), 64, 82 (n. 64)
Gordon v. Lance, 81 (n. 25)
Gordon, Stephen, 83 (n. 67)
Grant, Daniel R., 126 (n. 22)
Grant, William R., 132 (n. 166)
Grants-in-aid, 67, 71-75, 78, 135, 138-39, 145-53, 170
  education, 73-75
Graves, W. Brooke, 155 (n. 18)
Greenhouse, Linda, 128 (n. 54)
Governor's Commission on Metropolitan Area Problems, 114, 129 (n. 96)
Grodzins, Morton, 15 (n. 11)

Hanus, Jerome J., 154 (n. 1)
Harriss, C. Lowell, 82 (n. 54)
Hatch Act of 1887, 138
Hein, C. J., 108 (n. 84)
Helms, Jesse A., 143
Herbers, John, 106-07, 129 (n. 79), 157 (n. 82)
Herman, Robin, 83 (n. 92), 84 (n. 109)
Hines v. Davidowitz, 155 (n. 33)
Hogan v. City of South Charleston, 15 (n. 17)
Home rule, v, 10, 47 (n. 66), 64
Homestead exemptions, 52-53, 58
Horton v. Meskill, 84 (n. 105)
Housing and Community Development Act of 1974, 156 (n. 71)
Hunter, Marjorie, 155 (n. 47)
Hurd v. City of Buffalo, 81 (n. 20), 126 (n. 17)
Hurley, Thomas L., 72-73, 83 (n. 96), 147-48, 156 (n. 69-70)

Illinois Constitution, 46 (n. 21)
Imperium in Imperio, 3, 26-28, 30, 43-45, 47 (n. 47), 163, 168
Income tax, 62-63, 79
Incorporation, 110-11, 125

Index of local discretionary authority, 37-42, 45
Indianapolis, 96, 124
Indirect federal mandates, 140
Ingraham Company v. City of Bristol, 81 (n. 9)
Initiative, 59-62, 80, 160
  direct, 59
  indirect, 59
Insurance pools, 95-96
Intergovernmental service agreements, 14, 86, 91, 93
Interlocal contracting, 86, 91
Interlocal cooperation, 14, 86, 91, 167
Interlocal equity mandates, 65
Interlocking directorate, 99, 103
International Association of Assessing Officers, 81 (n. 12), 126 (n. 11)
Interstate Commerce Act of 1887, 135
Investment pools, 94-95

Jefferson v. State, 47,(n. 52), 170 (n. 3)
Joint Economic Committee, 126
Joint enterprises, 86
Judicial interpretation, 3, 136, 154 (n. 10)
  doctrine of the continuous journey, 136
  doctrine of implied powers, 136
  Gibbons v. Ogden, 136
  McCulloch v. Maryland, 136, 154 (n. 10)

Kansas State Board of Tax Appeals, 53
Katzman, Martin T., 127 (n. 30)
Keys, Joyce M., 108, 129 (n. 84)
Knapp v. O'Brien, 129 (n. 76)
Koch, Edward, 73
Kolderie, Ted, 107-09, 129 (n. 80-82, 87)

Ladd, Helen F., 54, 81 (n. 18)
Lance v. Board of Education, 81 (n. 25)
Lane County Local Government Boundary Commission, 118-19, 130 (n. 140)
Layer cake federalism, 3
Leach, Richard H., 155 (n. 19)
League of Kansas Municipalities, 10
Lease purchase agreement, 55, 90
Legates, Richard T., 114, 130 (n. 118-19)
Legislative courtesy, 20
Legislative delegation, 20
Legislative Research Council, 32-33, 47 (n. 66), 79, 84 (n. 123-24)
Levitt, Arthur, 101-02
Levy limits, 53, 89, 166
Lindsay, John V., 86, 144
Loan restrictions, 52, 55, 80
   credit, 52, 55, 80
   property, 55, 80
Local affairs agencies, 91-92
Local agency formation commissions, 114-15
Local assistance fund, 77
Local concerns, 10
Local discretionary authority, v, 5-6, 25-34, 36-45, 70, 89, 147, 160-70
   defender of, 168-69
   determinants, 5-6
   expansion of, 160-68
   indexes of, 37-42, 175-82
Local government boundary commission, 110-20
Local government expenditure review board, 71-72
Local nonproperty taxing authority, 62-63
   income tax, 62-63
   sales tax, 63
Logue, Edward J., 100, 128 (n. 46, 48)
Long Island State Park Commission, 103

Loss of local tax base mandates, 65
Louiselle v. City of East Providence, 47 (n. 60)
Louisiana
   Association of Business and Industry, 70-71, 83 (n. 83)
   Constitution, 68-69, 83 (n. 75)
Lynn, Massachusetts, 24

Macchiarola, Frank J., 27, 46 (n. 41), 51, 80 (n. 5)
Madden, Richard L., 94 (n. 98)
Maeroff, Gene I., 154 (n. 16)
Magavern, James L., 36
Maine v. Thiboutot, 48 (n. 79), 136-37, 154 (n. 13-14)
Maintenance of effort, 147
Mandates, 11, 14, 64-70, 80, 140, 165-66
   fiscal notes, 67-68, 80
   pass-through, 14
   rationale, 65-66
   state reimbursement, 66-69, 80
   survey of, 66-67
   typology, 64-65
Manlove, George, 155 (n. 31)
Marion County, 96, 124
   Health and Hospital Corporation, 96
Marion-Polk County Local Government Boundary Commission, 119
Martin, Roscoe C., 86, 126 (n. 2), 133-34, 154 (n. 3-5)
Maryland Environmental Service, 102-03, 121
Massachusetts, 30, 33, 46 (n. 22, 24), 47 (n. 68), 68-69, 83 (n. 76), 122, 131 (n. 156)
   Bay, 2, 18, 45 (n. 1-3)
   Bay Colony, 2, 18
   Bay Company, 18
   Constitution, 30, 46 (n. 22, 24), 47 (n. 68), 68-69, 83 (n. 76), 131 (n. 156)

Department of Community Affairs, 33
Supreme Judicial Court, 122
Mathewson, Kent, 129 (n. 82)
Maxwell Graduate School, 97, 127 (n. 34)
McCullogh v. Maryland, 136, 154 (n. 10)
Medicaid, 72-73
Merriam v. Moody's Executors, 45 (n. 6)
Metropolitan Boundary Commission, 116
Metropolitan District Commission, 97
Metropolitan financing district, 79, 84 (n. 123)
Metropolitan Land Planning Act, 105, 128 (n. 73)
Metropolitan Parks and Open Space Commission, 106, 109
Metropolitan planning commissions, 91-92
Metropolitan Revenue Distribution Act, 110, 125
Metropolitan services financing district, 79, 84 (n. 123-24)
Metropolitan Sewer Board, 106
Metropolitan study commissions, 91-92
Metropolitan Transit Commission, 106-07
Michelin Tire Corporation v. Wages, 15 (n. 9)
Michigan
    Constitution, 21, 44, 45 (n. 11)
    Municipal League, 50-51
Milliken, William G., 124
Minnesota, 105, 110-13, 130 (n. 106-07)
    Municipal Board, 105, 111-13, 130 (n. 106-07)
    Supreme Court, 110
Missouri Constitution, 26, 46 (n. 34)
Moral obligation bonds, 101
Moynihan-Holtzman Amendment, 144-45

Municipal affairs, 10
Municipal assistance corporation, 76-77, 120
Municipal Bankruptcy Act, 75, 84 (n. 113)
Municipal bond banks, 91
Municipal corporation, 19, 23, 28, 64
Municipal equity account, 110
Municipal Finance Officers Association, 89, 126 (n. 12)
Municipal insurance pools, 91, 95-96

Naftalin, Arthur, 108-09, 129 (n. 83, 85)
Nathan, Richard P., 149, 157 (n. 77)
National Academy of Public Administration, 77-78, 84 (n. 119)
National League of Cities, 47 (n. 46)
National League of Cities v. Usery, 137, 155 (n. 41)
National Municipal League, 26, 47 (n. 47)
National powers, 134-37
    constitutional amendments, 134-35
    expansion of, 134-37
    judicial interpretation, 136-37
    statutory elaboration, 135-36
Need-fiscal resource mismatch, 78-79, 85
New Hampshire Bureau of Solid Waste Management, 66
New Jersey Water Supply Authority, 103
New Mexico Municipal Boundary Commission, 115-16
New York City community school districts, 122-23
New York State, 15 (n. 12, 30), 45 (n. 12), 46 (n. 19, 28, 36, 42), 47 (n. 53, 71), 51, 54-55, 57, 65-66, 75, 80 (n. 6), 81 (n. 26, 29, 35), 83 (n. 66), 88, 90, 98, 126 (n. 7, 15, 20), 128 (n. 49)
    Air Quality Implementation Plan, 145, 156 (n. 52)

Constitution, 15 (n. 12), 30, 45
  (n. 12), 46 (n. 19, 28, 36, 42),
  47 (n. 53, 71), 51, 55, 57, 80
  (n. 6), 81 (n. 26, 29, 35), 83
  (n. 66, 88, 90), 126 (n. 7, 15,
  20), 128 (n. 49)
Constitutional Convention, 65-66
Court of Appeals, 27, 54-55, 75,
  90, 98
Educational Conference, 74
Municipal Assistance Corporation,
  76-77, 120
Supreme Court, 74
Temporary State Commission on
  the Powers of Local Governments, 82 (n. 61), 100
Nineteenth Amendment, 141
Noise Control Act of 1972, 141
Nonproperty taxes, 62-63
  income tax, 62-63
  sales tax, 63
Nonrecallable bonds, 103
Noscitur a sociis, 26

Office for Local Government, 92
Ohio Constitution, 82 (n. 55), 88,
  126 (n. 8)
Olson, Gerald W., 37, 48 (n. 83)
One person, one vote, 54, 86, 89
O'Neill, William, 73
Open town meeting, 2
Opinion Research Corporation, 1
Optional charters, 7, 23, 163
Optional county government law, 24
Oregon, 31-32
  Constitution, 31-32, 47 (n. 56)
  Supreme Court, 32
Oregon v. Mitchell, 155 (n. 39-40)
Ostrom, Vincent, 170 (n. 1)
Owen v. City of Independence, 48
  (n. 79), 136-137, 154 (n. 15)
Owen, Henry, 155 (n. 25)

Payroll tax, 79
Pennsylvania Constitution, 68-69, 83
  (n. 77)

Pension funds, 56-57
  actuarial system, 56-57
  cash system, 56
People v. Hurlburt, 45 (n. 7)
Perkins v. Matthews, 142, 155 (n. 44)
Permanent Commission on Public Em-
  ployee Pension and Retirement
  Systems, 57
Permissive statute, 7
Personnel mandates, 65
Petersen, John E., 126 (n. 12)
Pisani, Joseph F., 75
Plural-headed authorities, 104
Police power, 141
Political culture, 5
Political decentralization, 122-24
  education, 122-24
Port Authority of New York and
  New Jersey, 98
Portland Metropolitan Area Boundary
  Commission, 119
Poulos v. Caparrelli, 47 (n. 63)
Pound, Cuthbert W., 27
Powell, Lewis F., Jr., 137
Preemption, 3, 7, 67, 80, 121, 125,
  133, 135, 138-45, 153, 162,
  168-69
  formal, 3, 153
  impact, 138-45
  informal, 138-39, 153
  partial, 3, 80, 121, 133, 135, 153,
  169
  total, 121, 133, 135
Privileges and immunities, 135
Procedural requirements, 22, 24
Prohibition of special laws, 4, 18, 21-
  24
Property, affairs, or government, 27,
  30
Property assessment, 49, 52, 58, 61,
  80
  fractional, 52, 58
  full valuation, 52, 58, 61, 80
  use value, 53
Property tax, 49-51, 57-62, 80
  assessment, 49-50, 58, 89

exemptions, 52-53, 80
limits, 89
senior citizen circuit breaker laws, 58-59, 61
Property tax base sharing, 79
Proportional representation, 123
Proposition 2½, 60-61, 82 (n. 51)
Proposition 4, 60, 68-69
Proposition 9, 60
Proposition 13, 58-60, 81 (n. 12), 126 (n. 11)
Proprietary functions, 19
Public authorities, 96-105
Maryland Environmental Service, 102-03
Metropolitan District Commission, 97
New Jersey Water Supply Authority, 103
New York State, 97-102
single-purpose, 125
state-controlled, 96-105
Urban Development Corporation, 98-102
Public choice theory, 160
Publius, 3, 15 (n. 10)

Quasi-municipal corporations, 4, 18, 56, 160

Radiation Control for Health and Safety Act of 1968, 140, 155 (n. 29)
Rampton, Calvin L., 14, 15 (n. 18)
Ravitch, Diane, 123, 131 (n. 164)
Ray v. Atlantic Richfield Company, 155 (n. 37)
Reagan administration, 76, 92, 145, 148
Reapportionment, 86
Reeves, H. Clyde, 155 (n. 19)
Referendum, 50, 54-55, 59, 81 (n. 25), 82 (n. 46), 89-90, 93, 100-02, 105, 111-12, 115-16, 160
extra majority requirements, 54-55

First National Bank of Boston et al. v. Bellotti, 82 (n. 46)
Gordon v. Lance, 81 (n. 25)
Lance v. Board of Education, 81 (n. 25)
Regan, Edward, V., 36
Regional planning commissions, 91-92
Regressive tax, 63
Reserved powers, 3, 33
Residual powers approach, 29
Revenue Act of 1926, 151, 157 (n. 86)
Revenue bonds, 55, 97
Revenue sharing, 38, 67, 71, 78, 145, 150-51
general, 38, 145, 150-51
special, 145, 148-50
Reverse option law, 7
Rhode Island Supreme Court, 32
Rice v. Santa Fe Elevator Corporation, 155 (n. 34)
Rich, Spencer, 156 (n. 48)
Ripper laws, 4, 22
Robbins, G. M., 108, 129 (n. 84)
Robertson v. Zimmermann, 46 (n. 40), 127 (n. 39)
Rockefeller, Nelson A., 86, 98, 127 (n. 36), 144
Rosenberg, Philip, 157 (n. 77)
Rowell, David T., 131 (n. 157)
Ruben, Elisabeth A., 131 (n. 158-59)
Rules of the game mandate, 64-65

Sacks, Seymour, 156 (n. 59)
Safe Drinking Water Act, 140, 155 (n. 32)
Sale-leasebacks, 151
Sales tax, 63
San Antonio Independent School District v. Rodriguez, 84 (n. 104), 137
Santa Clara County Agency Formation Commission, 114, 130 (n. 112)

Schmandt, Henry J., 91, 127 (n. 24)
Schultze, Charles L., 139, 155 (n. 25)
Seattle v. Long, 47 (n. 54)
Senior citizen circuit breaker laws, 58–59, 61
Separate entity approach, 26–27
Serrano v. Priest, 84 (n. 103)
Service agreements, 93
Service mandates, 65
Shannon, John, 81 (n. 17)
Shestack, Jerome J., 104, 128 (n. 70)
Shurtleff, Nathaniel B., 45 (n. 1–3)
Sixteenth Amendment, 135
Smith, Adam, 61, 82 (n. 53)
Smith, L. Kinsley, 74–75
Smith, William French, 143, 156 (n. 49)
Social Security Act of 1935, 157 (n. 87)
Spain, Catherine L., 126 (n. 12)
Special charters, 18
Special city acts, 22
Special districts, 55, 92, 167
    multi-purpose, 92
    single purpose, 92
Special fund legal doctrine, 55
Special laws, 4, 7, 18, 20–23, 33–34, 47 (n. 67), 161–62
Special revenue sharing, 148–50, 153
Spicer, George W., 53–54, 81 (n. 16)
Spillover or service mandates, 65
Stallings, Wayne, 126 (n. 12)
Standard setting, 120–21
Standing, William H., 91, 127 (n. 24)
Stapleton v. Pinckney, 46 (n. 16)
State agencies for local affairs, 91–92
State aid, 70–79
State Appeals Committee, 121–22
State Boundary Commission, 116–17
State Charter Commission for New York City, 123, 131 (n. 163)
State concern doctrine, 27
State-controlled public authorities, 96–105
State dominance, 1
State ex rel. Bowker v. Wright, 46 (n. 18)

State ex rel. Brelsford v. Retirement Board, 47 (n. 64)
State ex rel. Heinig v. City of Milwaukee, 47 (n. 57–58)
State ex rel. Perry J. Sloane et al. v. Thomas Reidy et al., 47 (n. 62)
State financial assistance, 70–80
    acute fiscal distress, 75–76
    fiscal resource equalization, 78–79
    grants-in-aid, 72–73
    grants for education, 11, 73–75
    revenue sharing, 71–72
    targeting assistance, 76–78
State and Local Fiscal Assistance Act of 1972, 38, 150
State Land and Conservation Development Commission, 118
State-local relations model, 160–68
    areawide governments, 167
    classified legislation, 164
    code of restrictions, 164
    devolution of powers, 162–63
    recodification of state laws, 162, 165
    removal of constitutional restrictions, 166
    special legislation, 161–62
    state boundary commissions, 166–67
    state mandate reimbursement, 165–66
    state minimum service levels, 167–68
State mandates, 11, 21, 50, 64–69, 140, 165–67
    fiscal notes, 67–68, 80
    state reimbursement, 66–69, 80, 165–66
    survey of, 66–67
    typology, 64–65
State restraints, 20–21
State role, 14, 87–124, 169
    facilitator, 14, 87, 90–96, 124, 169
    inhibitor, 14, 87–90, 124
    initiator, 14, 87, 96–124, 169
Statutory elaboration, 135–36

Stein, Jane L., 131 (n. 149)

Stenberg, Carl W., 146, 156 (n. 61–62), 157 (n. 72)

Stephens, G. Ross, 37, 48 (n. 81–83)

Strikes, 121

Study commissions, 91–92

Sublegislative powers, 19

Substitute administration, 75, 96, 120

Sullivan, Joseph F., 84 (n. 111–12)

Sun Printing & Publishing Association v. Mayor, 81 (n. 28)

Sunshine laws, 52, 57
open meetings, 57
public records, 57

Supercession of state laws, 4, 29, 140

Supremacy clause, 3

Supreme Judicial Court, 24

Suspensory veto, 4, 22, 162

Sutton, Robert W., Jr., 47 (n. 61)

Targeting assistance, 76–78, 96, 146

Task Force on Local Government Reform, 119–20, 131 (n. 145–46)

Task Force Report on Public Employee Retirement Systems, 81 (n. 31)

Tax base sharing, 110

Tax credits, 138, 151–54

Tax and expenditure cap law, 59, 67

Tax limits, 43, 51–54, 80, 89–90, 166

Tax rate limits, 53–54

Temporary State Commission on Constitutional Tax Limitations, 82 (n. 61)

Temporary State Commission on the Powers of Local Governments, 82 (n. 61), 100

Temporary State Commission on State and Local Finances, 83 (n. 87)

Tennessee Constitution, 68–69, 83 (n. 78), 88–89, 126 (n. 9)

Tenth Amendment, 3, 18, 29, 135, 142

Texas Municipal League, 96

Texas Water Rights Commission, 119

Thompson v. Kenosha County, 46 (n. 26)

Tiebout, Charles M., 170 (n. 1)

Tippett, Frank, 156 (n. 60)

Titles of nobility, 3

Town Bonding Act, 55, 81 (n. 27)

Town-colony relations, 18

Town of Lockport v. Citizens for Community Action at the Local Level, 126 (n. 10)

Town meeting, 2

Transfers of functions, 87, 167

Triborough Bridge and Tunnel Authority, 103

Turner, Wallace, 82 (n. 50)

Twin Cities Metropolitan Area, 79, 105–10, 125
Council, 105–10, 125
tax base sharing, 79, 110

Ultra Vires Rule, 4, 17–18, 43, 49, 51, 87, 163, 168–69

Uniform law application, 23–24

United States
Advisory Commission on Intergovernmental Relations, v, 37, 42, 47 (n. 48), 48 (n. 84–86), 51, 56, 64–65, 67–68, 70, 76–77, 80 (n. 3), 81 (n. 7, 12, 23–24, 32), 82 (n. 60, 62), 83 (n. 65, 68, 70, 80–82, 84–86, 93–95), 84 (n. 100, 115, 119–20), 86–87, 92, 104, 110–11, 119, 126 (n. 4–5, 11–18), 127 (n. 25, 27, 29), 129 (n. 95), 131 (n. 144), 138–39, 146, 149, 154 (n. 6)

Bureau of the Census, 80 (n. 1), 81 (n. 8, 10–11, 30), 82 (n. 38–41), 150, 157 (n. 83–84)

Constitution, 2, 15 (n. 3–7), 128 (n. 67), 135, 137, 142, 153, 155 (n. 45)

Department of Housing and Urban Development, 35, 76, 82 (n. 42–43), 84 (n. 114), 148

General Accounting Office, 56–57, 81 (n. 33), 146–47, 150–51, 156 (n. 58, 64), 157 (n. 73, 85)

Grain Standards Act, 140, 155 (n. 29)

Office of Management and Budget, 48 (n. 87)

Supreme Court, 3, 20, 36–37, 54, 59, 74, 86, 89, 136, 140–41, 143

Untouchables, 104

Urban Development Corporation, 98–99, 102, 127 (n. 43)

User fees, 97

Vermont Constitution, 5

Veto, suspensory, 22

Village of Burnsville v. Onischuk, 129 (n. 89)

Virginia v. Tennessee, 15 (n. 8)

Voting Rights Act, 135, 142, 155 (n. 43)

Walker, David B., 87, 126 (n. 6), 146, 156 (n. 63)

Washington, 31, 47 (n. 49), 98
Constitution, 47 (n. 49), 98

Supreme Court, 31, 98

Water Quality Act of 1965, 135, 154 (n. 6)

Weissman, Marsha, 127 (n. 34)

West Virginia, 54
Constitution, 54
Supreme Court, 54

Williams, Constance, 131 (n. 158–59)

Williamsburg Savings Bank v. State, 128 (n. 51)

Wilson, Woodrow, 136, 154 (n. 11)

Winston v. Spokane, 127 (n. 38)

Wisconsin, 23, 29, 31–32, 46 (n. 25)
Constitution, 23, 46 (n. 25)
Supreme Court, 29, 31–32

Woonsocket City Charter, 32

Wright, Deil S., 155 (n. 19)

Yates, Charles B., 75

Young, Coleman A., 124

Zimmerman, Joseph F., 46 (n. 35), 47 (n. 50), 48 (n. 86, 88, 90), 82 (n. 37), 126 (n. 21, 23), 127 (n. 26–27, 29, 31, 35), 131 (n. 150, 160), 154 (n. 1), 155 (n. 19, 43), 156 (n. 66–68)

ABOUT THE AUTHOR

JOSEPH F. ZIMMERMAN is a professor of political science at the Graduate School of Public Affairs of the State University of New York at Albany and also serves as research director of the New York State Legislative Commission on Critical Transportation Choices. He previously taught at Worcester Polytechnic Institute and Clark University.

Dr. Zimmerman is the author of *State and Local Government, The Massachusetts Town Meeting: A Tenacious Institution, Pragmatic Federalism, State Mandating of Local Expenditures, Measuring Local Discretionary Authority,* and *The Government and Politics of New York State.* He is coauthor of *The Politics of the Veto of Legislation in New York* and editor of several books, including *Government of the Metropolis* and *Subnational Politics.*

Professor Zimmerman received a B.A. at the University of New Hampshire and an M.A. and Ph.D. at Syracuse University.